MW01102242

TEEN SMART!

Ready-to-Use Activities to Help Teens Build Positive Relationships with Peers and Adults

Saundrah Clark Grevious

ILLUSTRATED BY KATHY BARON

JOSSEY-BASS
A Wiley Imprint
www.josseybass.com

Published by Jossey-Bass
A Wiley Imprint
989 Market Street, San Francisco, CA 94103-1741   www.josseybass.com

This publication is not associated with the TEEN SMART crash reduction program distributed by Advanced Drivers Education Products and Training, Inc.

Poetry for Activity 2–7, "Your Freedom to Be...To Become," and for Activity 2–14, "Spread Out Beauty," was written by Saundrah Clark Grevious.

Jossey-Bass books and products are available through most bookstores. To contact Jossey-Bass directly call our Customer Care Department within the U.S. at 800-956-7739, outside the U.S. at 317-572-3986 or fax 317-572-4002.

Jossey-Bass also publishes its books in a variety of electronic formats. Some content that appears in print may not be available in electronic books.

Library of Congress Cataloging-in-Publication Data
Grevious, Saundrah Clark.
     Teen smart! : ready-to-use activities to help teens build positive
relationships with peers and adults / Saundrah Clark Grevious
          p.   cm.
     Includes bibliographical references.
     ISBN 0-13-022652-1
     ISBN 0-7879-6641-X (layflat)
     1. Interpersonal relations in adolescence.   2. Teenagers—Conduct
of life.   I. Title.
BF724.3.I58G74   1999
158.2'0835—dc21   99-24033

FIRST EDITION
HB Printing 10 9 8 7 6 5 4 3 2 1

DEDICATION

For my precious grandchildren
Njeri Kamilah
and
Nkosi Themba
and
Njioma Chinyere.

For all of my students
past, present and future.

For the young people
of America who go forth,
hopeful, into the new
century and the new
millennium; hopeful that
they, together with the
adults in their lives,
can make a positive
difference.

ACKNOWLEDGEMENTS

I extend my deepest appreciation to my family for the love, moral, and spiritual support that made the completion of this book possible. I am especially appreciative to my husband, Herbert, for believing in me and encouraging me to pursue my dreams. Through it all, he has been my patient champion and my constructive critic. Thank you, Herb.

My children not only lent their love, moral, and spiritual support, but, weary of the "dinosaur" upon which I processed my "projects," they brought their mother into the 21st century with a gift of advanced technology. Kevin, Steven, Mark, Shannon, and Sharon, my new computer, related hardware and software mean so much to me as you know, but the strength, love, and encouragement that were my daily fare from you were as necessary as air. Thanks to all of you.

From Corinne Clark, my mother, who taught me so much through her lovely singing, vivid dramatizations, and value-laden stories, to my siblings, Frances, Dan, Meredith, Preston and Donnie, there was complete understanding of my need to "hibernate," yet a readiness to listen and respond whenever I sought their support. I extend my heartfelt thanks to all of you.

Laura Grevious Gaskins saw possibilities beyond any I had ever dreamed of and encouraged me to write for wider audiences. Thank you Aunt Laura.

Evan Holstrom, my developmental editor, was diligent in her meticulous review of the manuscript. Her skill, advice, and attention to minute details were crucial in the interest of clarity during the earliest stages of production. Thank you, Evan.

My artist, Kathy Baron, has an incredible ability to interpret social and academic concepts accurately and artistically. Her lively illustrations simultaneously capture the intent and tone of the lessons and convey the underlying themes that are designed to enrich the lives of the students. Thank you, Kathy.

Winfield Huppuch, Vice-President and Publisher at Prentice-Hall, approached me with the idea for this book for secondary students. I extend my deep appreciation to Win for both his insight and foresight and for giving me the opportunity to develop what he envisions as a necessary tool for secondary educators as we enter the dawn of the next millennium. Thank you, Win.

Susan Kolwicz, my Education Editor, was the driving force behind this project. Her coordination of all of the elements from the conceptual through the production phases was skillful and logical. Her knowledge, expertise, and perseverance, have brought the organization and content of the book into sharp focus. Thank you, Susan.

ABOUT THE AUTHOR

Saundrah Clark Grevious received her Bachelor of Arts degree from Chicago Teachers College and her Master of Education degree from the Harvard University Graduate School of Education. She has done postgraduate work at the University of California at Berkeley and was trained there as a Teacher consultant for the Bay Area Writing Project. She is certified in grades K–12 and has taught all of these grade levels. In addition, Mrs. Grevious has directed a Headstart Program and worked as a Consultant in Curriculum and Instruction for the New Jersey State Department of Education. During this time, her responsibilities included not only monitoring federally funded programs in school districts around the state, but doing the research for and writing the initial product for the State Plan for Basic Skills.

Most of her teaching experiences have been in culturally, racially, and ethnically diverse environments in cities such as Chicago, Baltimore, Boston, Fairbanks, Minneapolis, and Oakland. Mrs. Grevious has also done volunteer work in cross-cultural communication strategies with adult community groups and with middle school, high school, and college level students. Mrs. Grevious has written many educational materials including, *Ready-to-Use Multicultural Activities for Primary Children, Teaching Children and Adults to Understand Human and Race Relations, All-Write: A Quality Control Writing Competency Program,* a script for a film "Once Upon a Chalkboard" for the University of Minnesota, and two plays "The Peraltas" and "My Sister, My Twin," the latter of which she has recently developed into a novel. She conducts in-service programs in an effort to raise the awareness of educators to the power that they have to change the world for the better. Saundrah Clark Grevious currently teaches in the Piscataway Township Public Schools in Piscataway, New Jersey.

ABOUT THIS RESOURCE

High school students are on the brink of adulthood and on the cutting edge of the many human conflicts that rage about them. Inner strength and a willingness to work with others to resolve problems are crucial attributes for young people if they are to be prepared for their adult roles in the new millennium. *Teen Smart!* is an invaluable resource designed as a survival guide. It is a collection of student-centered strategies to help secondary students confront, control, resolve, and prevent conflicts at home, school, and in the community. Only when they are able to function responsibly in these environments will students have the self-confidence and the levels of mutual respect they need to assume their future roles in an increasingly complex and diverse society. Adults who work with young people deserve a meaningful tool to help them prepare the future citizens of America for their roles in the twenty-first century. This comprehensive, educationally sound resource is exactly what discerning educators need.

Each of the five sections—Family Bonding, Character Development, Community Involvement, "It Takes a Whole Village to Raise a Child," and Choices, Changes and Challenges—is filled with activities that raise the awareness of students to the need to be proud of their heritage and that help them to better understand what it means to be responsible, compassionate, knowledgeable, and self-reliant teenagers. Moreover, students learn that one's level of self-confidence and one's ability to maintain a positive attitude have as much to do with one's outlook, attitude, and behavior, as with the kinds of relationships one has with family, friends, teachers, and other members of society. Through these activities, students learn that self-esteem does not exist in a vacuum. They come to understand that young people's personal characteristics, good feelings, accomplishment, and wisdom are attainable attributes that emanate from the adults with whom they interact—beginning with the people in their homes.

These lessons help students to recognize and respond appropriately to "good strokes"; however, the concepts will also help them to transcend the temporary, "feel-good" aspects of self-esteem and find the wisdom to look within for shortcomings that need correcting. Exposure to these educationally-sound activities, therefore, will help students to practice skills in self-improvement and to collaborate with others for the building of more peaceful environments. One important concept in *Teen Smart!* helps young people really see that there is a difference between *true self-esteem* and *arrogance*: They learn and demonstrate that positive self-esteem does not lead one to "put down" other people, but positive or true self-esteem results in one's ability to acknowledge, respect, and celebrate the good in others.

Teenagers grasp the significance of the impact that the family has on the early building of positive self-concepts in **Section 1, Family Bonding.** As the students work on these lessons, their appreciation for their families increases, and they begin to tap into the richness of their heritage and the source of their values—the people closest to them. Students will come to understand that it is most often from their parents and other close family members that they first learn the meanings of love, loyalty, generosity, trust, honesty, hard work, respect, self-discipline, justice, and kindness. These family-based values are inherent in these activities and provide a significant foundation for strengthening students' self-confidence.

Lessons in **Section 2, Character Development,** reinforce the positive values that family members have passed on to their children. Students learn that they will need these positive values as they move in and out of various environments and encounter personal and societal conflicts. There are many opportunities for students to reflect on personal characteristics that help them to establish methods of combating negativity and to form harmonious relationships with peers and adults outside the home. Essentially, students practice the giving and receiving of the kinds of values that benefit themselves and other members of society. In addition to strategies that help students to internalize positive values, many activities are effective in steering them away from the negative options that result in violence, racism, prejudice, hatred, materialism, irresponsibility, and selfishness. Furthermore, students understand why they must reject negative value systems that ultimately erase self-esteem, destroy character, create conflict, and prevent an awareness of the positive roles they must assume in society.

Student exposure to lessons in **Section 3, Community Involvement,** helps them to continue to develop an aversion to injustice, violence, and intolerance. After internalizing the concepts, they want to become part of the solution to the problems of rejection that currently plague society. In addition, these comprehensive lessons will give hope to some young people whose lives are demoralized from personal experiences that invalidate their existence. Students who have higher levels of self-esteem are challenged to verify the sources of their confidence to ensure that their high self-esteem does not result in pain for others. Once they are certain that they have self-confidence levels that are considerate of others and are not based on arrogance or pride, they are encouraged to extend hope to peers who have low self-esteem. Young people who have yet to develop higher levels of self-esteem gain inner strength when they are shown how to find the good inside and the confidence to combat conflict in their lives. Activities in this section of *Teen Smart! Ready-to-Use Activities to Help Teens Build Positive Relationships with Peers and Adults* foster the development of competence, confidence, caring, commitment, feelings of belonging, and the natural desire that all young people have for success and fulfillment.

Techniques to help students develop, maintain, and extend the results of having positive self-esteem abound in **Section 4, "It Takes a Whole Village to Raise a Child."** Parents, teachers, counselors, school administrators, and members of the community often work together to help young people to establish a meaning and a purpose for living. The activities are designed to show teenagers that many of the people with whom they interact have their best interest at heart—that they want young people to be less vulnerable to negative forces. Also in this section, students learn that they, too, are a part of the village and as such, have a responsibility to follow rules and regulations and support the safety of other village members. As a result of participation in these activities, most students become less willing to give in to temptations that might cause them to destroy their lives and those of others. Increased strength comes from students' knowing why they chose the "best" options and from their experiencing the satisfaction that comes from building rather than tearing down the "village." These lessons lead young people to see the value in becoming givers rather than takers, and participants in the processes that bring justice, equality, peace, and happiness to everyone, regardless of who or what you are.

The slant and tone of the lessons in *Teen Smart!* help young people to appreciate racial, ethnic, and cultural diversity while simultaneously valuing human commonalties. Because we are in a state of perpetual turmoil as society is on the verge of entering the twenty-first century, teenagers must be decisive for they are at the focal point of the search for harmonious human relationships. **Section 5, Choices, Changes, and Challenges,** brings students to the point where they have to make decisions regarding the paths they will take in pursuing self-esteem and satisfaction in life. As young people move into position to take over the reins of society in the next millennium, they must be capable of self-examination; maintaining mental and physical health; contributing to improved human relationships among various racial, cultural, and ethnic groups; and pursuing academic excellence. These lessons will help each participating student to develop a stronger sense of self, an ability to identify and prioritize goals, and the skills to formulate a plan of action for his or her future. If young people are adequately trained to be competent, confident, compassionate, and more socially and academically responsible, they will have the ability to weigh and test options when faced with difficult challenges and conflicts. Moreover, they will be able to validate the existence of people who are different, and because they have true self-esteem, they will be inclined to bring others alongside as they pursue success.

Finally, *teens crave time* with the adults in their lives. Therefore, adults must invest the necessary time and energy in preparing the future adults for their roles in society. *Teen Smart!* provides adults who frequent the lives of teenagers with a meaningful tool to help accomplish the goal of a stronger, saner, more just society. Young people who work on the character-building lessons in this book will emerge with true self-esteem, constructive attitudes, and behaviors that help them work to increase positive human interaction and reduce conflict and divisiveness. This student-centered resource makes the task of training a society of givers not only possible, but easy, engaging, and enjoyable for students and the adults with whom they interact.

Saundrah Clark Grevious

CONTENTS

SECTION 1
FAMILY BONDING

===== ACTIVITIES =====

SECTION 2
CHARACTER DEVELOPMENT

―――――――――――――――――― **ACTIVITIES** ――――――――――――――――――

SECTION 3
COMMUNITY INVOLVEMENT

━━━━━━━━━━━━━━ **ACTIVITIES** ━━━━━━━━━━━━━━

SECTION 4
"IT TAKES A WHOLE VILLAGE TO RAISE A CHILD"

═════════════════════════ **ACTIVITIES** ═════════════════════════

SECTION 5
CHOICES, CHANGES, AND CHALLENGES

===================== **ACTIVITIES** =====================

BIBLIOGRAPHY

APPENDIX
READY-TO-USE ENRICHMENT ACTIVITIES

WHAT ARE THE OBJECTIVES OF *TEEN SMART!*?

Fortunately, our students are very aware of the many societal problems all around them. Unfortunately, they have anxieties about the extent to which they can handle the problems that they will inherit as they take over their adult roles. Despite the fact that adults do not always know how to solve societal problems, we must ease the anxieties of our children as they discover what to do about problems in their own environments. The solutions to these problems are found in education. The focused objectives found in *Teen Smart!*, therefore, provide leverage for educators who want to encourage young people to deal constructively with conflicts in their homes, schools, and communities. Through their use of these activities, teens will:

1. Explore family origin as a means of gaining self-identity.

2. Understand influences of family values, goals, and emotional, physical, and mental health.

3. Differentiate between positive self-esteem and arrogance.

4. Accept responsibility for helping to improve human relationships in personal environments.

5. Appreciate the similarities and differences among various races and cultures.

6. Respect the rights of others in making decisions.

7. Affirm the ongoing need for adopting acceptable forms of behavior.

8. Set meaningful goals and work toward them.

9. Analyze individual roles in protecting the welfare of all members of the community.

10. Maintain personal identity, promote diversity, and value human commonalties.

11. Identify specific causes of conflict and seek ways to prevent, mediate, or resolve them.

12. Understand functions of social institutions in meeting the needs of individuals and groups.

13. Create harmony in their various environments in which one moves.

14. Prepare to assume adult roles in the larger society.

15. Recognize the impact of early lifestyle choices on physical and mental health and well-being later in life.

16. Analyze the impact of stress and violence on physical and emotional health.

17. Accept opportunities to "start over" after suffering the consequences of past mistakes.

18. Promote the causes of freedom and equality for all ethnic, racial, and cultural groups.

19. Share feelings of positive self-esteem with others.

20. Value true self-esteem over materialism, and set goals, accordingly.

21. Develop critical-thinking skills via reading, writing, discussion, debate, and personal reflection.

22. Understand historical and contemporary perspectives on public and private issues.

23. Accept challenges to make positive contributions to society.

24. Experience personal and academic growth and development.

25. Develop leadership skills and awareness of emerging adult roles in society.

These objectives will help equip students to analyze and resolve conflicts that they really can do something about. Human relationships can be a source of many conflicts that would not normally occur if people had more respect for one another. However, people must feel good about themselves before they can begin to treat others with respect. These objectives are designed to begin the process of self-awareness and provide a rationale for using new levels of confidence to extend tolerance and respect to others.

Development of self-awareness is a multifaceted process that includes a personal value system. Knowing where we and our families stand on right and wrong, for example, helps us to establish what our action will be when faced with a choice between these two options. Because students need to internalize positive value systems and develop the intrinsic motivation to change negative behaviors, reinforcement of concepts is crucial. Subsequently, socialization and educational concepts that foster critical thinking skills are woven throughout the lessons.

As each student develops keen personal awareness, she or he will be ready to take control of and improve her or his circumstances, including relationships with other people. Altogether, the objectives provide a reason for students to consider others as important as themselves and to see this as the first step to extending mutual respect. Finally, the objectives are varied, engaging, and academically sound, and designed to ensure that all students will be able to accept the challenge of protecting the human dignity, freedom, and rights of all, including themselves. Exposure to these objectives and related activities, therefore, will encourage the development of positive attitudes—those needed for violence-reduction and improved human relationships in the new millennium.

FAMILY BONDING

INTRODUCTION

The activities in the "Family Bonding" section are designed to show young people that each individual's life has purpose and meaning; meaning that is first conveyed within the context of the family. The development of positive self-concepts occur within the family structure and decrease the vulnerability that many young people have to negative forces in society. Lessons are also designed to help students evaluate and validate who they are as well as honor their family heritage and traditions through interviews and interactions with family members. Specifically, students discover that it is within the family structure that they experience joy and develop self-esteem, self-determination, values, emotional support, and the survival skills that will help them as they venture out beyond the protection and the security of their homes. As they explore family culture, race, ethnicity, and accomplishments, students will recognize that their own personal identities, potential, and value systems emanate from the people closest to them.

In addition to developing and extending strong family connections, this section includes social skills to help students interact with people who are not immediate family members. The importance of emotional stability, intact lifestyles, and positive values to future generations is also addressed. As they work on the concepts, young people come to understand what is expected of them: the necessity of following rules, making sound decisions, controlling their environments, and planning for the future. The internalization of the concepts in this section of the book contributes to each young person's ability to do what is expected by increasing his or her level of self-confidence and preparing him or her for life in the larger community.

═══ ACTIVITIES ═══

TEACHER DIRECTIONS FOR SECTION 1 ACTIVITIES

1–1 WHEN I WAS YOUNG

Elicit from students memories of their very young years. Discuss some of the commonalties of their experiences—those things that transcend racial, ethic, and cultural lines. Have them share specific information regarding birth dates, weights, family traditions, first ice cream cone, favorite games or toys, learning experiences, siblings, and so on. *Give each student a copy of Activity 1-1, When I Was Young.*

1–2 DEFINING WHO I AM

Elicit from students some of their admirable traits and write a few examples of them on the board. Students will more than likely be happy to describe themselves as **kind** or **honest.** Then, ask them to share some traits that are not so admirable. For example, some students might admit to being **moody** or **selfish.** Have volunteers give definitions for and compare and contrast these traits. Ask students to consider their relationship with various people and indicate which traits are positive and which are negative. Discuss the fact that human relationships based on how concerned each person is about the feelings of other people are preferable to uncaring relationships. Ask students to share their opinions as to what could happen in society if every person began to show his or her positive traits more often. *Give each student a copy of Activity 1-2, Defining Who I Am.*

Then, ask each student to reflect on his or her personality and list and define a maximum of ten traits. From these, have each young person select five words to place on the Mind Map. Students should be able to write a composition based on their lists, definitions, and the completed mind maps explaining specific reasons why these traits reveal who they really are. Have students complete the activity sheets and write their compositions on the back of the activity sheets. Then ask students to share their written personality assessments and indicate how their positive traits will foster better human relationships at home, at school, and in the community. Encourage students to be creative in displaying their favorite personal attributes by making ID bracelets or by decorating notebook covers, brown lunch bags, ribbons, and so on.

1–3 AUTOBIOGRAPHICAL QUESTIONNAIRE

Ask students why the information that a person gathers about his or her family background is useful in gaining a stronger self-image. Have students use what they have learned from family interviews and their own personal experiences, hopes, and dreams to complete an autobiographical questionnaire. Engage the class in a time of sharing to reveal the richness of their commonalties and diversities. *Give each student a copy of Activity 1-3, Autobiographical Questionnaire.*

A final activity could be the writing and publication of the autobiographies— *but only if students are willing to publish them.* Invite them to share various aspects of their backgrounds, and have them draw inferences as to the richness of both their common and their diverse experiences. Assure students that if they note on their autobiographies that they do not want other students to read them, their autobiographies will be kept strictly private.

1–4 FAMILY NOTES

Students' ability to communicate with family members and the need to discover more about their own heritage provide the focal points of this activity. Elicit from students how family bonds can be tightened during the times when members can talk about who they are and how they feel about one another. Emphasize the value of family members being available to one another to talk and listen.

  Note: Encourage the sharing of positive family relationships. Personal issues that might have negative results for students and their families should be discouraged or referred to counselors or parents. *Give each student a copy of Activity 1-4, Family Notes.*

1–5 FAMILY GRIOT

Read a portion of Alex Haley's ROOTS to the class. (Have a few copies on hand for any students who might want to read it.) Identify the source of his knowledge about Kunta Kinte, his African ancestor. Point out that Alex Haley's aunt and grandmother had heard the stories from their parents—much as he was hearing them. They all carried the history of their ancestors in their heads; it was not written down. Introduce and define griot (gree-o). The griot was the family and/or village member who memorized and recited the stories of families in the African village where Haley's ancestor was born. Ask the students if there is someone in their family who knows about the history of their ancestors up to the present day. Have them identify this person as a "griot" and plan to set up an interview with this person and compile and disseminate the information to extended family members. If there is no family griot, read the details about Alex Haley's griot. Then, have each student act as the "griot" in his or her own family setting. *Give each student a copy of Activity 1-5, Family Griot.*

1–6 WHAT MY NAME MEANS TO ME

Share the origins and meanings of various given names. Ask students to interview parents and other family members about cultural traditions in choosing names. Elicit from students the difference between being able to select your child's name and being forced to accept someone else's choice of a name. Discuss the plight of slaves in early America who had little or no choice in the selection of their names. Have students tell what their names mean or their experiences with their names.

  (**Caution:** Be sensitive to genealogical information that might cause anxieties for some children or their families.) *Give each student a copy of Activity 1-6, What My Name Means to Me.*

1–7 GENEALOGY IDEAS AND RESEARCH YOUR ROOTS

Open the lines of communication about individual students' growth and development by having them investigate the genealogy of their families. Elicit from students the connections in their own family structure and the physiological, sociological, and geographical relationships among all humankind. *Give each student a copy of Activity 1-7, Genealogy Ideas and Research Your Roots.*

1–8   FAMILY MENU INTERVIEW

Extend the interview of family members to include specific kinds of foods that are indicative of the individual cultures of students in the class. Discuss foods that are family favorites: traditional dishes in that recipes have been passed down from one generation to another. Some dishes are just consumed because they taste good. In other cases, ethnicity or culture dictates the kinds of foods eaten in a family. Ask students to share information about those foods that have something to do with religious beliefs, for example, kosher foods in the Jewish tradition. Have students interview a family member about foods served in their families. Suggest that favorite recipes can be brought in and shared with the class. Consider the publication of a multiethnic recipes cookbook. *Give each student a copy of Activity 1-8, Family Menu Interview.*

1–9   ROOTS FOR FUTURE GENERATIONS

Elicit self-knowledge information from each student. Ask students to respond to such questions as: "How do you spend your time? What are your hobbies? Do you have special skills or talents? What are some things that are very important to you? What do you know about your ancestors, including your grandparents? What kinds of artifacts do you possess that would reveal unique information about your family history and culture?" Ask students to give one word, idea, or article that, if saved, would provide their offspring with information and insight about them. Indicate to students that concrete, purposeful actions are paramount to words. Therefore, encourage students to actually begin to put things away in a safe place for future generations. Discuss the words: heirloom, memento, antique, collector's item, and others that you may think of. Discuss how people react to historical discoveries today and how their current possessions will be history for their children. *Give each student a copy of Activity 1-9, Roots for Future Generations.*

1–10   FAMILY FAVORITES

The experiences of each student result in the development of his or her cultural heritage. Validate each student by encouraging him or her to share family favorites. (**Note:** Be aware of the need for students to keep private family matters to themselves.) *Give each student a copy of Activity 1-10, Family Favorites.*

1–11   START A FAMILY TRADITION: WRITE A PROGRESSIVE FAMILY LETTER

Discuss the fun of receiving letters, as indicated by the letters that many students write to each other during the course of every middle school and high school day. Elicit from students how families enjoy learning about the good things that are happening with various members. List some of these ideas on the board. (**Note:** This is not the same thing as a chain letter. Chain letters are usually from strangers and threaten negative consequences for those who fail to send them on. This is a letter to be sent from one relative to another with no threats or penalties attached.) Ask students to start a tradition in their family by writing the first letter, which will go around to all members. *Give each student a copy of Activity 1-11, Start a Family Tradition: Write a Progressive Family Letter.*

1–12 ACCENTUATE THE POSITIVE

Choosing friends and deciding with whom one wants to spend time are very personal choices. Elicit from all students the criteria they use for selecting friends. Encourage them to discuss how they feel about the people they've chosen to spend time with. Challenge them to attach meaning to their feelings by using certain kinds of punctuation. For example, a friend who is very important to someone might be described with excitement or enthusiasm. If this description were in writing, it might be punctuated with an exclamation point. For example, "I really like having Jane as a friend because she is always there for me!" or "My mother sees to it that I have enough food to eat every day." Note that this statement of fact is punctuated with a period. Discuss that individuals can communicate a great deal in their human relationships with the kinds of emphasis (punctuation) they use in speaking and in writing. *Give each student a copy of Activity 1-12, Accentuate the Positive.*

1–13 MY GIFT TO YOU

Elicit from students the variety of ways that people can show appreciation and the extent to which saying "thank you" can be mutually beneficial. Have them identify specific gifts of appreciation, especially those that cost nothing to give (a smile, a handshake, a letter, an original story or poem, a pretty seashell or stone, a box decorated with foil or comics, a song recorded on cassette, a videotaped message, time, etc.) Ask students to develop a list of people in their families or community to whom they would like to show appreciation. Suggest parents, nurse, custodian, secretary, teachers' aides, bus drivers, principals, friends, librarians, or coaches. Have them indicate some reasons that they want to show appreciation: the coach because she believed that I could make the team and told me exactly what I needed to do, the teacher's aide because he came to me every day and asked me in what areas of study I needed help, my parents because they are always supportive, even when I make mistakes. *Give each student a copy of Activity 1-13, My Gift to You.*

1–14 MY PORTFOLIO

Ask students to share their most positive personal talents, skills, accomplishments, and attributes. Discuss family influences on the development of their skills and talents. Elicit from them specific and tangible examples of some of their accomplishments and inquire as to the value of sharing these things with other people. EXAMPLE: ITEM 1—WINNER OF POETRY AWARD; POSITIVE ATTRIBUTE— CREATIVITY. Discuss the importance of including these positive things in their résumés and job or college applications. Emphasize the need for recognizing and rewarding symbols of the talents of young people who will someday use their positive attributes as members of adult society. Have students share how their talents and skills should form the basis for résumés and other documents. *Give each student a copy of Activity 1-14, My Portfolio.*

1–15 WHAT MAKES YOU TICK?

Ask students to share times when they might have been misunderstood or wrongly accused. Elicit from them the impact that these experiences might have on people who find themselves targets of distrust and suspicion. Discuss feelings of anger, disappointment, regret, and revenge. Ask students whether or not these feelings are destructive. Write the words "Ticks Me Off" on the board and ask for definitions. Then, pose a scenario to which most teenagers can relate. "When you and some of your friends are gathered at the mall, a police officer stops and threatens to take the whole group to jail. How will you react to the suspicions of the police officer? Will you let anger overcome reason and make the situation worse, or will you ask for permission to call and get help from home?" Discuss this and other kinds of experiences (at home and in the larger society) that cause some young people to become angry and resentful. Have students compare these times to the positive feelings they get when they are valued by adults and peers. Elicit from them the need to handle these situations wisely, rather than becoming "ticked off" and causing more trouble. *Give each student a copy of Activity 1-15, What Makes You Tick?*

1–16 You've Got the Power!

Inquire as to whether students have heard of the V-chip, which is designed to help parents prevent their children from tuning in to inappropriate television programs. Ask students to imagine that they are counselors and can protect their peers and others from becoming victims of dangerous or uncomfortable experiences. As part of this protective power, each student would also be able to provide sound advice for peers who might otherwise make poor choices. Indicate that they all have the power to exhibit and encourage modesty, personal pride, and high expectations on the part of their counselees. Have them recognize, as well, that their advice will have the power to protect their counselees from physical, emotional, and spiritual harm. Pose the following scenario for students to consider: One of Harry's friends has asked him to join in with him and two other people in spray-painting offensive slurs on a local religious institution. Harry has never been involved in anything like this; however, he really doesn't want to lose friends or risk being called a coward. What advice will you give to Harry? Allow students to discuss the details and project a logical outcome. *Give each student a copy of Activity 1-16, You've Got the Power!*

1–17 Just Do What's Right!

As observers and participants in human relationships, students can be challenged to put themselves in another person's place as a way to decide how to treat someone. When it comes to each person's ability to make someone else feel good or bad, it's important to know what to say, how to say it, or not to say anything at all. In addition, it might mean that a person who has a tendency to "show off" should be aware of how such behavior could make another person feel inferior. Ask students to consider the fact that not one person on earth is perfect, but that everyone can, based on his or her values, select from a series of actions and choose those behaviors that are right. Doing what is right can range from getting involved in certain situations to ignoring and staying out of other situations. Give students the opportunity to respond to each of the following scenarios: A student attending classes at your school is a dwarf and is subjected to daily teasing and taunting. What is the right thing for YOU to do? Recent newscasts have reported an influx of immigrants into the state and immigrant students in your classes are being rejected by others. What is the right thing to do? Someone has been writing racial slurs and drawing hate symbols on the walls of the bathrooms in the school. What is the right thing to do? *Give each student a copy of Activity 1-17, Just Do What's Right!*

1–18 BOTTLED MESSAGES

Many students write letters to friends during school and convey their personal feelings on many issues. Discuss how important communication is in human relationships, and have students offer various ways that people learn about one another. Ask them to give their opinions regarding the most effective methods of communicating in today's world. List E-mail, express mail, telegrams, long-distance and local telephone calling, beepers, and any other methods you or they come up with. Ask each student to write a letter describing some exciting or important aspects of his or her life for a stranger. *Give each student a copy of Activity 1-18, Bottled Messages.*

1–19 COLD STARES AND WARM SMILES

"Actions speak louder than words" is a motto that many students will recognize. Offer them an opportunity to tell what it means to them and to share experiences that prove this statement true. For example, most people have had the experience of a parent's looking at them a certain way—and they know exactly what that look means. Others know what it means to have someone place his or her finger over closed lips, indicating the need to be quiet. (**Note:** Caution students not to hesitate to use words when necessary, especially in emergency situations.) Discuss the fact that there are people who cannot speak and must always rely on nonverbal communication. Elicit from students how they can become more aware of those who have special needs. Discuss ways that nonverbal communication can be used to give both comfort and pain, and the need for people to be considerate of others in order to reduce pain and increase comfort. *Give each student a copy of Activity 1-19, Cold Stares and Warm Smiles.*

1–20 WHY ARE YOU SPECIAL?

Ask students about their preferences in music, food, dance, vacation spots, amusement parks, sports, or other entertainment. Indicate the beauty of their individual choices. Human diversity makes life richer, for example, as people get to taste a variety of ethnic foods, learn a variety of types of music, and enjoy many different types of ethnic attire. Ask how they as individuals are special people and valuable as resources for those who want to learn more about them and the richness of humankind in general. *Give each student a copy of Activity 1-20, Why Are You Special?*

NAME _____ DATE _____

WHEN I WAS YOUNG

Teenagers often think of themselves as young adults with their childhood far behind them. Most teens can remember a special birthday party, an athletic or academic competition, a recital, a spelling bee, a dramatization, a family outing, or a number of other pleasant experiences. Often, family members take pictures of these events.

Paste a copy of a picture of yourself engaged in a special activity when you were younger. If you don't have a photo, you can draw a picture. Describe the event and how your childhood was made memorable because of it. Be sure to identify family members, friends, and acquaintances who were with you. Have fun sharing your memories with your peers. If you need extra space, use the other side of this page.

Date of Picture: _____

Event: _____

Names of People: _____

_____

Description: _____

_____

_____

© 1999 by John Wiley & Sons, Inc.

8

NAME _____ DATE _____

DEFINING WHO I AM

What are your personality traits? Which words above best describe how you are when you are alone and when you are with other people? Using a dictionary or your own knowledge of word meanings, briefly define a minimum of 8 of the words. Then, from this list, select a minimum of 5 words that define YOU. Write these words on my MIND MAP and explain why they represent the kind of person you are.

Leader • creative • musical • funny • impulsive • agreeable • honest
shy • spiritual bad • thoughtful • loving • family-oriented • energetic
upbeat • brave • hardworking dependable • moody • realistic • haughty
friendly • vulnerable • aggressive • compassionate • kind • biased
independent • greedy • happy • unkind • fearless • peaceful • tolerant
respectable • violent • focused

WORD	DEFINITION	WORD	DEFINITION
1. _____	_____	5. _____	_____
	_____		_____
2. _____	_____	6. _____	_____
	_____		_____
3. _____	_____	7. _____	_____
	_____		_____
4. _____	_____	8. _____	_____
	_____		_____

MY MIND MAP

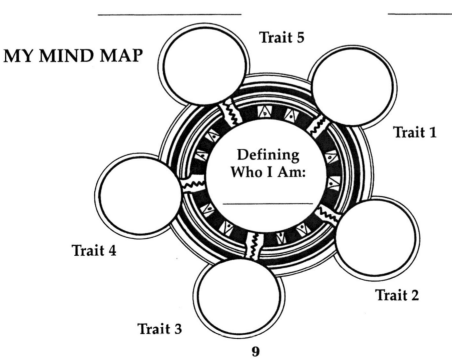

Trait 5

Trait 1

Defining
Who I Am:

_____

Trait 2

Trait 3

Trait 4

1–3

NAME _____   DATE _____

AUTOBIOGRAPHICAL QUESTIONNAIRE

When people see something about themselves in writing, they have a clearer idea of who they are, and they know more about how others see them. The first step in the process of writing your autobiography or your life story is to complete the questionnaire below. Once finished, write your autobiography on the computer or in your notebook.

1. Name _____

2. Birth Date _____

3. Place of Birth _____

4. Language(s) _____
   _____

5. Parents or Guardians _____
   _____

6. Siblings* _____
   _____
   _____
   _____

7. Other Family Members and Friends
   _____
   _____
   _____
   _____

8. Religion _____

9. Hobbies _____
   _____
   _____

10. Favorite Book(s) _____
    _____
    _____

11. Favorite Sport(s) _____
    _____
    _____

_____
* Brothers or sisters.

10

NAME _____ **DATE** _____

12. Talent(s) _____
_____
_____

13. Other _____
_____
_____

14. Educational/personal goals _____
_____
_____

15. Five words that describe me best _____
_____

16. Someone I would trust with a personal problem _____
_____

17. Activities I would like to do in school _____
_____
_____

18. My best friend is _____

19. If I had three wishes they would be _____
_____
_____

20. My outlook on life _____
_____

21. The person I most admire _____

22. If I had only one piece of advice to give, it would be _____
_____
_____

23. I am most confident when _____
_____

24. Other _____
_____
_____

NAME _____ DATE _____

FAMILY NOTES

Interview your mother, father, or other family members about how they felt when you were born. *Feel free to add your own questions to those below. As you talk with your parents or guardians, think about the importance of the time that you're spending together. Record responses of the interviewees on the lines.

1. How did you feel the day I was born? _____

2. Did you know anything about me before I was born? _____
_____

3. Who came to pick us up at the hospital, or was I born at home or in an unusual place?
_____

4. Do you remember my birth weight, length, your reactions, and so on? _____
_____

5. What were the reactions of other family members? _____
_____

6. What were my first words? _____

7. What sorts of things made me smile or giggle? _____

8. How did I happen to first crawl, stand up, or walk? _____

9. What five words would you use to describe my early personality traits?
_____

10. What are some of your fondest memories of me? _____
_____

*ADDITIONAL QUESTIONS

1. _____
2. _____
3. _____
4. _____

NAME _____ DATE _____

FAMILY GRIOT

Alex Haley, author of ROOTS, listened to his aunt and grandmother when he was a little boy. He loved the stories they told of his early African relatives. Alex especially liked to hear them talk about Kunta Kinte, who was snatched from his African village by slave traders and brought to America. Listening to these stories made Alex curious about his African homeland and his African ancestors, so when he grew up, he searched for information about his past. He went to Africa and again he listened.

Alex Haley heard a village storyteller, a griot (gree-o), recite the history of his family. The griot's mind was like a computer as he told of important events—births, deaths, wars, slave traders, and so forth. When the griot said the name Kunta Kinte, Alex Haley knew that he had found his roots.

Do you have a griot in your family? Do you listen to people who talk about your family's history? How many things can you remember about family events, celebrations, births, vacations, inventions, surprises, and so on? Become the griot in your family by completing the information below:

MY FAMILY HISTORY AS TOLD BY _____ , FAMILY GRIOT

_____

_____

_____

_____

_____

_____

_____

_____

_____

_____

_____

_____

_____

_____

_____

_____

CHALLENGE: Read Alex Haley's novel ROOTS and discuss emerging family themes with peers. Consider writing your family's history, and use these notes as your first piece of research.

NAME _____ DATE _____

WHAT MY NAME MEANS TO ME

Explore the origin of your name with a family member. For example, were you named for a close relative, friend, celebrity, or special occasion? Is there a cultural tradition regarding the naming of babies in your family?* Discuss these questions with a parent or guardian. Write your full name on the lines below.

First Name _____

Middle Name _____

Last Name _____

1. What is the origin of my name? _____

2. What cultural traditions contributed to your selection of my name?

_____

_____

In the greatly acclaimed saga, ROOTS, by Alex Haley, the main character was taken from his homeland of Africa and renamed by slavemasters. He found it difficult to give up his real name of Kunta Kinte. In the story, he was beaten as the slavemasters tried to force him to take the name "Toby." They called him "Toby," but he never forgot who he was. Describe what your name means to you on the lines below. What would you do if someone tried to force you to change your name? Share your comments with your peers.

WHAT MY

NAME

MEANS TO ME

_____

_____

_____

_____

_____

© 1999 by John Wiley & Sons, Inc.

* Many Native Americans had different names at different points in their lives. Some names were based on character traits, talents, accomplishments, or nature. If you were to choose a name for yourself right now, what might it be? Why would you enjoy having that name now?

NAME _____ DATE _____

GENEALOGY IDEAS
BACKGROUND INFORMATION

It can be fun to find out more about your family—your roots! Here are some ideas to get you started:

1. Begin by asking questions of older members of the family. Get a notebook and record their answers.

2. Be a very good listener. As people talk, try to remember what they say and how it relates to you and your history.

3. Be an observer. Whom do you look like? Find family photographs. Ask permission to organize them. If you are adopted or live with guardians, don't be afraid to ask questions, observe, and work to get more information. The people you live with are your family.

4. Take your time and find out about ONE BRANCH of the family at a time.

5. Your country has a history. America is filled with immigrants from countries all over the world. Ask people in your family about their national origin. Their answers will give you more information about your country.

6. Begin your search for your roots by asking questions about the family NAME.

7. Next, ask about DATES and PLACES OF BIRTH.

8. Find out about MARRIAGES.

9. Find out about OFFSPRING (children).

10. Find out about DEATHS.

11. Find out about MOVES TO OTHER LOCATIONS.

12. Write letters to out-of-town relatives for more information. Have a special place for your notebook and letters.

13. Go to the courthouse and look up historical documents about your family.

14. Use technology as well. Find appropriate places on the Internet to trace your family history.

15. Read about genealogy in the book DO PEOPLE GROW ON FAMILY TREES? GENEALOGY FOR KIDS & OTHER BEGINNERS (The Official Ellis Island Handbook), by Ira Wolfman, with a foreword by Alex Haley. New York: 1991. Workman Publishing, Illustrations by Michael Klein.

Name _____ Date _____

RESEARCH YOUR ROOTS

Complete this genealogy chart, beginning
with yourself. Work backward in time to your
earliest ancestor who came to the United States.
If your family has recently come to America, include
as many of your ancestors as you wish, by recording
them on the back of this sheet.

MY FAMILY TREE

_____
My Name

_____   _____
Mother's Name   Father's Name

Born _____   Born _____
Where _____   Where _____
Married _____   Married _____
Where _____   Where _____

_____   _____
Grandfather   Grandmother

Born _____   Born _____
Where _____   Where _____
Married _____   Married _____
Where _____   Where _____
Died _____   Died _____
Where _____   Where _____

_____   _____
Grandfather   Grandmother

Born _____   Born _____
Where _____   Where _____
Married _____   Married _____
Where _____   Where _____
Died _____   Died _____
Where _____   Where _____

NAME _____ DATE _____

FAMILY MENU INTERVIEW

Interview a member of your family who knows something about foods that have been eaten in your family for many years. Share the results with your classmates. Use the questions below, or write some of your own.

Name of the family member (friend, guardian, etc.)

_____

Date of the interview _____

1. What are some of the foods that have been eaten in our family for many years?

   _____   _____
   _____   _____
   _____   _____

2. Which of these dishes is your favorite? Why?

   _____
   _____
   _____

3. Do you have other favorites? Is so, describe them and give the reasons for your choices.

   _____
   _____
   _____
   _____

4. How have you been able to keep these and other dishes as traditions in the family?

   _____
   _____
   _____
   _____

NAME _____ DATE _____

5. Have the traditional foods we eat in our family been "Americanized," or are they just like they were in the "old country" (authentic)?

_____

_____

_____

6. On what occasions are ethnic foods that reflect our cultural heritage used in our family?

_____

_____

_____

SUMMARY OF INTERVIEW

Favorite Foods	Origin	Occasion	Authentic (Yes or No)
1.			
2.			
3.			
4.			
5.			

NOTE: Flavors in some ethnic foods have been changed because some foreign spices and ingredients are not available in America. When original spices and other ingredients are replaced with American substitutes, the dishes become "Americanized."

Write a paragraph explaining something new that you learned as a result of this interview. Also, indicate how you and your family have contributed to the richness of the various types of foods eaten by Americans.

_____

_____

_____

_____

_____

_____

_____

_____

NAME _____   DATE _____

ROOTS FOR FUTURE GENERATIONS

Begin to save things that describe who you
are as a person. Someone just might be
interested someday. Plan a display of
your collection. Use the checklist as you collect items:

_____ 1. Save some personal items such
as letters, cards, pictures, a favorite
poem, an old keepsake, your baby shoes,
a toy from a Cracker Jack box.

_____ 2. Save a family tree; include pictures of yourself and other family members.

_____ 3. Write down some of the things you like to do—painting, dancing, hobbies,
quilting, reading, traveling, singing, playing games.

_____ 4. Record your voice on a cassette tape. You could be reading a story, singing a
song, or having a conversation with someone. Identify yourself and give the
date. It might be fun to give the weather and one or two news reports.

_____ 5. Locate your family's name in the telephone book. Include this page in your
collection.

_____ 6. Include honors, awards, news articles, trophies, publications, invitations, and
certificates.

REMEMBER TO:

• ALWAYS ASK PERMISSION BEFORE YOU INCLUDE FAMILY ITEMS WITH YOUR
OWN.

• FEEL FREE TO EXPAND THIS LIST. FOR THE SAKE OF FUTURE GENERATIONS,
KEEP YOUR COLLECTION GOING.

• FIND A SAFE PLACE FOR YOUR MEMENTOS . . . . . . HAVE FUN!!!

NAME _____ DATE _____

FAMILY FAVORITES

You are a product of the experiences you have in your family. Although families have lots of things in common, your family is not exactly like any other. This is because each family has its own routines, traditions, ethnic heritage, and other things that make it special. Make a list of things below that shows how your family is unique.

1. Favorite words your family uses often. Include idioms, quotations, one-liners, and phrases that describe your family members (sense of life, e.g., "Bill always knows how to fix things.").

    _____

    _____

    _____

2. Favorite family foods

    _____

    _____

    _____

    _____

3. Favorite family stories

    _____

    _____

    _____

    _____

4. Favorite family events and activities

    _____

    _____

    _____

    _____

5. Favorite family pastimes

    _____

    _____

    _____

Compare and contrast your preferences with those of your peers. Then, take your list home to share with family members.

NAME _____ DATE _____

START A FAMILY TRADITION: WRITE A PROGRESSIVE FAMILY LETTER

With the cost of telephone calls soaring, friends and relatives can keep in touch by writing to each other. When people live far apart, it is fun to write notes, letters, or E-mail. Letter writing can even be fun when family members and friends live in the same neighborhood or in the same house.

Write to someone in the space provided—or get another sheet of paper, a postcard, or a blank greeting card. Then, begin to write your first entry in your progressive letter. (Some people like to record messages on cassette tapes; you might choose this method of communication.) The greatest benefit of a progressive letter is that it can be passed around until every inch of space is filled. Remember to date your entries. When the first sheet is complete, start a new one. Include as many writers as you can. What great mementos these letters can be five to ten years from now! Assign one person to keep "completed" letters in a binder for future reference.

Date _____

Dear _____,

_____

_____

_____

_____

_____

_____

_____

_____

_____

_____

Love,

_____

P.S. I like the idea of writing back and forth using one sheet. Let's see how fast we can cover the empty spaces. Oh, I forgot to tell you . . . !

NAME _____ DATE _____

ACCENTUATE THE POSITIVE

As you relate to other people, you have many different kinds of reactions based on several premises—your individual experiences, your values, your preferences, your goals, your hopes, your accomplishments, and so on. Think about several people with whom you regularly come into contact, including family, friends, acquaintances, bosses, and teachers. Consider the most positive comment that you can make about these people. Then, use specific types of punctuation to describe your ideas about, feelings and concerns for, or your overall relationship with these individuals. Include information about how they have influenced you. Use the following types of punctuation to vividly convey your descriptions.

Period (.) for a statement of fact

Comma (,) for a series of ideas

Question Mark (?) for a question

Exclamation Point (!) for excitement

Semicolon (;) for connecting two related ideas

Colon (:) for a list

My Grandma understands me!!

ACCENTUATING THE POSITIVE PEOPLE IN MY LIFE

Person 1	Person 2	Person 3
Person 4	**Person 5**	**Person 6**

Explain how and why punctuation helps to communicate your feelings accurately.

NAME _____ DATE _____

MY GIFT TO YOU

Birthdays, holidays, anniversaries, reunions, graduations, and other celebrations often require gifts for loved ones. Has it ever occurred to you that gifts do not have to cost money? Some of the best gifts cost nothing. People spend money on things that might break, wear out, or get lost. The memory of a smile, however, lingers on, as do precious time, good conversation, or a cheerful letter. A senior citizen was elated at receiving a Certificate of Honor from people who loved her and celebrated her life. Think of someone you would like to honor or celebrate and present this person with a Certificate of Honor. Then, make a list of gifts that cost no money but give much joy.

Certificate of Honor

Presented to _____

in appreciation for _____

_____

_____

_____

_____

Signed _____   Date _____

MY LIST OF GIFTS THAT COST NO MONEY

_____   _____   _____

_____   _____   _____

NAME _____ DATE _____

MY PORTFOLIO

As you grow and develop into adulthood, what accomplishments represent who you are and what you are capable of? If in applying to prospective colleges, you were to send certain tangible items to the Admissions Office to persuade them to accept you, what items would be in this special collection? Your portfolio should have only the most important symbols: those things that advertise your academic, social, and personal achievements.

Label the tab of each portfolio with specific notations that signal who you are, what you have accomplished, and your potential for success. Include awards, report card grades, certificates, news articles, photos, essays, poetry, standardized test scores, artwork, and so forth. Be certain to highlight how each item reflects YOUR POSITIVE ATTRIBUTES.

PORTFOLIO ITEM 1:
_____
Personal Attribute: _____
_____

PORTFOLIO ITEM 2:
_____
Personal Attribute: _____
_____

PORTFOLIO ITEM 3:
_____
Personal Attribute: _____
_____

PORTFOLIO ITEM 4:
_____
Personal Attribute: _____
_____

PORTFOLIO ITEM 5:
_____
Personal Attribute: _____
_____

Share your portfolio with classmates, family, and mentors.

© 1999 by John Wiley & Sons, Inc.

NAME _____ DATE _____

WHAT MAKES YOU TICK?

Do you mean what ticks me off?

What things make you glad to be alive? What experiences cause you to try a little harder? On the other hand, what makes you angry, unhappy, or willing to give up? Rate the things on the list below according to the following:

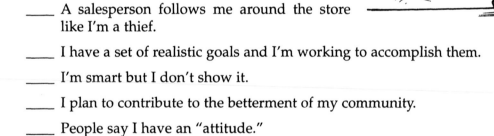

1 For things that make you really happy and excited about contributing to your own progress

2 For things that make little difference to you

3 For things that cause great trouble for you—cause you to become angry, aggressive, embarrassed, or withdrawn

_____ A salesperson follows me around the store like I'm a thief.

_____ I have a set of realistic goals and I'm working to accomplish them.

_____ I'm smart but I don't show it.

_____ I plan to contribute to the betterment of my community.

_____ People say I have an "attitude."

_____ I get A's and B's on my report card.

_____ People I admire give me compliments.

_____ I am able to think for myself.

_____ People misunderstand me.

_____ I wanted to ask this guy out, but a more popular girl beat me to it.

_____ Because I'm an honest person, I can live with myself.

_____ Some people scalp tickets.

_____ I didn't make the football team.

_____ The career I'm thinking about has many opportunities.

_____ My heart beats so fast when I ask a question in class.

_____ A lot of towns have curfews for teenagers.

_____ People who cheat on tests get better grades than I do.

NAME _____ DATE _____

YOU'VE GOT THE POWER!

Pretend that you have reached adulthood and that you are one of the many responsible people in society. As an adult, you have the wisdom and the power to give teenagers advice when they face different kinds of problems. Read each scenario and select a letter to indicate the kind of advice that is appropriate for each situation. Write the letter on the lines.

YOU CAN MAKE A DIFFERENCE

ADVICE	SITUATIONS/PROBLEMS
	1 _____
A. Talk to a priest, a minister, or a rabbi.	Jan's mother and father have restricted her TV viewing time, especially on weekends. Jan resents this decision.
	2 _____
B. Speak to your teacher.	As a foster child, Josh has never been a candidate for adoption. He feels that various foster parents have used him. He wants someone to love him for who he is.
	3 _____
C. Listen to a supportive friend.	Sam has a crush on Amy, and she knows it. She doesn't really like him, but she flirts with him and laughs at him when she's with her friends. Sam is hurt.
	4 _____
D. Talk to an older relative.	The American flag is important to Kim as a symbol of freedom for all U.S. citizens. He is disappointed and upset when some of his fellow students don't say the Pledge.
	5 _____
E. Explain your feelings to the other person(s).	A new boy has moved next door to you. His dislike for some races and ethnic groups is obvious by the things he says. While he does not seem to be violent, he is spreading hate.

Share with your peers times when you've offered sound advice with good results.

NAME _____ DATE _____

JUST DO WHAT'S RIGHT

No person is perfect. No one knows all of the answers to the questions of life, but we all have the ability to do our very best to make life better for ourselves. Doing what is right and doing your best require caring for others as well as for yourself. Caring might mean that you need to get involved and act on someone else's behalf. Based on your beliefs and values, decide whether you would get involved in the events described below. Use the codes to indicate the right choices.

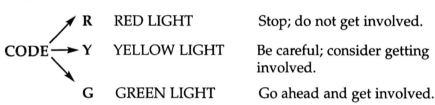

CODE

R	RED LIGHT	Stop; do not get involved.
Y	YELLOW LIGHT	Be careful; consider getting involved.
G	GREEN LIGHT	Go ahead and get involved.

1.____ A computer whiz at your school knows how to break into the system and change report card grades.

2.____ A student from another state enrolls in your class and some bullies want to beat him up.

3.____ The teacher has forgotten to collect the homework assignment, and you haven't done it. Some kids are upset when one student reminds the teacher about the homework.

4.____ A friend's parents have gone away for the weekend. He knows that it would be wrong to have a party, but others have talked him into having a party.

5.____ A community group wants to raise funds for blankets for the homeless, and they've asked teenagers to volunteer to help.

6.____ The media often promote inappropriate programming that includes violence, disrespectful behavior, and sexual activities.

7.____ Nadia doesn't have the nicest clothes to wear to school, and some of the kids make fun of her.

8.____ Several people in your neighborhood are trying to drive an immigrant family away.

9.____ A girl that you don't particularly like is being picked on. They say she's a show off and deserves it.

10.____ Because the baseball team lost the championship game, they are being called "the Losers."

NAME _____ DATE _____

BOTTLED MESSAGES

Imagine that you are walking on a beach and a bottle washes up on the shore. You notice that there is a piece of paper in the bottle, and you open it and begin to read about the life of a person your age. Somehow, you feel connected to this person from another time and another place.

Consider who you are and the many experiences you've had since your early childhood. Think about vivid, humorous, and interesting things you've experienced. Describe your environment, your family, and your neighborhood. Try to capture some of the most exciting images in the world around you and write your own message. Plan to place it in a bottle and send it out to sea.

MY MESSAGE FOR A BOTTLE

_____

_____

_____

_____

_____

_____

_____

_____

_____

_____

_____

_____

NAME _____   DATE _____

COLD STARES AND WARM SMILES

"Actions speak louder than words." This statement can be used to convey the idea that people don't always have to use words to get their messages across. If you want some-one to leave you alone, you might walk away without saying a word. If a person you know well makes you very angry, you might try a long, cold stare to communicate your feelings. A smile and a handshake are universal signals of friendliness.

   Think about how you might handle the following situations without having to use words. Select from among these choices:

    A. I would walk away

    B. I would stare coldly

    C. I would ignore him or her

    D. I would shake his or her hand and smile

    E. I would _____

_____ 1. Someone you have a crush on looks at you for the first time.

_____ 2. It's your brother's turn to do the dishes, and he asks you to do them.

_____ 3. A person approaches you with drugs.

_____ 4. A friend asks you to let him copy your homework because he hasn't done his.

_____ 5. The principal of the school compliments you because your report card grades are steadily improving.

_____ 6. A person accidentally brushes up against you and doesn't apologize.

_____ 7. Your mother insists that you must clean your room before you can go to the mall.

_____ 8. A person contacts you on the Internet and asks you out.

_____ 9. A member of a gang is trying to recruit new members and asks you to meet the gang after school.

___10. An acquaintance told her parents that she was invited to your house for dinner. Her parents called your house looking for their daughter and she was not there. You will see her at school in the morning.

NAME _____ DATE _____

WHY ARE YOU SPECIAL?

You are a special person; you are unique among the millions of human beings on the earth. Even though commonalties exist among us, individual qualities, experiences, and preferences make it possible to distinguish one person from another.

    Within each category on the chart, identify specific things that YOU prefer. Include the reasons for your preferences.

HOBBIES	TRAVEL	SPORTS/RECREATION
FOOD	**BOOKS/MAGAZINES**	**ENTERTAINMENT**

    Discuss individual preferences with your peers. Note that many preferences and experiences transcend racial, gender, and cultural lines.

CHARACTER DEVELOPMENT

INTRODUCTION

Self-discovery is basic to positive changes in one's character. The activities in the Character Development section reveal some of the turbulence and stress of adolescence. Because conduct, current value systems, and personality traits can be indicators of the kind of citizens teenagers will be in the future, young people must explore their own viewpoints, character, and reactions to outside influences. These explorations or self-examinations will help them to get a sense of who and what they are today, and get a firm grasp on how their current identities and standards of behavior might influence the kind of adults they will become. This section offers ways of identifying negative traits that might become entrenched and learning how to control and/or change attitudes and behaviors that might eventually prove detrimental. Students will explore their perspectives on such issues as right or wrong, violence, nonviolence, work, leisure, education, materialism, honesty, compassion, deceit, relationships, and environment.

The activities in the Character Development section also advance students' knowledge of the concept of character and their ability to recognize and develop positive character traits. Self-discovery and self-examination are crucial elements in character-building. Moreover, lessons in original and contemporary prose and poetry convey the significance of inner strength and encouragement for students to become good, contributing members of society. Ultimately, students who are able to identify with and embrace the ideas and concepts that challenge them to think and act rationally will be less vulnerable as they make the transition from adolescence to adulthood.

Strategies for combatting temptations and avoiding some of the challenges of adolescence are inherent in these character-building lessons.

ACTIVITIES

ACTIVITIES
Continued

TEACHER DIRECTIONS
FOR SECTION 2 ACTIVITIES

2–1 BUILT-IN CONTROLS—YOU'RE IN CHARGE!

Write the following question on the board and give students a few minutes to think about it. "Which means more to you as a teenager—the opportunity to be a group member or the opportunity to be an individual and think for yourself?" Discuss their viewpoints and pose the scenario of two teenagers faced with the dilemma of breaking a rule. One implies that it would be okay to do something wrong or dangerous, and the other teenager has to consider his value system, which tells him that he shouldn't. He faces the possible loss of a friend if he doesn't break the rule. Pose a specific conflict and have the students role-play the dilemma. Elicit from students the need for people to have the kind of character that causes them to decide *not* to do something wrong because they have *self-control* and *the ability to resist peer pressure*. Discuss the extent to which people who don't have self-control infringe upon the rights and freedoms of other citizens. Have them think about the large measures of responsibility that each person must assume if "freedom and justice for all" is to become a reality. Does this quote indicate that individuals should also think of personal freedoms and the right to say NO when asked to participate in dangerous, unwise, or unhealthy activities? Have students reflect on the kind of society that could prevail if people considered not only their own rights but those of their fellow citizens as well. How can self-control contribute to self-esteem for individuals? Discuss this question before and after the worksheets are completed. *Give each student a copy of Activity 2-1, Built-In Controls—You're in Charge!*

2–2 THE WORDS YOU SPEAK

Have students comment on ways in which mental stress can add to or subtract from the quality of life. Have them give a few examples of internal stress that might result in external conflicts. For example, taking a test, trying out for a team or the band, auditioning for a play, learning how to drive, or getting an after-school job. What are some words or actions that can be expected if these stressful situations do not work out well for the individuals involved? Instead of reacting negatively, what are some appropriate words and actions that can improve the situation or, at least, make the person feel better? Discuss how people need to think before they speak or act. Place the words INAPPROPRIATE and APPROPRIATE on the chalkboard, and ask students to focus on the kinds of things people should say in response to harsh, negative words. Write one or two inappropriate statements and have students provide one or two appropriate statements to help counteract the impact of the negative words. Two examples are:

INAPPROPRIATE	APPROPRIATE
1. That new kid has a big nose.	1. Maybe he has, but he's the best football player on the team.

INAPPROPRIATE	APPROPRIATE
2. I failed that Math test. It was too difficult.	2. Now I know that I have to ask for extra help if I don't understand something completely when it is taught.

Give each student a copy of Activity 2-2, The Words You Speak.

2–3 TOUCH MY TONE

So often young adults wonder whether their opinions or ideas matter to adults or their peers. Offer each student an opportunity to bring up an issue that is very important to him or her and to explain why his or her position would help to improve life. Elicit from students some of the questions they would ask other people about issues that cause societal conflict. Then, ask students to share their responses to these questions. For example, the questions regarding doctor-assisted suicide for terminally ill patients need answers from reasonable people. Have them consider the fact that doctors take an oath that requires them to try to heal people. What are the contradictions between this oath and the effort of a physician to help people end their lives? Ask students to share what they would put on a recording to powerful politicians who could pass laws in support or nonsupport of this and other controversial issues in society. Encourage them to include persuasive techniques that could help to change the attitudes of those who do not share their opinions. Have students discuss the extent to which their views might impact on themselves and others as they mature and become adults. *Give each student a copy of Activity 2-3, Touch My Tone.*

2–4 WHAT'S YOUR POINT OF VIEW?

Extend the concepts of providing opportunities for students to express personal views on controversial issues. Have students compare and contrast their views with one another. Encourage enthusiasm but ask students to extend courtesy and politeness as they exchange ideas. *Give each student a copy of Activity 2-4, What's Your Point of View?*

2–5 COLOR ME HAPPY . . . SAD . . . ANGRY

Have students acknowledge that people react to their experiences with emotions that transcend racial, cultural, and ethnic origin. Encourage them to express their feelings during any given day in a story or poem. Have them share, if they wish. *Give each student a copy of Activity 2-5, Color Me Happy . . . Sad . . . Angry.*

2–6 HOW TO SURVIVE LIFE'S ROLLER COASTER RIDES

Elicit from students their experiences with roller coasters. Most will have had fun at amusement parks and can support the fact that roller coasters ascend and descend at top speeds—this is the source of the thrills for most riders. Draw an analogy between the anxiety that comes with these "dangerous" rides and the vivid contrasts in life. Ask students to consider how they are able to cope with the devastating challenges and to think of how they try to savor the most enjoyable experiences. Explain that the UPS and DOWNS in life have been expressed in music and poetry. Play the song *Turn, Turn, Turn (to Everything There is a Season)* by Judy Collins or read the words by King Solomon (Ecclesiastes 3:1-8). Have students infer the meanings in each line and how individuals should react to the various situations. Ask students to share some of their successes and failures or joys and sorrows. Emphasize examples of how they face reality, use survival techniques, and cope. Do they talk to other people, walk away from confrontations, keep quiet, laugh, or cry? (**Note:** Be aware of and sensitive to students who might be suffering from emotional, psychological upheavals. These students might need privacy, encouragement, and help.) *Give each student a copy of Activity 2-6, How to Survive Life's Roller Coaster Rides.*

2–7 YOUR FREEDOM TO BE . . . TO BECOME

Write John Donne's quote "No man is an island" on the board and ask students to explain what it means. Discuss the fact that human beings are interdependent and that young people, especially, need the help of older people as they grow and develop. Ask them to share the extent to which family, community members, and government have responsibility for providing for and protecting them. Have them consider what responsibility individuals have for themselves, even when they are young. Ask each student to think of several people who have made a contribution to his or her progress. Elicit from students why such individuals are necessary for young people as they try to succeed and learn what it means to really be free. Have students share information about mentors who are established and have had the will to help others achieve success as well. Ask students to respond to these questions:

1. When one person helps another to reach his or her goals, how is his or her own life enriched?

2. How can preventing another person from reaching his or her goals hurt both parties?

3. How can offering equal opportunities for progress increase the extent to which everyone enjoys freedom?

Have students consider how people who have positive self-concepts are able to extend a helping hand to those who are less fortunate. Ask them to explain how this positive self-image differs from arrogance. Which person is really *Free to Be . . . To Become*—the person who has true, positive self-esteem and feels good about bringing others along as he or she pursues success, or the person who is arrogant and unwilling to help others? *Give each student a copy of Activity 2-7, Your Freedom to Be . . . To Become.*

2–8 WHEN I AM ALONE

Have students acknowledge that they are the only ones who know what is in their minds. (If students offer God or another as one who knows what we are thinking, allow this.) Have students acknowledge also that personal reflection is a wonderful opportunity to develop a positive self-image and discover some of our hidden talents. Everyone desires time alone when it is possible to relax and indulge in personal reflections. Ask students to share some of their favorite activities when they are alone. (Note: The character of individuals is often evident in what they do when they think that no one is looking.) Explore with students the fact that individuals like chances to do what they want when no one is there. Discuss the benefits of having time to reflect on personal concerns. *Give each student a copy of Activity 2-8, When I Am Alone.*

2–9 WHO AM I WHEN NO ONE IS LOOKING?

Personal reflection is a significant way to build a positive self-image. People need to examine their motives in decision making, human relationships, and goal setting. It is when people are alone that their innermost thoughts are revealed and true personality traits emerge. Ask the students to share what they are like when no one else is around. Have them share whether they are happy with themselves in their private, self-reflective moments. (Note: Students must not be asked to share personal information that might prove painful, destructive, or embarrassing to themselves or their families.) Encourage them to share the most positive aspects of their reflections on themselves, life in general, and relationships with peers, family, and acquaintances. Have them focus on specific personality traits that are evident in their human interactions. If students state that they do not have thoughts, actions, and personality traits of which they can be proud, suggest that they concentrate on turning negatives into positives. (You might also want to talk to a counselor or parent in such cases.) Ask students to agree or disagree with the following:

1. People who are the same in public as they are in private get along better with others.

2. People who try to be someone other than who they really are in private have difficulty relating to others.

3. People who are self-confident when they are alone find it easy to support and empathize with others.

4. Individual character is often evident in what people do when they think no one is looking.

Student responses to riddles will vary. *Give each student a copy of Activity 2-9, Who Am I When No One Is Looking?*

2–10 MY BRAG SHEET

Elicit from students their views on the connections that exist between one's desires, abilities, and efforts to learn and one's eventual success. Ask students to contribute to a Class List of Accomplishments and to use this same strategy in developing Personal Lists of Accomplishments. (This information should be used when developing résumés or filling out job and college applications.) Have students acknowledge one another's talents and the extent to which EVERYONE has something to BRAG ABOUT. Ask students if it's okay for people to brag about themselves. Elicit from them the mixed messages we receive when we are told: "Be modest . . . humble . . . self-effacing" and "If you don't blow your own horn, nobody else will." What do these two messages mean? To what extent do they help people to build self-esteem? To what extent do they keep people from developing higher self-esteem? What effect do the messages have? What do they say about society? Discuss the various viewpoints of students and ask if informing people of your positive attributes and, in return, listening to their positive attributes helps to create MUTUAL RESPECT and SELF-ESTEEM simultaneously. *Give each student a copy of Activity 2-10, My Brag Sheet.*

2–11 ARROGANCE OR SELF-ESTEEM—WHICH IS IT?

Write the words ARROGANCE and SELF-ESTEEM on the board, and ask volunteers to define them. Have the rest of the class indicate similarities and differences between these terms. Discuss with students how arrogance often manifests itself in negative actions, while positive actions and concern for others are usually evident in people with true, positive self-esteem. Give examples of "negative self-esteem," or arrogance, when people are very quick to "put down" others. Compare and contrast this with examples and benefits of positive, or true, self-esteem in which people are happy to lift up or encourage others. Challenge students to think of the consequences of the negative aspects of high self-esteem emanating from individuals who have *no respect* or *concern* for people. In many instances, these individuals display airs of superiority that result in the victimization of the people they consider inferior to themselves. Based on this, elicit the types of human relationships that might develop. For example, historically, individuals who have thought too much of themselves have relegated others to positions of subservience, slavery, or other forms of oppression; they have perpetrated crimes resulting in the untold horrors of holocausts, ethnic cleansing, terrorism, and other murderous actions. Have students reflect inwardly regarding their own positions on these issues and decide for themselves where positive self-esteem ends and negative self-esteem, or arrogance, begins. Discuss their opinions and specific instances where arrogance and oppression have negated mutual respect, and have them offer solutions to the inequities. *Give each student a copy of Activity 2-11, Arrogance or Self-Esteem—Which Is It?*

2–12 "THE CATASTROPHE OF SUCCESS"

Have available a copy of the essay by Tennessee Williams entitled *The Catastrophe of Success*. Write the title on the chalkboard and have students explain the contradiction. Elicit from them the literary term, OXYMORON. Based on the inferences and the reading of the essay, the themes in this work can often be used to help students understand the complexities of materialism. Present this scenario to them: "Suddenly, you become famous; you've written a best seller, won the lottery, become a movie star, or recorded a hit song. You're an overnight sensation; people follow you around asking for your autograph, and money is rolling in. Your bank accounts are swelling and you have long-lost friends and relatives 'coming out of the woodwork' now that you're wealthy and famous." Elicit from each student how he or she would act if this scenario became a reality. Have students share whether they would remain the same or change. Give each student an opportunity to respond to the scenario, or hold small-group discussions that give students a chance to dialogue. Then, talk about how the news media often portray famous or wealthy people. Help students to recognize that real life often mirrors the experiences Williams describes in *The Catastrophe of Success*. Help students to see the need to remain in control of their own life choices and not succumb to the trappings of success. *Give each student a copy of Activity 2-12, "The Catastrophe of Success."*

2–13   TRUE SELF-ESTEEM IN ROLE MODELS

Elicit from students various personality traits they look for in a role model. Discuss which traits are most beneficial and explain why this is so. (Role models should help to foster self-confidence and encourage those who admire them to pursue excellence.) Indicate the extent to which athletes, movie stars, singers, and other famous people are imitated and admired by their fans. Discuss the fact that, although many people try to model their lives after them, the rich and famous are not accessible to the ordinary public. Ask how realistic it is, therefore, to look to these people for encouragement, caring, or guidance on how to live and how to accomplish one's goals. Have students name a person who would make a good role model for them; one who is close enough to call on the phone, to write a note to and expect a reply, or to talk to at the dinner table. Ask them to identify the specific characteristics of this person they have selected as a role model. Also, have them consider the various environments in which they would find their heroes or heroines, such as home, school, or community. Have students share their ideas as to the kind of guidance, caring, or encouragement they might receive from this individual and the extent to which this person might help to foster their self-esteem, motivate them to pursue well-thought-out goals, and be there for them through the long haul. *Give each student a copy of Activity 2-13, True Self-Esteem in Role Models.*

2–14   SPREAD OUT BEAUTY

Show students pictures of attractive models of various races and colors (male and female). Discuss the fact that these individuals have a right to earn their living as models. Pose the question: "What happens when these models age or get out of shape?" Relate this idea to other professions in which outward beauty is necessary. Then, have students share other professions in which a person's intellect, expertise, and other internal attributes are important—not how she or he looks. Have students reflect on superficial and internal characteristics of people and compare and contrast the drawbacks or benefits of each. Discuss the meaning of the statement, "Beauty is only skin deep." Elicit from them the idea that what's inside a person's heart comes out and reveals that person's true character, and that people can have either lasting or temporary beauty. Ask students to think of "A" as a symbol for Appearances or Attitude and "S" as a symbol for the Soul or Spirit. Discuss the extent to which these ideas hold true for people who are visibly disabled or physically challenged. Ask students to explore other "A" and "S" words that are relevant to the themes in the poem. These words can be positive or negative (i.e., Arrogance or Superiority). *Give each student a copy of Activity 2-14, Spread Out Beauty.*

2–15   LEARNING FROM MISTAKES OF THE PAST

Individual students must think of ways in which one person can begin the process of healing divisions among various racial and cultural groups. Viewing errors in judgment by powerful people and observing what the consequences of their choices are provide important lessons for young people. Both print and visual media rush to get sensational news out when celebrities have personal and public problems. Elicit from students the extent to which they are deterred from certain actions based on their observations of negative consequences. If students are not able to make the connections between mistakes or errors in judgment and the kinds of consequences suffered by famous people, have them personalize the possibilities within their own lives. Vivid connections can be made by students between their behaviors and choices and the punishment or rewards given to them by parents or guardians. Have students share some of the mistakes or errors in judgment they have made followed by the consequences they suffered. Give them opportunities to indicate how they, as adults, might have handled a mistake or error in judgment by their children. *Give each student a copy of Activity 2-15, Learning From Mistakes of the Past.*

2–16 ON MY HONOR

Write the following statement on the board: "I didn't think it was cheating unless I got caught." Ask students to respond to this statement by revealing whether they agree or disagree with it. Then ask them to define the term CHEATING. Challenge students to consider what the phrase ON YOUR HONOR means and how they can uphold this in a world where people seem to make progress even when they do not behave with honor or honesty. Elicit from them the extent to which each individual has to internalize how important it is for himself or herself to behave with honor— no matter what other people do. *Give each student a copy of Activity 2-16, On My Honor.*

2–17 A BULLY GETS HERS

In schools across America, there are students who like to fight. They'll do anything they can to start trouble, especially if they can emerge with the victory. In the process of their aggressive behavior, they create frightening and violent environments for classmates, teachers, and other school personnel. Elicit from students how bullies can be controlled in school and in the community. (Note: Feel free to share personal experiences that will benefit students in helping them to make non-violent choices of behavior and to practice rational conflict-resolution strategies.) Discuss the consequences of unwise choices and actions. *Give each student a copy of Activity 2-17, A Bully Gets Hers.*

2–18 L'S ADVICE COLUMN

Each person must find joy and self-esteem within, but many people depend on others for their self-esteem. While it is good to care about what others think, it is more important to have guidelines for life that contribute to one's own personal growth, development, and self-satisfaction. In the absence of personal, confidence-building traits, too many people spend more time wondering what others think of them rather than living according to their own value systems and pursuing their own goals. Ask students to respond to the following: Is it good or bad to follow your own value systems, and should one's efforts to become a better person be the foundation for higher levels of self-esteem? Discuss pros and cons. Have students clarify their opinions as to whether a strong self-image ought to come from inside each individual or from the people with whom they interact. Have them indicate if they have mixed emotions on this topic. *Give each student a copy of Activity 2-18, L's Advice Column.*

2–19 TAKING CARE OF MY MIND AND BODY

Discuss the word "longevity"—the amount of time people might live—and how the care of their bodies adds to or takes away from the length of life. Discuss the choices people can make regarding nutrition and lifestyles, including stress-reducing activities. *Give each student a copy of Activity 2-19, Taking Care of My Mind and Body.*

Extend the concepts of taking care of both the mind and the body by having students acknowledge that they are the only ones who can determine the quality of their mental and physical well-being. Have them write a short composition describing how well they take care of their physical and mental health.

2–20 MY KEEPSAKES FOR LIFE

No matter what their age, race, culture, size, shape, or gender, the world is dangerous in many ways for human beings. Positive changes can be expected only when each person begins to see himself or herself as the answer to the problem and works to create safe environments for everyone. Propose to students the possibility of their assuming the responsibility of changing the negative behaviors in environments in which they have some measure of control; their homes, schools, and neighborhoods. Ask them to describe the morals, values, levels of tolerance, motives, and purposes that should prevail in safe environments. Inquire of each student his or her motivation for wanting safer, more enjoyable surroundings in which to interact with peers, family, and friends. Discuss ways in which acceptable morals, values, and behaviors can be learned, lived, and passed on to future generations. Have students define the slogan "Stop the Cycle of Violence" and the term "keepsake." What significance do these words have in the goals of individuals who want to live in safer environments? *Give each student Activity 2-20, My Keepsakes for Life.*

2–21 NEVER EAT ROTTEN APPLES!

Ask students to verify the importance of the senses in helping people determine dangerous substances before they are ingested. Have them agree that physical harm can be caused by poisons getting into the system. Therefore, people do what they can to make certain that the food they eat and the beverages they consume are free of contamination. Ask students to consider the physical harm that can occur from dangerous substances taken into the bloodstream. In the same way, violent and negative behavior and attitudes can contaminate an individual's mind and heart.

Elicit from students the fact that their senses of SIGHT, SMELL, HEARING, TASTE, and TOUCH must be trained to discern the subtle invasion of foreign substances. Expand this concept to the need to use their senses to detect the dangers of such ills as racism, intolerance, greed, violence, and dishonesty. Have each student share where some of these destructive things might be found as they go about their daily lives, and ask each student to share how she or he would avoid these things. Because the lines between right and wrong or good and evil can be blurred, suggest that it's fine for people to ask others to help when they have difficulty detecting and destroying the culprits. Discuss how much healthier human interaction would be if each individual became more aware of the ways to avoid entrapment. *Give each student a copy of Activity 2-21, Never Eat Rotten Apples!*

2–22 TWENTY WAYS TO SAY, "YOU'RE THE GREATEST!"

Elicit from students the responses they have when someone yells or screams at them or calls them bad names. Have them share internal as well as external reactions. Discuss the extent to which some people might use their dissatisfaction with their own lives as an excuse to be mean, nasty, and disrespectful to others. Ask students to decide how to reverse negative trends in human relationships. If talk radio and television shows thrive on guests attacking each other, what can counteract the emerging distrust, dislike, and pain? Have students consider the positive responses they have when someone says something nice to them, or treats them gently, or uses terms of endearment. Discuss both the internal feelings and the external reactions. Have them project how people who receive positive reinforcement will—based on their own good feelings—pass positive feelings on to others. Suggest this as a way of reducing racism, hate, and prejudice among diverse groups of people. *Give each student a copy of Activity 2-22, Twenty Ways to Say, "You're the Greatest!"*

2–23 SPELLBOUND!

In observing the world around us, we've all had times when we were totally awestruck. We've seen things that are so incredible that we say, "That's unbelievable!" Wonder is an important aspect of life that helps all of us to focus on what is good about being alive. If there are ever reasons for unhappiness, reflecting on the wonder of life can make human beings feel better. Ask students to share some of the most awesome natural phenomena they have encountered. For example, how many have seen the Grand Canyon, Niagara Falls, or a hummingbird extracting nectar from a flower? How many have seen the athletic prowess of famous athletes and been in awe? Ask students to use vivid word pictures as they describe different things. Most of us wonder about the intricate technological feats that have made computers, space flight, and undersea exploration possible. Discuss the importance of preserving a sense of wonder in their world. *Give each student a copy of Activity 2-23, Spellbound!*

2–24 THE MOST BEAUTIFUL THING IN MY LIFE TODAY

Challenge each student to become her or his own best friend. Discuss the need for people to reflect inwardly in order to discover personal desires and potential. Have students focus on this beautiful beginning to self-acceptance as the basis for finding friendship outside themselves. Discuss the need for self-acceptance and self-affirmation—the importance of feeling good about themselves. Then, have students decide whether they need to look inside or outside for a person, thing, or place that can help to bring inner joy and beauty to them. Elicit from students the need for daily experiences of beauty and encouragement. Ask each student to reflect on one thing or experience and list all of the encouraging, self-affirming feelings that emerge as a result of focusing only on good, positive things. Discuss ways that beautiful experiences can be enjoyed, day after day. *Give each student a copy of Activity 2-24, The Most Beautiful Thing in My Life Today.*

2–25 THE CONTENT OF ONE'S CHARACTER

Read or play a recording of an excerpt from Martin Luther King's "I Have a Dream" speech. Focus upon the lines in which he speaks of wanting his children to be judged by the ". . . content of their character, not the color of their skin." Have a student define the word CHARACTER. Discuss the fact that what is inside a person's heart comes out as he or she interacts with others. If a person is cruel, racist, kind, or tolerant, these things are obvious in the words the person speaks, his or her attitude, and related actions. Ask for examples of things in the heart that cannot help but come out. Elicit from students how some people create hatred and lies; these people are really NOT ATTRACTIVE, for often they act on these words. Discuss, as well, how some people are truly ATTRACTIVE when the words that come out of their mouths are filled with concern, admiration, and truth—and when their actions reflect what they say. Discuss the importance to society of people who have a good work ethic, believe in upholding the rights of their fellow citizens, and try to create harmony in their environments. Have students agree that *all* people are ATTRACTIVE when their character reflects the concern that they feel toward others. (**Note:** Elicit from students how ordinary people can be leaders when they act on the premise that "All men and women are created equal.") *Give each student a copy of Activity 2-25, The Content of One's Character.*

2–26 "BUT YOU . . . !!"

Elicit from students how they feel when their peers get to do things that they are not allowed to do. Discuss the source of their limitations and the reasons behind them. Discuss the fact that parents want to protect their children from physical, emotional, and psychological dangers; thus, they have rules for various activities in which their children might be involved. Ask students if they ever place limits on themselves. Discuss the extent to which their personal limitations compare with those placed on them by others, including parents, teachers, community agencies, and so on. Have students suggest specific activities that might warrant personal or adult limits on their participation. (Suggestions: X-rated movies, surfing the Internet or chatting with strangers on the computer, drug use, drinking alcohol, smoking cigarettes, talking back to parents or other adults, breaking a curfew, going somewhere without permission, hanging out with the wrong people, not doing homework, etc.)

Inquire as to the role peer pressure might play in making decisions whether to participate in these or other risky activities. Take a poll of the class regarding how many appreciate adult limitations on their activities. (Note: If some students' parents allow their children to participate in certain behaviors or activities that might be considered "risky," discuss parental authority, and the difference between life choices emanating from parents and those resulting when children begin to make their own personal decisions.) Try to find out how many students really like the protection of adult rules that take the sting out of being teased when they say, "My parents won't let me . . ." Discuss specific rules that some parents have for their children: a time to be home helping with household chores, saving money, showing respect to adults, and so on. *Give each student a copy of Activity 2-26, "But You . . . !!"*

2–27 WASHING AWAY SAND CASTLES

Ask students to describe or give the attributes of a "strong" person, and indicate the extent to which a strong person can stand up for what is right. Write the following on the board and discuss each point:

- ☞ Strong people do not blame others for their problems.

- ☞ Strong people can maintain true friendships.

- ☞ Strong people can resist the urge to be arrogant.

- ☞ Strong people have no problem cleaning up their own mess.

- ☞ Strong people go out of their way to make sure that others are safe around them.

- ☞ Strong people can think for themselves.

- ☞ Strong people can compliment others without feeling that this subtracts from their own worth.

Ask students to add other truths to this list and explain why these are positions of strength. Have them claim those attributes that are true for them and add others, if they can. Discuss, as well, how these attributes and others can be developed and maintained in the life of a teenager: How can teenagers be strong in their environments? Pose this question, as well: What would happen if a young person has only a superficial strength as he or she interacts with others and begins to pursue life goals? *Give each student a copy of Activity 2-27, Washing Away Sand Castles.*

2–28 WHAT'S YOUR WORTH?

Show students articles about the salaries of corporate executives, athletes, politicians, educators, and so on. Ask for their opinions regarding the fairness of the money people earn for various jobs. Discuss the training required for certain professions and whether there is equity in the earnings. Have them share their career goals, plans they have for training, and expected earnings. Discuss the extent to which people are motivated to work hard on training in anticipation of higher earnings in the future. Ask them to weigh this option against going right into the work force out of high school and not pursuing higher education or training. (Note: Extend the meaning of these concepts by having students work in small groups to convert hourly *and* weekly wages to yearly take-home pay. Ask them to compare the results to the salaries that people earn and ask which they prefer—wages or salaries?) *Give each student a copy of Activity 2-28, What's Your Worth?* (ANSWER KEY: 1. H, 2. K, 3. E, 4. G, 5. L, G. C, 7. B, 8. F, 9. I, 10. D, 11. J, 12. A)

2–29 LAUGHING MATTERS?

Elicit from students the pleasure that comes from laughter. This universal human trait is beneficial unless it is at the expense of another person. Discuss the fact that laughing with people provides rich, mutually beneficial pleasure. On the other hand, laughing at people causes internal pain and embarrassment for people who are the brunt of cruel jokes or laughter. Have students consider what might be going on inside a person who gains pleasure from laughing at and causing pain for another human being. Ask students to volunteer their experiences with being the brunt of teasing or joking, and how others might or might not have come to their rescue. Also have students share their experiences with "pleasurable" laughter. Then, challenge them to come up with a list of ways to increase the frequency of pleasurable laughter that lifts rather than crushes one's feelings. *Give each student a copy of Activity 2-29, Laughing Matters?*

2–30 THE NIGHT TIME IS THE RIGHT TIME

Ask students to share how they spend time during the week and on weekends. Also ask them to indicate whether some of their activities or behaviors are more appropriate for day or night. Inquire as to what kinds of activities or behaviors are never appropriate, no matter what the time. For example, it is *never* appropriate to drive a car without a license or to take drugs. Have students agree that there are certain behaviors and activities that are *never* appropriate during school hours but would be perfectly fine after school. Certain clothing, for example, is appropriate for after school but should not be worn in school. (**Note:** After school is considered NIGHT TIME.) *Give each student a copy of Activity 2-30, The Night Time Is the Right Time.*

2–31 BE YOURSELF—GET RID OF YOUR MASK!

Ask students to think of times when they have wanted to hide but couldn't. Inquire as to how they might have coped with being embarrassed about incidents in which peers were aware of their shortcomings. (**Note:** Students do not have to reveal their indiscretions in order to agree that every human being experiences temporary embarrassment over a variety of situations.) Discuss the fact that most people are able to get over feeling ashamed enough to want to hide. Also, explain that human beings need to know that others approve of them and often feel obliged to disappear when they are guilt-ridden or when they don't feel that they have "measured up" to the expectations of those with whom they interact.

Elicit from students the fact that when people cannot find a balance between what they, as individuals, want and what other people expect, they might not like themselves and might try to create a new, external identity. In these cases, people do everything they can to please others rather than trying to be who they really are; they try to hide their low self-images behind "masks." Have students share some of their opinions about the reasons people might want to pretend they are someone other than who they are. These reasons might include: FEAR OF REJECTION BY OTHERS, A FALSE SENSE OF SUPERIORITY, EXTREME SHYNESS, or LOW SELF-ESTEEM.

Ask students to consider writing a letter of advice to someone who might wear a mask of AGGRESSION, for example, but in reality is very shy and frightened. Challenge students to offer suggestions that might help this person to accept his or her personality. Ask students about the tone of the advice that they give; how might this be related to the willingness of the person to receive and consider using some of their suggestions? Ask students to consider the tones of kindness, comfort, caring, and acceptance, and invite them to write the letter of advice to themselves, if necessary. *Give each student a copy of Activity 2-31, Be Yourself—Get Rid of Your Mask!*

2–32 RIGHT OR WRONG?

Ask three questions of students: Where does the responsibility lie for keeping order in society? Who decides whether certain actions are right or wrong? Does it matter whether an action is right for the individual or right for the larger group? Discuss student responses. Then write the words LAWS, RESTRICTIONS, LIMITATIONS, VOWS, RULES, and STANDARDS on the chalkboard. Ask students to define each term and indicate what would happen if we did not have them in such situations as marriage vows, keeping promises, signing contracts, and any others that emerge from the discussion. Then, have them reflect on personal standards that they have for dress, talk, habits, friends, school, and so on. Discuss how their personal standards might carry over to the daily environments in which they find themselves. For example, what is expected of every person who drives a car, uses the public library, borrows money from a bank, or eats in a restaurant? Discuss both written and unwritten laws, standards, or rules that might apply in these and other situations. Inquire as to whether individual U.S. citizens can be made to say the Pledge of Allegiance to the American flag. Where does personal responsibility end and support for the nation begin? What is the outcome of having restraints, rules, laws, and standards in society? (**Note:** Students will most likely agree that society would be in chaos were it not for standards, laws, rules, and/or restraints that encourage people to do the right thing. *Give each student a copy of Activity 2-32, Right or Wrong?*

2–33 SORRY, WRONG NUMBER!

Ask students how young people decide on how they are going to behave. Read the following statement to them and ask them to agree or disagree with it. "When young people begin to make their own decisions, they do so based on observations of those around them, including family and friends. In addition, many teenagers imitate the actions of real-life or fictional people. While many of their observations and experiences are positive, teenagers do see many, many negative things in the movies or on television and think that such behaviors are fine." Give students an opportunity to discuss all aspects of the statement and to explain why they think their positions are valid. Have them indicate the extent to which they imitate family, friends, actors, or other celebrities. Ask them to share how they react when they hear of the downfall of famous people and whether this changes any tendency they might have to emulate these people. Discuss what lessons are learned from observing the mistakes of others and whether they are stronger and more able to resist temptations when they see the negative consequences. Ask students to consider appropriate positive responses for negative messages. *Give each student a copy of Activity 2-33, Sorry, Wrong Number!*

2–34 SNAPSHOTS: LOOK WHAT DEVELOPED!

Photographs can preserve a moment in time and bring joy to observers many years after they were first taken. Ask students to think of an important moment in their lives that was captured on video or in still photography. Recall important events in human history that have recorded—for example, the landing of man on the moon, the Holocaust, the March on Washington, Dr. Martin Luther King's "I Have a

Dream" speech, the assassination of President John F. Kennedy, or the 1996 Olympic Games in Atlanta. Then, have students share specific information about everyday, ordinary events that they know of—things that should have been recorded in writing, on video, or still photography but were not considered important enough.

Discuss the fact that many ordinary, everyday occurrences are more meaningful to us because we can relate to them more readily. For example, people do good deeds for their fellow human beings, and others are unaware of them. Have students imagine that they are roving photographers, looking for situations that make life better for the ordinary person. They are to photograph or videotape at least one incident involving someone who would not be recognized by the news media. Have them indicate the area of the incident and describe the people involved. Ask each student to explain how his or her imaginary event helps to make the life of ordinary people better. *Give each student a copy of Activity 2-34, Snapshots: Look What Developed!*

2–35 THE TRUTH AS THE LIGHT

Ask students if people can be too smart for their own good. Have them give examples to back up their opinions. Infer that smart people usually know how to avoid traps and are aware that in life there are those who earn money by causing problems for their fellow human beings. Many smart people, however, have become victims of subtle entrapments. Discuss various ways that people who are very aware have ruined their health, become criminals, and lost all of their money as a result of trying to "make a fast dollar," not thinking for themselves, jumping on the bandwagon, deserting the value system by which they were raised, trying to get something for nothing, choosing immediate gratification over patience, being selfish, and so on.

Ask students if people can make life harder for themselves by following through on certain decisions. Elicit from them what people who are really smart do when faced with choices that are not in their own best interest. Write the words: TRUTH, HONESTY, and INTEGRITY on the chalkboard and have students explain them. Discuss the fact that these are the only options for truly smart people. Telling lies causes people to get confused, and those who want to set traps for you know this. The old saying "Honesty is the best policy" is true. Have students come to a consensus that truly smart people follow and are enlightened by this old adage. Specifically, people who tell the truth develop self-confidence, and they get the best out of life. Discuss the reasons for this. *Give each student a copy of Activity 2-35, The Truth As the Light.*

2–36 HIDDEN TREASURES

Elicit from students their awareness of people who make the lives of others better as a result of the kindness of their hearts. Indicate that there are many people whose hearts and minds lead them to generously share their love, material goods, and concern without telling everybody about their gifts. Often givers are very private people who just want to keep a low profile and know within themselves that they have made it possible for someone else to survive. Discuss the fact that there are young people in the class and in the school who are good-hearted and who are concerned not only about their families, but also about their fellow students and members of the community. People don't tell everything they do for others, and perhaps there are students in the classroom who are in disguise—hidden treasures in that they do wonderful things in their homes, schools, or communities. Stress that it is not important to dig these treasures up and reveal them, but it is important to encourage them and to let them know that they are needed in a society in which many people are skeptical and suspicious of one another's motives. Suggest that these "hidden treasures"—young people who care about human life—are really the leaders and the hope of society. *Give each student a copy of Activity 2-36, Hidden Treasures.*

2–37 WHO AM I? A HUMAN BEING

Inquire of students the extent to which they need approval from those with whom they live, work, learn, have fun, or worship. Listen closely for indications of acceptance or rejection. For students who have experienced rejection, ask if there has ever been a time when they have rejected another human being. Elicit from students that to reject another human being is to invalidate that person's very existence. Suggest that this kind of invalidation is more painful than physical blows because it burrows into the heart and the mind and lasts. (**Note:** Discuss the counterproductive risks, however, of assuming the role of "victim.")

Ask students what it would take for all human beings to begin to accept each other despite color, racial, and ethnic heritage. Ask them to indicate their racial, ethnic, and cultural backgrounds and share their pride in their heritage. Then, ask them why they are glad to be human rather than any other species of life on earth. (**Note:** Be sensitive to anxieties of students of all racial backgrounds, but especially those of mixed racial heritage who might have difficulty with labeling.) Indicate that the only label we should focus on is our humanity. This activity is designed to get students to share their concerns and then to develop a course of action in their *Personal Message* and the *Think About This!!!* responses. Suggest that students share these activities with family and community members. *Give each student a copy of Activity 2-37, Who Am I? A Human Being.*

2–38 SPEAK ABOUT THE RIGHT TO BE FREE

Write this statement on the board: "No one can be truly free if his brother or sister is in bondage." Have students explain and then discuss their opinions regarding the validity of the statement. Define the word FREEDOM. Then, locate a written copy, a recording, or a film of Dr. Martin Luther King's "I Have a Dream" speech. Discuss the impact of the speech on individual listeners. Ask students to describe Dr. King's tone (passionate, sincere, focused, heart-felt, and so on). Elicit from students some of the famous or familiar lines from the speech, and discuss why people remember these particular words. Clarify the fact that the speech was given to help solve racial problems in America and to help U.S. citizens to look at themselves—their personal value systems and their personal character.

One of the most famous lines from the speech has been memorized by the youngest of children: "I have a dream that my four little children will one day live in a nation where they will not be judged by the color of their skin but by the content of their character." Elicit from students some of Dr. King's vivid imagery; for example, he used sound and sight in the lines, "Let freedom ring from Stone

Mountain of Georgia! Let freedom ring from every hill and molehill of Mississippi!" Dr. King also used the senses of sight and touch as he appealed to people of different colors and religions to come together, "black men and white men . . . Jews and Gentiles, Protestants and Catholics, will be able to join hands . . . " Dr. King threads the imagery of dreams as a metaphor for HOPE throughout the speech and, in the process, he appeals to the imagination, the faith, and intelligence of his audience. In short, Dr. King has asked people to be reasonable in their relationships with one another and, thereby, protect rather than violate everyone's human rights.

Have students explore the emotion—the passion—in the use of repetition in the closing lines of Dr. King's speech: "Free at last, free at last, thank God Almighty we're free at last." Ask students to listen to the speech again and to begin to formulate the structure for a speech that can be modeled after Dr. King's "I Have a Dream" speech. Also, give them opportunities to listen to or read human rights speeches by others. Ask students to think of one aspect of freedom, justice, or equality that needs improvement in today's society. Indicate that their goal is to come up with ideas to help solve this problem and to write a speech for an appropriate audience. Ask them to plan to deliver this speech at some future date. *Give each student a copy of Activity 2-38, Speak About the Right to Be Free.*

NAME _____ DATE _____

BUILT-IN CONTROLS—YOU'RE IN CHARGE!

To develop and maintain a positive self-image, you can never allow anyone to undermine your attempts to follow or live by your value system. You know right from wrong, you know what your parents have taught you, and you know when to say NO to things that might pose great danger or harm to you or to other people. As a responsible individual, you have built-in controls or warning systems that keep you from getting into trouble. "Red flags" go up when you even THINK about doing something that would violate your principles! If this is NOT TRUE for you, what should you do to develop internal controls that would urge you to make the right decisions regarding your life? As you work on this activity, consider your individual strengths.

Create a dialogue, or conversation, between two teenagers that reveals their awareness of self-control and right and wrong. Use the Word Bank and your own ideas to help these teens express their ability to make good, productive decisions. The dialogue begins with the first teen asking the leading question shown below. For his response, consider how the second teen, who is aware of his or her value system and needs to do the right thing, would answer this leading question. If you think the first teen has not made up his mind, decide what else he will say and write it in the bubble on the far left. What would you do if someone asked you to attend an adult club where liquor is served?

WORD BANK FOR DIALOGUE

responsibility	peer pressure	safety	purpose	punishment
yes	future	dependability	reward	personal decisions
curfew	jail	alcohol	trust	home training
danger	fake ID cards			
Other _____		Other _____		Other _____

DIALOGUE/CONVERSATION

Hey man, did Jeff ask you to go with him to that adult club on 21st Street tomorrow night?

First Teenager   Second Teenager

THE WORDS YOU SPEAK

Are there appropriate and inappropriate places for using abusive or offensive language? Should language that shocks or hurts never, ever be used? What would life be like in schools, courts, offices, theaters, or restaurants if the only words ever spoken were caring, soft, and encouraging? Is it realistic to think that people will use courteous language to one another every single day?

Respond to the following statements with A for Agree or D for Disagree. Then, write your own opinion regarding the use of violent or abusive language vs. courteous or encouraging language in society.

1. _____ It's okay to verbally abuse someone rather than throwing a punch.

2. _____ Another person's personal air space should not be polluted with curses and/or abusive language.

3. _____ It is possible for everyone to speak kind words instead of violent ones.

4. _____ Harsh language is an acceptable way for people to release tension.

5. _____ There should be a law against swearing in public.

6. _____ Physical conflicts often start with the use of combative or abusive language.

7. _____ Courtesies have been developed by cultures to prevent violence among members of the society.

8. _____ Young people learn abusive language from adults.

MY OPINION ON ABUSIVE VS. COURTEOUS LANGUAGE IN SOCIETY

_____
_____
_____
_____
_____
_____
_____
_____
_____
_____

NAME _____ DATE _____

TOUCH MY TONE

What personal attitudes or attributes reveal WHO YOU REALLY ARE INSIDE? Imagine that people could dial your special telephone number and listen to recordings that convey to them your feelings and opinions about social, environmental, economic, educational, or personal issues. It's your opportunity to tell people what you think without having to defend your position. However, be sure to develop valid opinions for future opportunities in order to reach wider audiences.

Record your message for some important issues in the spaces below. (Write other issues on the blanks):

"Hi! This is _____ and I'm not at home to take your call. Please select your options and listen to my very personal messages to you. I feel deeply about these issues and hope to discuss them with you in person."

CALLER OPTIONS

PRESS 1 for my ideas on THE YEAR-ROUND SCHOOL PROPOSAL:

_____

_____

_____

_____

PRESS 2 for my opinion on BOOT CAMP FOR TEEN OFFENDERS:

_____

_____

_____

_____

PRESS 3 for my opinion on AFFIRMATIVE ACTION:*

_____

_____

_____

_____

_____

*Affirmative Action—An active effort to improve the educational and/or employment opportunities for minority groups and women.

Name _____ Date _____

PRESS 4 for my opinion on CROSS-CULTURAL DATING:

_____
_____
_____
_____

PRESS 5 for my ideas on mandatory PLEDGE TO THE FLAG:

_____
_____
_____
_____

PRESS 6 for my opinion on THE INCREASE OF IMMIGRANTS IN OUR NEIGHBORHOOD:

_____
_____
_____
_____

PRESS 7 for my ideas on VIOLENCE IN FILMS:

_____
_____
_____
_____

PRESS 8 for my opinion on GOAL SETTING FOR MY FUTURE:

_____
_____
_____
_____

PRESS 9 for my opinion on _____:
                                 (Other)

_____
_____
_____
_____

PRESS 10 for my ideas on _____:
                                (Other)

_____
_____
_____
_____

NAME _____ DATE _____

WHAT'S YOUR POINT OF VIEW?

Opportunities to work out problems can occur only if the lines of communication are opened. People who talk to each other can reach an understanding about issues of controversy and ideas on which they have divergent points of view. Furthermore, sharing views in an open forum provides ways to air differences and eliminate the likelihood of conflicts.

Read the scenario below and consider the options listed:

SCENARIO

Paul's parents expect him to get all A's on his report card every marking period throughout the school year. He is really a very good student, but the yelling over grades is getting on Paul's nerves. For example, on the last report card, he earned four A's and two B's. His parents insisted that he should have had straight A's because they want him to become a doctor. Paul feels that if he had a friend to talk to, it would help. In the meantime, he's thinking about cheating on his midterm exam as a way of making sure that he gets all A's. Another alternative is to talk to his parents and a counselor. Can you help Paul with his dilemma?

CHOOSE A SOLUTION FOR PAUL

Circle One:

A. Confront your parents and explain that you're doing the best that you can do.

B. Cheat on exams and copy homework from classmates whenever you can.

C. Try to ignore your parents, and rebel against them and authority in general.

D. Really look at your work habits—the way you spend your time; correct weaknesses.

E. Discuss the criteria for grading with your teachers, counselor, and your parents. Then, set reasonable goals for yourself that include periodic reviews before it's time for report cards. That way, there will be no surprises! Also let's discuss your lack of friends and how to improve this situation.

Explain why you selected _____ (A, B, C, D, E) and tell how this choice could help to solve Paul's dilemma. Also, describe your motivation for selecting that solution. Compare and contrast your point of view with those of your peers. Use the separate sheet provided for your response.

NAME _____ DATE _____

_____

_____

_____

_____

_____

_____

_____

_____

Compare and contrast your point of view with those of your peers.

_____

_____

_____

_____

_____

_____

_____

_____

_____

NAME _____ DATE _____

COLOR ME HAPPY . . . SAD . . . ANGRY

People know when you are happy or sad because you laugh, smile, look sad, or cry. Often, however, people have feelings inside that they are careful to hide from observers.

How are you feeling today? Complete the sentence frankly and write a short composition or a poem telling why you feel this way today. Then, identify ways in which you share joy or resolve pain or sadness. Include specific actions such as: talking to a friend or family member, getting exercise, praying, listening to music, or singing.

Today, I feel _____ .

I feel this way because _____

_____

_____

_____

_____

_____

_____

_____

_____

_____

_____

_____

_____

_____

_____

_____

_____

I share POSITIVE FEELINGS by: _____

_____

I eliminate NEGATIVE FEELINGS by: _____

_____

HOW TO SURVIVE LIFE'S
ROLLER COASTER RIDES

In life, we all experience a variety of ups and downs. How do you handle the downside of life? How do you handle those times when you are scared, upset, or sad? How do you handle the peaks of joy and happiness in your life? Do you talk about and share your reactions to these life experiences with others, or do you just keep them to yourself?

Read the following regarding life's ups and downs. It reveals the wisdom of King Solomon. In these words, he highlights the themes of TIME, LOSS, GAIN, AWARENESS, ACCEPTANCE, and PREPARATION for the inevitable.

A TIME FOR EVERYTHING

For everything there is a season, and a time for every matter under heaven:

- A time to be born, and a time to die;
- A time to plant, and a time to pluck up what is planted;
- A time to kill, and a time to heal;
- A time to break down, and a time to build up;
- A time to weep, and a time to laugh;
- A time to mourn, and a time to dance;
- A time to cast away stones, and a time to gather stones together;
- A time to embrace, and a time to refrain from embracing;
- A time to seek, and a time to lose;
- A time to keep, and a time to cast away;
- A time to rend, and a time to sew;
- A time to keep silence, and a time to speak;
- A time to love, and a time to hate;
- A time for war, and a time for peace.

Through the wisdom of King Solomon's words (Ecclesiastes 3:1-8), it is obvious that we all have times of misery and times of joy. It is in the awareness of and the preparation for these emotions that we develop the ability to cope with and decrease the pain, and the will to increase and share in the joy. What are some UPS and DOWNS in your life that can be written using the structure of this poem? Think of some high points and some low points in your life. Then write your experiences on the lines. Identify and share commonalties that appear in your poem with those of others—peers, family members, teachers, or counselors. Discuss the extent to which any of these experiences are justified or valid. Also, discuss which of them should be eliminated in the interest of better human relationships.

NAME _____   DATE _____

MY ROLLER COASTER RIDE (Write your own title)

_____

_____

_____

_____

_____

_____

_____

_____

_____

_____

_____

_____

_____

_____

_____

_____

_____

_____

_____

_____

Written by _____
(Your Name)

NOTE: Try to put your poem to music, and plan to perform it before an audience.

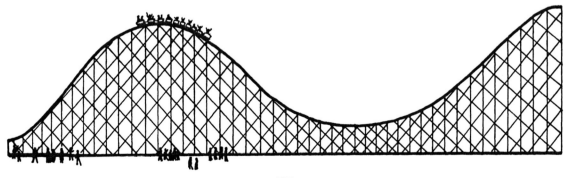

NAME _____   DATE _____

YOUR FREEDOM TO BE . . . TO BECOME

MY FREEDOM TO BE . . . TO BECOME

My freedom to be . . . to become
Is closely tied to the number of times you,
My mother, my father, my teacher, my friend . . .
Give me books, maps, charts and let me sing.
Tell me, show me, teach me, let me discover

That I and my ancestors,
We are as fine as you,
My teacher, my friend, my fellow human being.
Give me time, love, opportunity and let me wonder,
My co-inhabitor of this earth.

Take my hand, if only for a moment, my neighbor.
Lead me towards the sunlight, fill my empty pages.
Teach me to question, search for answers,
Meet new people, create new ideas, and grow in wisdom.

Through you, my teacher, my friend, my father, my mother,
I will learn to be . . . to become
More than I thought I could be.
Give me truth, trust, safety and let me dream.
Then, I'll win and because of you . . . I'll be free.

By Saundrah Clark Grevious

1. After reading the poem above, locate two main ideas regarding who is responsible for ensuring freedom for young people in a democracy. Underline these ideas.

2. Now, think of what these main ideas mean to you and write about them below:

MAIN IDEA 1

_____

_____

_____

NAME _____ DATE _____

MAIN IDEA 2

_____

_____

_____

3. Identify other ideas that are meaningful to you as an individual who desires to have the freedom to pursue your goals. Consider what messages are directed toward groups of people who often touch the lives of young people. What should the adults do for young people?

OTHER IDEAS:

_____

_____

_____

_____

4. Define the words FREEDOM and RESPONSIBILITY. Then, define the relationship between them. How can knowing what these words mean help you and other young people work to achieve positive goals?

_____

_____

_____

_____

5. What are some of the specific responsibilities of adults as they provide young people with what they need in order to experience freedom and success? Explain.

_____

_____

_____

_____

6. Which words suggest that the narrator recognizes that human dignity is part of one's heritage?

_____

_____

_____

NAME _____ DATE _____

WHEN I AM ALONE

What do you like to do when you are all alone? Do you like to daydream, play music, dance, or have complete silence? From the list of words below, circle ONE IDEA that you consider fun and fulfilling. Then, write a short description of how you would engage in this activity when you're alone.

- dance   • sing   • draw   • play music   • sleep
- eat   • laugh   • talk aloud   • daydream

_____

_____

_____

_____

_____

_____

Now, describe details of what you would be doing in each of the situations below if you were alone. Use your imagination and complete each item. See the example for eating.

☞ **Eating**   Reclining in my favorite chair, I would be eating cookie dough ice cream topped with whipped cream.

_____

☞ Pretending _____

☞ Flying _____

☞ Reading _____

☞ Listening _____

☞ Resting with my eyes closed _____

_____

☞ Eating _____

☞ Thinking _____

_____

☞ Looking in the mirror _____

_____

NAME _____   DATE _____

WHO AM I WHEN NO ONE IS LOOKING?

Read the riddles and decide which values must be learned and embraced by everyone in order to live honest, kind, and productive lives.

Read the values at the bottom of the page, and write your choices on the line next to the correct riddle. You do not have to use every word, and you might want to use a different form for some words. (Example: reliability, reliable, unreliable.)

1. I am able to control and correct myself for the sake of improvement. I have
   _____

2. Moral, legal, and mental accountability are a way of life for me. I am
   _____

3. I am sympathetic and conscious of others' distress and I try to help those who need it. I am _____

4. I have sustained physical and mental strength in an effort to perform a task or achieve an objective. I can _____

5. Resisting opposition, danger, and hardships, and firmness of mind in the face of danger are natural for me. I have _____

6. I am able to identify with the agony of a person who has endured racism, home-lessness, violence, and illness. I have _____

7. I persist in a state, enterprise, or undertaking in spite of opposition or discourage-ment. I have _____

8. I have the ability to comprehend the world and I value freedom. I am
   _____

9. I remember my home training when I am at school. I am _____

10. I have done something really stupid and only I know about it. What was I thinking? I am _____

VALUES

COMPASSION • FRIENDSHIP • HONESTY • EMPATHY • INJUSTICE • FEAR
BEAUTY • GREED • VIOLENCE • FORGIVENESS • LOVE • HAPPINESS • UNSELFISH-
NESS • TRUTH • WORK • FAIR PLAY • RESPECT • FREEDOM • RESPONSIBILITY
PERSEVERANCE • PEACE • EMBARRASSMENT • RELIABILITY • SELF-DISCIPLINE
LOYALTY • KNOWLEDGE • HOPE • VENGEANCE

Name _____ Date _____

Now, make up a riddle of your own using one of the values listed. Share your perspectives with your classmates and other interested people. See if anyone can guess which value you selected for your riddle.

YOUR RIDDLE

_____

_____

_____

_____

_____

_____

_____

_____

_____

NAME _____   DATE _____

MY BRAG SHEET

Keep track of all your successes—no matter how minor—as a way of preparing for your future. (Maybe you won a spelling contest in elementary school, or volunteered to help raise funds for the homeless. Maybe you sang a song or played an instrument for a church program or placed high in an athletic or art competition. Possibly, you've written a story or poem, and it was published in the school newspaper or literary magazine.) Try to remember EVERYTHING and ANYTHING you've accomplished up to this point in your life. NOTHING IS TOO SMALL to consider for your record of positive personal accomplishments.

THINGS I'VE ACCOMPLISHED

_____
_____
_____
_____
_____
_____
_____
_____
_____
_____
_____
_____
_____
_____
_____
_____
_____

NAME _____ DATE _____

ARROGANCE OR SELF-ESTEEM—
WHICH IS IT?

A positive self-image and healthy self-confidence allow for good relationships with others. Yet, there are self-centered people who have difficulty acknowledging that their fellow human beings also have a right to feelings of high self-esteem. Are such people arrogant? What is the difference between high self-esteem and arrogance? Knowing the difference requires observing the motives of people as they interact with each other. Several questions will help to reveal motives:

☞ Are there instances when a person who has high self-esteem might "put down" others?

☞ Are people who are likely to "put down" others always overbearing—giving the impression of superiority?

☞ Is it possible that some arrogant people are really insecure, lonely, or suffering from low self-esteem, and that they would find it difficult to be supportive of other human beings?

☞ To what extent might a so-called arrogant person lack communication skills?

☞ What can people who are victims of "put downs" do to avoid giving in to the attacks of others?

☞ What actions would help to begin the processes of mutual respect, tolerance, and acceptance among people who have either verbally attacked—"put down"—or been the receivers of negativism? How can people "lift each other up"?

Study the examples of the different traits that are evident in individuals who have positive self-esteem, insecurity, and negative self-esteem (arrogance). Then, based upon the words beneath the examples and your own observations and experiences, identify specific behaviors for each category and write them in the appropriate places on the chart.

EXAMPLES OF TRAITS EXHIBITED IN:

POSITIVE SELF-ESTEEM	INSECURITY	NEGATIVE SELF-ESTEEM
Always Supportive	Unsure or Low Self-Esteem	Self-Centered, Support Nonexistent

© 1999 by John Wiley & Sons, Inc.

NAME _____ DATE _____

COMPLETE THE CHART BY USING
THE ADDITIONAL TRAITS EXHIBITED

put-downs • support confined to specific people or groups • shy • colorblind
overbearing • smiles in your face, stabs you in the back • questionable motives
same behavior, no matter what • airs of superiority • always friendly • jealous
overly competitive • helpful • gossips • gives benefit of doubt • deceitful
affirms self at the expense of others • largely harmless • affirms self and others
sometimes up and sometimes down • doesn't take sides • creates conflict

POSITIVE SELF-ESTEEM	INSECURITY	NEGATIVE SELF-ESTEEM
1.		
2.		
3.		
4.		
5.		
6.		

"WE'RE ALL THE GREATEST!"

On the lines below, describe how people can listen to, validate, and celebrate one another's existence. Conclude with a statement of opinion regarding whether there is a place for arrogance in human relationships. You might want to record your ideas on videotape or cassette, as well.

THINK ABOUT IT!

_____

_____

_____

_____

_____

_____

_____

_____

_____

_____

DOES EVERYONE HAVE SOMETHING GOOD TO OFFER THE WORLD?

NAME _____ DATE _____

"THE CATASTROPHE OF SUCCESS"

Success is a worthy goal and everyone should strive to achieve those things that will make him or her happy. However, the playwright, Tennessee Williams, noted in his essay *The Catastrophe of Success* that wealth and fame can be seductive. He admitted the extent to which he succumbed to the trappings of success by allowing people to clean up after him, brag about his accomplishments, and treat him as if he were better than they. He didn't like what happened to his heart after he received critical acclaim. Initially, he felt that the people who were catering to him were insincere, hypocritical, and shallow. Then, Williams found that he was cynical and his heart was no longer pure. He ends his essay by saying that he no longer wanted to be spoiled and put on a pedestal. Williams sought to regain his former state of individual responsibility, sincerity and PURITY OF HEART.

Using the statement "Purity of heart is the one success worth having" as a guide, convert all of the negative attitudes below to positive ones that can be used to develop acceptable character traits. Then read the positive attitudes and explain why they reveal PURITY OF HEART.

NEGATIVE TRAITS/ATTITUDES

1. Failure to realize that other people are important, too

   _____

   _____

2. Development of selfish attitudes and not ordinarily volunteering to help another person

   _____

   _____

3. Difficulty accepting the answer "No" when asking for something

   _____

   _____

4. Reluctance to work hard for wages, grades, or basic needs of food, clothing, and shelter

   _____

   _____

5. No desire to have others share in the benefits of life

   _____

   _____

NAME _____ DATE _____

6. Not generous towards those who are in need

_____

_____

7. Possible difficulties for those who refuse to meet their demands

_____

_____

8. Must make sure that someone else is responsible for their well-being

_____

_____

POSITIVE TRAITS/ATTITUDES

1. Open to the needs of others

_____

_____

2. Welcome opportunities to share with other people some of the joy they experience.

_____

_____

3. No hesitance to serve others; their success doesn't "go to their heads"

_____

_____

NAME _____ DATE _____

TRUE SELF-ESTEEM IN ROLE MODELS

Where do you find your role models—those people you admire and most want to be like, or emulate? Think of someone you know personally that you admire. This person, a relative or a community member, could serve as a model or mentor as you begin to plan your future. What are the characteristics you most admire in this person—those traits that you want to develop in your own life? Identify at least three people and use the Word List to find admirable traits. Feel free to add other traits that are observable in these individuals.

ROLE MODEL AT HOME	ROLE MODEL IN THE COMMUNITY	ROLE MODEL OTHER
_____	_____	_____

WORD LIST

sensitive • ego/image • curious • virtuous • hopeful • unconditional love • wise
family-oriented • industrious • dependable • positive • humble • truthful
strong • lifelong learner • confident • sense of humor • high goals • talented
good disciplinarian • flexible • brave • supportive • keeps promises • listens
powerful • kind heart • cautious • dreams • open-minded • patient
other traits: • _____   • _____   • _____

1. In what environment do you find your Number 1 Role Model?

   Circle one: HOME   SCHOOL   COMMUNITY   SPORTS   MOVIES

2. Why is this person your TRUE ROLE MODEL? Explain in one or two sentences.

   _____

   _____

   _____

   _____

3. Use the Word List to write five of the most obvious SELF-ESTEEM traits that make this person your favorite role model.

   A. _____   B. _____   C. _____   D. _____   E. _____

NAME _____ DATE _____

SPREAD OUT BEAUTY

There are two kinds of beauty . . .
There is ALL AT ONCE BEAUTY . . .
Stunning, drop dead breathtaking . . .
The kind that "A" had when we were young.
Hair falling in silkened waves around a
Carmel complexion . . . a sweet-faced
Succulent morsel of a girl . . . a DREAM.

Then there's SPREAD OUT BEAUTY that
Takes years . . . coming a little at a time . . .
Slowly revealing itself in stages . . .
Deep and warm, faultless and ever present . . .
The kind that I had when "S" said to me
When I was 12, "You're going to be so
Pretty when you grow up." And I waited.

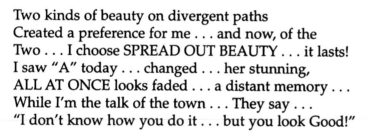

Two kinds of beauty on divergent paths
Created a preference for me . . . and now, of the
Two . . . I choose SPREAD OUT BEAUTY . . . it lasts!
I saw "A" today . . . changed . . . her stunning,
ALL AT ONCE looks faded . . . a distant memory . . .
While I'm the talk of the town . . . They say . . .
"I don't know how you do it . . . but you look Good!"

As they stare at the glow of my skin and they
Wonder about the mysterious secret in my eyes,
I remember "S" and how he saw clearly . . .
Beyond appearances . . . into my soul . . . There is no
Secret! I tell them as I'm telling you . . .
SPREAD OUT BEAUTY is the best kind of beauty . . .
Timeless . . . joyful . . . deep . . . that's what I know!

By Saundrah Clark Grevious

1. Who is the speaker in the poem?

2. What is the main idea?

3. Define the poet's concept of beauty and life.

4. Compare and contrast the two kinds of beauty.

5. Besides the fact that "A" and "S" are the initials of people, what inferences can be drawn from them regarding the two kinds of beauty? What other words that begin with "A" or "S" reinforce the themes in the poem?

6. What is the preferred state of beauty, and why?

69

NAME _____   DATE _____

LEARNING FROM MISTAKES
OF THE PAST

Read the list of mistakes and errors of judgment, and related consequences. Think of yourself as a counselor. What additional consequences or advice would you add? Identify the number of each item and write your advice on another sheet of paper. Discuss the question of whether lessons learned in childhood carry over into adulthood.

© 1999 by John Wiley & Sons, Inc.

MISTAKE OR ERROR IN JUDGMENT

1. I hit my sister.

2. I agreed to call my parents when I reached my destination and I didn't.

3. I rode my bike down a slide.

4. I slipped out of the house at night.

5. We had a laundry chute and I used to get inside and slide down.

6. I hit a girl who was bigger than I.

7. My friend and I played with matches.

8. I put a bean in my 1-year-old brother's diaper.

9. I talked about someone in a critical way.

10. I kicked a hole in the wall.

11. I flunked Spanish three times.

CONSEQUENCES SUFFERED

1. My parents "returned the favor" and I felt bad about it.

2. I upset my parents and scared them and myself when they called the missing persons bureau.

3. I hurt myself very badly.

4. I got caught by my dad.

5. One day I got stuck inside . . . I never did that again.

6. She picked me up, bounced me, and then tried to make a free throw with me.

7. One day, we almost set the house on fire when some bushes caught fire.

8. He cried when he sat down. I felt guilty, and I will be nicer to my brother.

9. Someone was listening and it came back to me.

10. I had to pay a lot of money to have it repaired.

11. I had to spend more hours studying Spanish.

NAME _____   DATE _____

MISTAKE OR ERROR IN JUDGMENT	CONSEQUENCES SUFFERED
12. I made a prank call.	12. The person dialed *69, and I got into trouble.
13. I lied to my mom about where I was going.	13. I got caught, and it was not fun suffering the consequences.
14. I roller-bladed up a ramp.	14. I fell.
15. I pierced my navel with a safety pin.	15. It really hurt, and then it became infected.
16. I was watching TV while curling my hair. I reached for the wrong side of the curling iron.	16. I burned my whole hand, and the next day it was covered with blisters.

Question: Do the lessons learned from the mistakes of childhood carry over into adulthood?

Possible Answers:

☞ "Some mistakes or errors in judgement occur innocently."

☞ "The consequences suffered early in life help to make adult life less troublesome. However, some people don't learn from their mistakes."

☞ "Consequences help us not to repeat mistakes. We remember unfortunate actions better than good ones. If we recall a bad thing relating to an action, we will not repeat that action."

☞ "When you do something wrong, there are usually consequences. These consequences help us to learn right from wrong. Some consequences come too late to learn from."

Your Answer:

_____

_____

_____

_____

_____

_____

_____

_____

_____

ON MY HONOR

Alei was caught cheating on a test, and his teacher chastised him for his wrongful act. His response to the teacher was, "I didn't think it was cheating unless I got caught." Getting caught was more stressful to Alei than the actual cheating! Think about this line of reasoning as it would apply to the stealing of someone's wallet. With Alei's point of view, it would be okay as long as the thief did not get caught. What if everyone in society held the point of view that unless your wrongful act is discovered, it's fine? What might the effect be in terms of human relationships, personal trauma, business transactions, education, health, the law, and social issues? Unfortunately, many people agree with Alei and conduct their lives based on this faulty value system. What would it take to change these attitudes so that individuals feel the NEED TO BE HONEST—not for someone else but for themselves?

Use the words and phrases below to develop reasons for personal honesty and integrity. Then, share your ideas with others. Write your ideas on the back of this sheet.

FAIR • STRAIGHTFORWARD • UPRIGHT • HONEST • TRUTH • INTEGRITY TRUSTWORTHY • HONOR • REGARD FOR STANDARDS AND THE UPHOLDING OF THE LAW • INCORRUPTIBLE • RESPONSIBILITY • FAITHFUL TO PLEDGE/ PROMISE ENCOURAGEMENT • REPUTATION • ETHICAL CONDUCT • PRAISE EARN A RIGHT TO RESPECT • SELF-RESPECT • RECOGNITION • CONSISTENCY IN ACCEPTABLE BEHAVIOR • DUTY • VALIDATION • POSITIVE ATTITUDE • CON-TENTMENT • NONMATERIALISTIC • KEEN SENSE OF RIGHT AND WRONG ADHERENCE TO THE TRUTH • MORALITY • LOVE • TOLERANCE • SENSITIVITY ENTHUSIASM

THINK ABOUT THIS!

Words look good on a sheet of paper but how can your ideas be shared with others to really help to make a positive difference in human relationships?

What role can you assume to educate those who feel that it's okay to lie, cheat, and steal? How can you help to change their hearts and minds?

NAME _____   DATE _____

A BULLY GETS HERS

Deep inside, you have the power to make decisions about what you want to do in your daily life. As a young person, you've seen people your age get into trouble because they've made mistakes or unwise choices from a variety of options. Because none of us is perfect, everyone has made mistakes. The real problem is that all of us must learn from our mistakes. People who don't learn from poor choices will continue to get into trouble. The main character in the narrative you're about to read made an unwise choice that resulted in an important lesson for her. Read the story below and answer the questions.

Jane didn't like to fight. In fact, she was really afraid to fight. But, one day, Alice kept teasing her and pushing her around. She knew Jane was afraid to hit her back, so she just continued to bully her. Because of a big crowd encouraging Alice to hit Jane more, she did, and finally, Jane could not take it anymore. Unfortunately for Alice, she had underestimated Jane's skills at tripping and punching, and she lost the fight miserably. The crowd laughed and teased Alice for picking a fight and losing. Alice never bothered Jane again. However, Jane began to feel that she could beat anybody; she was "big and bad."

Although Jane still didn't like to fight, she felt that she had to keep up the reputation she had gained by having beat up the worst bully in the school. Also, she wanted to prove to herself that she had really won the fight with Alice, and that it was not just a fluke, so Jane selected a very shy girl as her target. Her name was Paula, and she never bothered anybody. Jane decided that she would follow Paula as soon as school was out. She expected that "the crowd" would be on hand to watch and cheer her on, just as they had Alice. The only difference is that she would win with her superior tripping and hitting skills. Paula was a nobody!

Paula had stayed after school for help with a project, and the crowd was gone when she came out. Jane almost changed her mind when she found that only she and Paula were on the scene, but she decided to "test" Paula and started her "bad girl" talk. Paula ignored her and walked faster. This angered Jane, and she threw a punch which landed on Paula's shoulder. Jane had never been sorrier for that unwise move. First, Paula slapped Jane across the mouth, surprising and stunning her. Then, she raised her foot and drop-kicked Jane in a karate move that rendered her helpless. It was over in about 10 seconds. "Shy, meek" Paula had beaten Jane mercilessly, still without saying one word. She whipped Jane at her own game and went home the victor. The only thing that made Jane happy was that "the crowd" was not there to witness the beating of a "bully." As she limped home, Jane thought about Alice and the times when she threatened her; she knew that she did not want to be like Alice. Therefore, Jane denounced her new-found status as a bully and decided to write Paula a letter of apology.

All alone with her thoughts, Jane made a conscious decision never to fight with her fists, feet, hands, or mouth. Her days of being a bully were over! Jane decided that nonviolent, peaceful interaction was the way she wanted to live.

NAME _____ DATE _____

QUESTIONS FOR RESPONSE

1. How did Jane feel about fighting at the beginning of the story?

2. What best describes Jane's change of behavior during her encounter with Alice?

3. What are the similarities and differences between Alice and Jane?

4. What are the similarities and differences between Jane and Paula?

5. What attributes does Paula have that allow her to take control of the situation with Jane?

6. Compare and contrast Jane's feelings before and after her fights with Alice and Paula.

7. What lessons did Jane learn from her fight with Paula? What did she discover about herself?

8. How can the events in this story be used to keep people from choosing fighting as a way to show power over other people?

9. What decision could Jane have made when she was threatened by Alice? How would you have reacted? Explain.

10. What do you think Paula will do when she receives Jane's apology? What will this reveal about her character?

THINK ABOUT THIS!

Are there positive ways of resolving conflicts rather than fighting and other kinds of aggressive and/or violent behavior?

NAME _____   DATE _____

L'S ADVICE COLUMN

"L" is his name and he knows exactly who he is. L allows no one to define his personal goals, his outlook on life, or his relationship with his peers. And yet, L is a good listener. He has had some hard times and feels a great deal of compassion for people who cannot find the answers to their problems. This is why he started his advice column, but before you begin to bare your soul to him, read L's own account of who he is and how he feels about himself. Then, write a response to the various points he makes, indicating whether you agree or disagree with his viewpoints on LOVE, FIGHTING, SELF-CONFIDENCE, and so on. Explain by giving specific reasons. Write your own analysis of L and share it with your peers.

L'S SELF-ANALYSIS

I want other people to understand me and what I really am. First of all, my attitude is that people should live up to their own beliefs and never apologize, defend, or, backtrack on decisions they make. Second, I don't think there is anything that is tasteless or wrong, if it is done in style.

When it comes to love, it is the most important thing in the world. Everyone wants and needs to be loved. The thing that is wrong in relationships today is that, too often, there is no real love. People are willing to break all the rules just to get what they want. Love is never selfish, it is giving and doesn't take advantage of other people.

I enjoy being the center of attention; I like to be seen. If people laugh at the way I dress, I feel sorry for them because they try to look like everyone else. I am my own person. Most people judge me by what they see on the outside. "There's much more to me than what people see. I'm not worried about what they say because I usually frighten them more than they frighten me."

There is no way that I would let someone hit me without hitting that person back, but I prefer not to fight. "My handshake is firm, and my manner is polite in public, but don't let me lose my temper. My feet are planted firmly in reality. I laugh at anyone who doesn't want to be my friend because, with or without friends, I can manage."

I live life in a unique way, and if people want to be with me, they had better see my view—or just back off. I am not an immoral person. Inside, I'm a rather conservative, moral, new-fashioned soul. I have a different way of expressing myself. Teenagers should open up and be proud of whoever they are. Have a good life. I plan to.

NAME _____ DATE _____

YOUR ANALYSIS OF L'S ADVICE COLUMN

Circle the words that accurately assess L's attitude, values, and outlook on life. Add your own words to this list.

L is:

hateful • loving • arrogant • admirable • frustrated • serious • humorous
desperate • violent • apologetic • comical • pathetic • powerful • concerned
superficial • angry • bitter • destructive • irresponsible • unscrupulous • negligent
spontaneous • impulsive • disappointing • condescending • scholarly • nostalgic
selfish • fascinating • unyielding • determined • persuasive • cultured
sophisticated • careless • despicable • aristocratic • generous • sensitive
greedy • wise • courageous • silly • creative • sad
other _____   _____   _____

_____   _____   _____

Use some of the words you've circled to write your opinion of L and his attitude, relationships, and outlook on life.

YOUR ANALYSIS OF L

_____
_____
_____
_____
_____
_____
_____
_____
_____
_____
_____
_____

POINTS FOR DISCUSSION: Is L capable of offering an apology to a person he might have insulted or treated unfairly? Is the ability to apologize a good trait for people to have? Why? Would L be able to listen to other points of view? Explain. Also, discuss with your peers what L means in this statement: "I don't think there is anything that is tasteless or wrong, if it is done in style." Would you write to L for advice on a personal problem? Why or why not?

NAME _____ DATE _____

TAKING CARE OF MY MIND AND BODY

The Special Olympics have proven to society that individuals who are physically challenged can compete in sports, law, politics, education, business, and other endeavors. Often, they are expected to contribute, and they want to contribute, to society. Despite the fact that some individuals lack the full use of their physical bodies, they have the same physiological structure as other human beings. All human beings have to take care of the systems of the body in order to live the highest quality of life possible.

On a scale of 1 to 5, with 5 being the highest, rate the extent to which you take care of the systems of your body. Then, complete the survey on taking care of your body. Place your rating on the lines, and total your score at the end of the series on questions. A perfect score is 50 points!

HOW AM I DOING IN TAKING CARE OF MY BODY?

Seldom	Sometimes	Usually	Frequently	Always
1	2	3	4	5

1. I treat my body well now so that I'll be healthy later. _____

2. I eat plenty of fruits and vegetables daily. _____

3. I exercise regularly. _____

4. I go to the doctor for regular checkups. _____

5. I refuse to drink alcohol, take drugs, or use tobacco. _____

6. I bathe or shower daily. _____

7. I brush my teeth regularly. _____

9. I get plenty of rest each day. _____

8. I drink at least 8 glasses of water daily. _____

10. I eat "junk food" only once in a great while. _____

USE THE CHART BELOW TO EVALUATE YOUR SCORE—Circle one

45–50   Don't Change a Thing!

35–40   You're Almost There!

25–30   Don't Give Up—You Can Make It!

20–25   Start Changing Your Lifestyle!

5–15   Let's Talk About What You Can Do!

NAME _____ DATE _____

Based on your evaluation/score, describe necessary lifestyle changes to help you to pursue optimum health. Complete your comments below. Be specific.

_____

_____

_____

_____

My score indicates that I need to _____

_____

_____

WHAT ABOUT YOUR MENTAL HEALTH?

Your body is the house that you live in. If you take good care of it, you will be happy and healthy. In many communities, illegal drugs, cigarettes, and alcohol are available. Some people buy these harmful substances and put them into their bodies. Many become very sick—and sometimes die—from the effects of these dangerous substances.

You can make the decision to live a happier life by avoiding things that destroy your health. Remember, good physical health contributes to good mental health. Write a short description of how you take care of your mind and body. Use some of the words below as you develop your description:

Rest	Laughter	Friendship	Relaxation
Pollution	Reading	Playing	Stress
Vegetables	Prejudice	Bulimia	Alienation
Cleanliness	Anxiety	Anorexia	Knowledge
Drugs	Unkind Thoughts	Alcohol	Fruit
Fighting	Kind Words	Fresh Air	
Power	Learning	Exercise	

HOW I TAKE CARE OF MY MIND AND BODY

_____

_____

_____

_____

_____

_____

_____

_____

NAME _____   DATE _____

MY KEEPSAKES FOR LIFE

Some people keep mementos for future generations. Sometimes, these things are stored in
trunks for safekeeping. Upon opening the
trunk, one finds surprises and insight into
the lives of those who have lived in another
time. What would you like to store away for
future generations? Think of things that will
not decay with age but will last because
they are valuable for making a POSITIVE
DIFFERENCE.

From among the words on the chart, select
FOUR that are most important to share with future
generations. Write the words on the lines inside the trunk and briefly explain why you want
to pass these treasures on to people who are yet to be born.

A TREASURE TRUNK FOR THE FUTURE

KEEPSAKES FOR GOOD

KEEPSAKE 1 _____

EXPLANATION _____

KEEPSAKE 2 _____

EXPLANATION _____

KEEPSAKE 3 _____

EXPLANATION _____

KEEPSAKE 4 _____

EXPLANATION _____

Family and cultural heritage • thoughtfulness • leadership • compassion • wisdom
confidence • loyalty • togetherness • confidence • acceptance • love • freedom
nonviolence • hope • courage • gentleness • honesty • possibility • fairness
joy • pleasure • charity • commitment • manners • consideration • virtue • faith
caution • positive leadership • kindness • purpose • reason • decency • spirituality
competition • self-esteem • blessings • potential • morality • consciousness • dignity
work ethic • generosity • reliability • genuine • integrity • autonomy • intelligence
mental strength • forgiveness • lifelong curiosity • wonder • self-control • confidence

NAME _____ DATE _____

NEVER EAT ROTTEN APPLES!

Only YOU can decide what kinds of things get into your body. Avoid anything that can dirty or contaminate your bloodstream and send poisons to all of your organs. You can really avoid becoming sick if you're trained to detect the signs of bad foods. The same is true if you're to avoid the effects of things in society that can contaminate your mind and heart. As a future contributor to society, you must recognize and avoid all things that have outer beauty and inner ugliness. Such things can ruin lives—young and old.

Avoid the hidden traps that catch unsuspecting victims. Learn to recognize subtle enemies that use money, fame, sex, beauty, food, success, and power to lure those who are not trained to see the negative outcome of immediate gratification.

- TRAIN YOUR EYES TO SEE
- TRAIN YOUR EARS TO HEAR
- TRAIN YOUR NOSE TO SMELL
- TRAIN YOUR HANDS TO FEEL
- TRAIN YOUR MOUTH TO TASTE
- TRAIN YOUR MIND TO DISCERN
- TRAIN YOUR HEART TO RECOGNIZE GOOD AND EVIL
- TRAIN YOUR FEET TO RUN FROM EVIL DISGUISED AS GOOD

HOW TO AVOID OBVIOUS TRAPS

Based on your experiences with traps in society, write a brief comment on what you, as a young person, must be aware of in order to avoid falling prey to dangers. What KNOWLEDGE should you demonstrate to remain SAFE? Use the back of this sheet to write your comments. Then, share your composition with your peers. Work alone or with others to plan a video of all responses to help train younger children.

NAME _____   DATE _____

TWENTY WAYS TO SAY,
"YOU'RE THE GREATEST!"

Too often, the talk we hear is negative. People use their voices to break up friendships, or to insult or tear others down. What are some ways that you can help improve the kind of talk we hear at home, at school, and in the neighborhood? What kinds of words would help us to express our positive desires and experiences, but would also encourage others and create more harmony in all areas of our lives? Is it possible to replace selfishness with kindness, just by the words we use? SHUT OUT UGLINESS . . . OPEN THE DOOR TO KINDNESS!

Think of positive talk as you develop your list of 20 ways to make someone else feel good!

1. _____   11. _____
2. _____   12. _____
3. _____   13. _____
4. _____   14. _____
5. _____   15. _____
6. _____   16. _____
7. _____   17. _____
8. _____   18. _____
9. _____   19. _____
10. _____   20. _____

Now, try some of these positive words on others and watch the reactions! Note the number of smiles—as compared to frowns or other responses.

NAME _____ DATE _____

SPELLBOUND!

In our hurried lifestyles, we often lose our sense of wonder or awe about the things we observe. When we are in awe of the mysteries of human, plant, and animal life, we can dream of the impossible. We can believe that life can be beautiful.

As you read each spellbinding event below, reflect quietly on the wonderful realities. Think of how these and other events provide opportunities for you, a young person, to dream of what you might become—of what you might do to make the world a better place.

Circle the experiences below that take your breath away and make you wonder about the possibility of the moment lasting forever. Then, make your own SPELLBOUND list and share it.

- Michael Jordan, seemingly flying on his way to a deft dunk of the basketball as an enthusiastic crowd watches and explodes in excitement over the artistry of the man.

- The migratory patterns of birds, seals, salmon, turtles—how they know when to start out, how to get where they are going, and when to return.

- The breaking of the dawn as the first rays of sunlight split the darkness and usher in the new day.

- A hummingbird hovering in midair—its wings rotating as it takes its fill of nectar from perfumed blossoms.

- Tiny, microscopic life forms compared with 100-ton whales.

- How our huge earth is only a small planet in our solar system, and how our galaxy is only a small part of the infinite universe.

- The fragrance of dinner simmering on the stove, and being invited to partake of the fare.

- A tree—beautiful, majestic, as its branches reach for the sun and its roots burrow deeply to find refreshment.

- The night concerts as insects and nocturnal creatures make their presence known.

- Our daily allowances of air and perfectly balanced H_2O.

- The beauty of a rose.

- The birth of a baby and its ability—never having been taught—to take in nourishment.

- Our five senses that allow us to interpret, react to, and enjoy our environments.

- The vast amounts of information that can be stored on a microchip.

- The perfect symmetry of a snowflake.

NAME _____ DATE _____

Now, using some of the ideas in the bubble, make your own SPELLBOUND list and write a short composition about ONE awesome natural phenomena or a wonderful human accomplishment:

SPACE • ART
MUSIC • LANGUAGE
TECHNOLOGY • PLANTS
LAND • OCEANS
ANIMALS • HUMAN LIFE
OTHER _____

MY LIST

Spellbound by:

1. _____ 2. _____ 3. _____

4. _____ 5. _____ 6. _____

MY COMPOSITION

Spellbound by:

_____
_____
_____
_____
_____
_____
_____
_____
_____
_____
_____
_____
_____
_____
_____
_____
_____
_____

NAME _____ DATE _____

THE MOST BEAUTIFUL THING
IN MY LIFE TODAY

 Reflect inwardly, calmly, and quietly. Think of the things that make you most self-assured, happy, and content. Pretend that everything you see today is a symbol for all that is beautiful. From among all of the symbols, select one thing that you can turn into a pleasurable reality. Now, describe the splendor and beauty of this ONE thing, person, place, or idea that captures your imagination and causes you to forget negative, bothersome things. Concentrate on TODAY; find the beauty in TODAY!

A DESCRIPTION OF BEAUTY

_____

_____

_____

_____

_____

_____

_____

_____

_____

_____

_____

_____

_____

_____

How can you make beauty a regular part of your life?

_____

_____

_____

_____

_____

NAME _____ DATE _____

THE CONTENT OF ONE'S CHARACTER

Most of us can tell if we want to become friends with another person, just based upon comments the other person makes. Read the comments made by the people below, and decide whether their tone or attitudes will attract friends or drive potential friends away. Also, which people do you think contribute to society? Write A for *Attract* or N for *Not Attract* on the lines.

Don't you ever call here again. I hate tele-marketers! _____

There's no one looking. I don't have to pay. I can slip behind the gate. _____

Thanks for the com-pliment! _____

I hate my job. It takes up too much of my time. _____

I don't want to see her ugly face. She told on me! _____

What? No, I'm not going to take it. That would be stealing. _____

May I help you? _____

Please forgive me. I didn't mean it like that. _____

We *can* go to the mall. Just call up sick! _____

Look, this is the best I can do. Take it or leave it! _____

That's not your bike. Take it back where you found it! _____

Why don't you try to talk to him? _____

I know I'm the most important person on the team. You don't have to tell me! _____

I'm sorry. You caught me at a bad time. _____

NAME _____ DATE _____

"BUT YOU . . . !!"

Parents want to protect their children from harm and sometimes say "No" to a child's request to participate in certain activities. A response from the child like "Joey's parents let him . . ." only gives the parents an opportunity to say, "But you . . . !" Often, personal value systems and the standards of society or of the family dictate whether a young person will be able to do some of the things he or she wants to do or not. Consider your own conscience, family rules, values, and societal expectations that would allow you to participate or not participate in certain activities. Complete the charts below based on the standards or limitations placed on you by your parents or guardians, yourself, the community, or the larger society. Then, set up a debate with your peers on the questions that follow the chart.

ACTIVITIES THAT ARE OK OR NOT OK?

View X-rated films • Work after school • Quit school • Take drugs • Date during the week • Phone calls after 11 P.M. • Do homework • Have company when parents are away • Eat junk food • Hang out at the mall • Smoke or chew tobacco Carry a beeper • Join a gang • Drink alcohol • Stay out after 9 P.M. on weeknights Chat on the Internet • Go out without parental permission • Other _____

ACTIVITIES ALLOWED	ACTIVITIES NOT ALLOWED
1.	1.
2.	2.
3.	3.
4.	4.
5.	5.

DISCUSSION QUESTIONS:

1. Do we have too many laws that infringe upon individual freedoms in America?
2. Is our society too permissive? What or who makes up the society?
3. Are parents too strict, or are they just concerned about their children's safety?
4. Are some parents too permissive?
5. At what age do young people become responsible for themselves?
6. Whose fault is it when children or teenagers get out of control?
7. What role should members of society play in the raising of children?
8. At what age do children need to learn the difference between right and wrong?

NAME _____ DATE _____

WASHING AWAY SAND CASTLES

Building castles or houses of sand is fun, and we laugh when the heavy rains or crashing waves wash them away. Because such temporary structures have no foundation, they disappear quite easily. Real houses and castles, if they are to last, must be built upon strong, deep foundations that will stand when stormy winds and heavy rains come.

Your mind and body have to last for your entire life span. What strong, deep foundations do you depend upon for your survival? In other words, what beliefs, values, habits, words, thoughts, and deeds are evident as you protect your mind and body from internal and external harm? Because you know that you must be emotionally strong to resist peer pressure, what lifestyle changes do you have to make to get rid of behaviors that could weaken your foundation?

Use the words below to make five statements that demonstrate your ability to do things that are beneficial to you and your peers, and that make you a strong person who can stand up when trouble comes. Place the letters of your choices on the lines to the left of the numbers. Then, make your comments.

____ 1. _____

_____

____ 2. _____

_____

____ 3. _____

_____

____ 4. _____

_____

____ 5. _____

_____

A. Friendship	B. Independence	C. Arrogance	D. Education	E. Creativity
F. Awareness	G. Blame	H. Trust	I. Anger	
J. Embarrassment	K. Threats	L. Wisdom	M. Betrayal	N. Morality
O. Wealth	P. Confidence	Q. Courage	R. Other _____	
S. Other _____				

NAME _____ DATE _____

WHAT'S YOUR WORTH?

People earn various wages in their chosen fields of work. Note the professions, salaries, and wages. Who earns the least? Who earns the most? Wages and salaries should reflect what the services or products are worth to consumers. Read the list of professions or jobs and educational requirements on the chart, and match them to the appropriate wages or salaries. Then write the correct letters on the left and the earnings on the right below:

A. $30,000 – $56,000 a yr. B. $285 – $585 per wk.
C. $200 – $12.00 per hr. D. $19,500 – $23,000 a yr.
E. $25 – $200 per session F. $24,800 – $44,500 a yr.
G. $640 – $715 per wk. H. $27,500 – $33,500 a yr.
I. $300 – $375 per wk. J. $18,000 – $24,000 a yr.
K. $4.25 – $10.00 per hr. L. $28,000 – $125,000 a yr.

PROFESSION/JOB	EDUCATION	WAGE/SALARY
1.___ Blood Bank Technician	College	_____
2.___ Housekeeper	None	_____
3.___ Personal Exercise Trainer	College	_____
4.___ Highway Contractor	High School, Technical School/College	_____
5.___ Physician	Advanced Degree and License	_____
6.___ Telemarketer	None	_____
7.___ Painter/Paperhanger	None	_____
8.___ Environmentalist	College	_____
9.___ Nanny	None	_____
10.___ Meter Reader	None	_____
11.___ Refuse Worker	None	_____
12.___ FBI Special Agent	College	_____

Select a profession that you might consider. What will be the worth of your work to other people? Write about it.

NAME _____   DATE _____

LAUGHING MATTERS?

How important is laughter in our everyday lives? Research has shown that laughter eases tension and provides a sense of health and well-being. How much and how often do you laugh? To laugh with others is one of the greatest pleasures. However, to be laughed AT is one of the worst kinds of pain or hurt. Laughter occurs in each of the situations described below. Identify those in which the laughter is beneficial and pleasurable because it is not hurting another person. Identify those situations in which laughter is humiliating, devastating, and painful.

USE: **P** – Pleasure
      H – Hurt feelings

_____ 1. Bluejays push their young out of the nest, and the babies begin to learn to fly.

_____ 2. Florence struggles with the words in the story. She stutters as she tries to complete the oral reading.

_____ 3. The baby reaches for the ball and claps as his father tosses it into the air.

_____ 4. The boy runs to catch the bus and trips and falls. Just as he picks up his bookbag, his lunch box opens and his food spills all over the ground.

_____ 5. Today, girls often ask boys to dance and some boys refuse.

_____ 6. Each house that slid down the hill during the mudslide was worth at least $500,000.

_____ 7. The dancers wore colorful attire as they swirled around the stage to calypso music.

_____ 8. The chimpanzee rushed back and forth in his cage as a crowd of people gathered to watch him spin, clap his hands, and yell at the top of his voice.

_____ 9. The boy's low-slung pants slipped farther and farther below his waist. Walking wide-legged helped him to keep them up for a while, but he waited too long to hitch them up and his pants plunged to the floor.

_____ 10. "You know you're going to get a detention for cutting class," the teacher told the boy. The boy replied, "Do what you gotta do!"

FROM JOY TO JOY

Contribute to a class list of ways to increase the frequency of beneficial laughter during your waking hours. Use literary works for ideas.

NAME _____ DATE _____

THE NIGHT TIME IS THE RIGHT TIME

Some students forget that certain behaviors, while not okay for school, are perfectly fine after school, at home, or in the "hood." Of course, there are other behaviors that are never okay. In fact, they might pose danger for those involved—and others, as well. From among the items below, circle those that are NOT OKAY FOR SCHOOL but are FINE FOR AFTER-SCHOOL HOURS. Put an X on those items which are NEVER OKAY AT ANY TIME. If you feel that some actions are fine for school, list them below and explain why you would approve of such behaviors in school. Use your own ideas to help complete the chart.

- wearing sunglasses in the classroom
- doing homework in the classroom on the day it's due
- sleeping in class
- using the cordless phone or a beeper in class
- calling someone "dumb"
- wearing earphones and listening to a tape during class
- cutting in front of other people in line
- tripping another person
- studying for exams
- recycling
- talking or writing notes in class

- playing video games
- smoking behind the school
- starting a fight
- pulling the fire alarm
- hanging out with your friends
- playing with your dog
- doing homework
- volunteering to read to younger children
- memorizing your part in a play during science class
- drag racing
- going on a date
- carrying and/or concealing a weapon

THE FOLLOWING ACTIVITIES ARE JUST FINE FOR SCHOOL

Activity	Explanation/Reason

Complete your list on the back of this sheet, if necessary.

NAME _____   DATE _____

BE YOURSELF—GET RID OF YOUR MASK!

Chris wears his sunglasses every day. If he's asked to remove them, he gets angry and says that his rights as a citizen are being violated. When Chris has his sunglasses on, he walks with his head high and takes long, confident strides. His shoulders swing back and forth and no one can tell him that he's not "cool." When he doesn't have his sunglasses on, he squints his eyes, hangs his head, and complains. Does Chris have two personalities, or does he really lack confidence unless he's wearing his glasses?

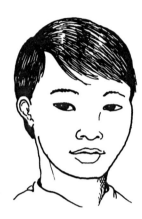

Many teenagers and adults hide their true feelings behind sunglasses, clothing styles, violent behavior, or a certain kind of talk. What makes people pretend that they are something other than what they are? What would make these people more comfortable with who they really are? To what extent do some people need to forget what others think and grow to love themselves? Write a letter of advice to Chris or any other person—including yourself—who needs to throw away the mask and find true joy in his or her reality. Be specific by explaining how to face insecurity, how to avoid hiding one's true identity, and how to develop and keep a positive self-image.

Date _____

Dear _____,

_____

_____

_____

_____

_____

_____

_____

_____

_____

_____

Sincerely yours,

_____

(Signature)

RIGHT OR WRONG?

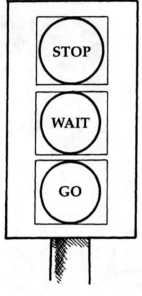

Are there standards, laws, or rules by which we can measure right or wrong? Or, in human society, can people just do whatever they want and decide whether their actions are good or bad? What if a person just decided that robbing a bank is not wrong because he needs money? What if another person decided that it would be fine to ask someone who is engaged to be married for a date? Should all drivers take driving tests and obey traffic signs? What would happen if there were no standards?

Based on your own sense of right or wrong, explain why the items listed below are necessary in everyday life. If you think that any of the items below are unnecessary, place an X on them and explain why.

1. Turnstiles/gates at the entrances to amusement parks, subway ticket booths, some stores _____

_____

_____

2. Banks _____

_____

3. Proctors for examinations _____

_____

4. Security systems _____

_____

5. Churches, synagogues, mosques, temples _____

_____

6. Dress codes _____

_____

7. Lie detectors _____

_____

8. Courts, judges, police officers _____

_____

NAME _____ DATE _____

9. Marriage vows, rings, weddings _____
   _____

10. Admission tickets _____
    _____

11. Conscience, feelings of guilt, shame _____
    _____

12. In-store video cameras _____
    _____

13. Jails, detention rooms _____
    _____

14. Licenses for driving, fishing, businesses _____
    _____

15. Check approval systems _____
    _____

NAME _____ DATE _____

SORRY, WRONG NUMBER!

Do you sometimes get the wrong messages from your observations of life? What negative impact do you think each wrong message could have on you? How do you decide what to heed or listen to—or what to shut out and ignore?

The following statements represent recorded telephone messages. Select those messages that should be ignored or heeded. Write I for IGNORE or H for HEED next to the recorded messages.

"Hi, this is Terese, I'm not home right now, but I have some very important tips for you."

____ 1. Work for and maintain good grades.

____ 2. Never walk away from an argument.

____ 3. Mean people always feel good inside.

____ 4. Marriage is temporary.

____ 5. Kindness is rewarded; you feel good inside.

____ 6. If it feels good, do it.

____ 7. Get rid of negative attitudes.

____ 8. Violence is not punished.

____ 9. Trust is not necessary in life.

____ 10. Bigger/stronger is always better.

____ 11. Modesty is an important characteristic.

____ 12. Don't expect too much of yourself or others.

____ 13. It's easy to remember truth; it's difficult to keep up with lies.

____ 14. Getting into other people's business is wise.

____ 15. True love does not exist.

Compare your list with those of your peers. Work together to come up with positive messages to replace all negative messages.

NAME _____   DATE _____

SNAPSHOTS: LOOK WHAT DEVELOPED!

Imagine that you are a photographer assigned to cover some of the most memorable examples of the best of the human spirit. Between your video camera and your 35 mm flash, you've been able to capture some of the gold-medal incidents that ordinary citizens have been involved in. Because of their kindness, strength, tolerance, and concern for others, you think that they should receive "Gold" medals. Read each incident. Then, describe the unforgettable scene you have observed and captured on video or with still photography.

GOLD MEDAL AWARDS

INCIDENT	VIVID DESCRIPTION	HONOREE
1. A relative of an airline crash victim is just hearing the news.	One woman, a stranger, held out her hand and whispered words of comfort to a mother.	One woman, who is unselfish
2. A physically challenged, wheelchair-bound student is sitting alone at lunch.		
3. Racial problems are dividing a community.		
4. Two teenagers are arguing, and a crowd gathers around.		
5. Stealing from the local convenience store is occurring nightly.		

Decide how, when, and where you will display your video or still photography in order to let others know about these gold-medal award winners.

NAME _____   DATE _____

THE TRUTH AS THE LIGHT

Any evidence of truth will make the tails of each firefly light up. Search the box and find the words or phrases that should be a regular part of every person's lifestyle. As you locate the words or phrases, think about what it means when individuals know the truth, tell the truth, and live by the truth. INDICATE EACH TRUTH by writing the identifying letter on the tail of a firefly.

a. It's okay to cheat.

b. We need friends.

c. Think for yourself.

d. Thankfulness is important.

e. Faithfulness is desirable.

f. Never set goals.

g. Speak the truth.

h. Know yourself.

i. Stay in the streets.

j. Destroy people.

k. Forgiveness is necessary.

l. One person can make a difference.

m. Stand up for what's right.

n. Stay in school.

o. Have faith in human beings.

p. Live by principles/ values/morals.

q. Make a good impression.

r. Peer pressure is beneficial.

s. Capitalize on your potential.

t. Encourage people.

u. Constructive criticism is beneficial.

NAME _____   DATE _____

HIDDEN TREASURES

Among the students in your school are some who go out of their way to be useful to other people. You don't usually hear about these young people; they really don't want other people to know that they are good, intelligent, and compassionate. When forced to face a challenge, however, they are not afraid to show their true colors. They have pride in their families, their friends, their school, and their community. They would risk injury to protect victims of violence in their schools and neighborhoods. Like hidden treasures, they have to be sought out by others, because they are content to go about their lives uninhibited by fame or fortune.

These young people are the heroes and heroines of the twenty-first century. From the list below, select the kinds of things they might do without telling anyone. Select the kinds of things they might do that others will find out about. Then, read the THINK ABOUT IT at the bottom of the page, and decide which of these qualities most represent you. Write the letter A by the hidden feats and the letter B by the obvious accomplishments of these promising, dependable human beings. Write the letter X by things that these young people would not be likely to participate in.

A. HIDDEN FEATS   B. OBVIOUS ACCOMPLISHMENTS   X. NO WAY!

THESE YOUNG PEOPLE:

_____ hate prejudice   _____ love without expecting anything in return   _____ show kindness and self-respect   _____give in to peer pressure   _____ have hope   _____ are willing to learn from other cultures   _____show tolerance and respect   _____ visit the sick or elderly   _____cheat on homework or tests   _____ do chores _____share their cultural heritage   _____ pull false fire alarms   _____follow rules _____ read to a young child   _____spend quality time with lonely peers   _____ do chores without being told   _____avoid idleness   _____ bully other people _____support injustice   _____ speak out for equality for all races and cultures _____act on a value system that supports mutual respect   _____ value their freedom _____say the Pledge of Allegiance even when others don't   _____ seek and pursue peace

THINK ABOUT IT!!!
HOW DO THESE CONCEPTS REFLECT *YOU?*
TURN THIS SHEET OVER AND WRITE ABOUT IT!!!

NAME _____ DATE _____

WHO AM I? A HUMAN BEING

Are there ever times when you feel as though you are not accepted by other people? What does this do to your self-image or self-esteem? Do you feel that you have to be of a certain background or have certain physical attributes in order to "fit in"? How fair is it that you have to even think about whether someone else approves of your very existence?

Everyone is worthy of acceptance, respect, and consideration by other people. Since not everyone receives these things, those who feel rejection or invalidation must begin the processes of self-acceptance, self-validation, and self-education. Think about your point of view on human beings rejecting each other and begin planning a solution that you will share with diverse groups of people. Higher levels of self-esteem will result from personal investigation and sharing of findings with others. Based on these ideas and your own experiences, respond to each item below:

1. People of mixed racial, religious, ethnic, or cultural origins want to be validated by their fellow human beings. If you or members of your family are racially, religiously, ethnically, or culturally mixed, describe specific aspects of this blending and the beauty of it. Include information regarding how these things confirm or validate your existence. You may also note invalidation or pain experienced, if you wish.

   _____

   _____

   _____

2. Some people like to be identified by their racial, ethnic, cultural, or religious heritage. Others do not want these labels and only want to be known as human beings. Describe your aversion to or acceptance of labeling.

   _____

   _____

   _____

NAME _____ DATE _____

3. Describe some of the benefits of being human despite one's specific racial, ethnic, religious, or cultural combinations.

_____

_____

_____

_____

4. Describe some of the benefits of being YOU because of or despite your racial, ethnic, religious, or cultural origins. Include attributes that transcend labels in your comments.

_____

_____

_____

_____

5. Discuss specific contributions that you are currently making to society or that you plan to make to society. Indicate whether your multiracial/multiethnic heritage enhances the skills or talents you possess. Write your message to society and share it with another person, a family, or members of the larger community. After writing your message, think about ways that you might accelerate your efforts to change societal attitudes towards intercultural relations. Write your message to society in a notebook or on the computer. Consider using the title below:

MY PERSONAL MESSAGE TO SOCIETY

THINK ABOUT THIS!!!

There are no pure races of human beings. Everyone is mixed, so where is the logic in racism, prejudice, and stereotyping? Accelerate your efforts to raise the level of awareness of others to these truths. Try some of these things:

WRITE A POEM • DESIGN A T-SHIRT • DRAW A PICTURE • INVENT A GAME
WRITE A SLOGAN • RUN FOR POLITICAL OFFICE • ORGANIZE A GROUP VISIT TO THE
SCHOOLS • WRITE A BOOK • WRITE A LETTER TO THE EDITOR • START A THEATER
GO ON A LEGITIMATE TALK SHOW • PLANT "GOOD SEEDS" IN THE COMMUNITY
OTHER _____ • OTHER _____

NAME _____ DATE _____

SPEAK ABOUT THE RIGHT TO BE FREE

Write a speech to deliver to an audience of racially, ethnically, and culturally diverse students, parents, or community members. Include concepts that reveal humanity's common need for freedom, justice, and equality. Focus on specific actions that you and other young people can take to improve intercultural and interracial relationships. Include the extent to which equal rights help in creating mutual respect. If necessary, consult resource materials and conduct interviews to validate the points you want to make.

   Set a date for the delivery of your speech. Choose audiences who need the messages you and your peers have developed.

EVERYONE HAS A RIGHT TO BE FREE
(Tentative title for your speech)

_____

_____

_____

_____

_____

_____

_____

_____

_____

_____

_____

_____

_____

_____

_____

_____

_____

_____

_____

Write on the back of this sheet of paper if necessary.

COMMUNITY INVOLVEMENT

INTRODUCTION

Students who work on the activities in the Community Involvement section develop an awareness of how and where they might function most effectively in their neighborhoods. Their roles and increasing responsibilities in communities outside their homes are revealed to students as they prepare to leave childhood and enter into the adult world. Because human relationships are often tenuous and unpredictable, especially for teenagers, discernment, wisdom, and self-confidence are necessary attributes for each young person. Moreover, students' prior knowledge and understanding of principles of morality and equity help them to reinforce positive self-concepts, standardize behaviors, and formulate positive human relationships.

In this section, students learn that a wide range of emotions accompany involvement in a community of human beings. Moreover, they learn that they have to increase positive and decrease negative emotions and reactions as they venture out into various environments. Ways of teaching students to recognize the importance of interdependence and forge peaceful interactions among diverse groups of people are integrated into these lessons. A significant challenge is that of students evaluating personal motives and deciding to what extent they want to participate in the building of a great community. Many strategies that will help to prepare students for their roles as responsible citizens exist within the lessons. Specifically, concepts inherent in these lessons help students to resist gang membership, enjoy interracial friendships, change negative attitudes, cultivate a strong work ethic, encourage peers, recognize and value encouraging adults, have compassion for others, and pursue peace in a world brimming with conflict.

ACTIVITIES

ACTIVITIES
Continued

TEACHER DIRECTIONS
FOR SECTION 3 ACTIVITIES

3–1 MAKING CHOICES IN THE COMMUNITY

Present the idea of making decisions in communities. Many neighborhoods have billboards advertising beer and other alcoholic beverages. Some students have seen drug dealers and the homeless who live in cars, in bus terminals, or in the streets. Elicit from students the fact that, while it is not always the fault of people who suffer, the reality is that some of these negative circumstances are the result of unwise and unhealthy choices that people have made regarding giving in to advertising or peer pressure to drink alcohol or to take drugs. Human beings of all races and cultures must have compassion for the homeless, unemployed, or hungry. Within a community, many people need attention, and there are not always enough volunteers to help the homeless, the elderly, the sick, and the disabled. Discuss the extent to which residents can cooperate and have a positive impact on their environments. Explain that many young people can be volunteers in their communities—with adult supervision, of course.

(Suggestions for volunteering: children's library, community soup kitchen, recycling centers, senior citizens center, hospitals, religious institutions). Ask students to think of things that they can do, as individuals, to help improve the lives of neighbors who might be less fortunate than they. *Give each student a copy of Activity 3-1, Making Choices in the Community.*

3–2 CHECKMATE!

Temptations and traps that take young people toward destructive ends exist in society. Elicit from students their experiences with resisting temptation and whether their escape from these traps was temporary or permanent. Have students relate metaphorically to the life choices they have to make. For example, their lives can be compared to a chess game, in which they have choices as to where to move the chess pieces. The idea is to win or survive the attack of the enemy or opponent. Emphasize the fact that each individual has the right and the power to select a piece and move it anywhere on the board. What does it take to see the whole board, anticipate the move of the opponent, and escape the traps that have been set by the opponents? Have students draw an analogy between the pieces in a chess game and themselves in the grip of negative forces or opponents such as drugs, crime, violence, hate, and other societal ills that are poised to catch, destroy, kill, violate, murder, kidnap, trick, deceive, the players—the chess pieces. Ask: What does it take to see the overwhelming destructiveness and to predict the impact on the lives of people who participate in at-risk behaviors? What does the person who wants to escape these dangers have to be aware of at all times? How does he or she win? *Give each student a copy of Activity 3-2, Checkmate!*

3–3 ADVICE FROM THE GANG

Elicit from students how some young people might get sidetracked, relate to the wrong crowd, or make errors in judgment that move them off the success track. Ask if negative trends can be reversed. Indicate how some people, including former gang members, have realized their mistakes and are working to correct them. Ask if people can abandon their former attitudes, behaviors, and practices, and adopt positive ones. *Give each student a copy of Activity 3-3, Advice From the Gang.*

3–4 CLAIMING THE CLASS CLOWN

Elicit from students ways that people who infringe upon the rights of others should be handled. For example, there are teenagers in high school classrooms who disrupt the learning of their classmates. How can these individuals be taught to respect the rights of others who really want to learn? Is there hope for the class clown, and who should intervene to curtail his or her behavior? How can students learn to respect authority AND retain their individual rights? Ask students what role parents should assume in resolving this issue. *Give each student a copy of Activity 3-4, Claiming the Class Clown.*

3–5 A QUESTION OF FAIR PLAY

Motivate students by asking three questions. Allow responses for each and discuss the various opinions.

1. Is it better to laugh at other people or with them? What is the difference between these two options? Which choice lends itself to tolerance?

2. Are the rules of society broken at the expense of the offender, or is everyone at risk? Who is responsible for ensuring that rules are not broken?

3. Would you help a bully out of trouble? Why or why not?

Elicit from students the kinds of people who become victims of intolerance, including people who might be physically disabled, overweight, extremely tall or short, ethnically diverse, poor, shy, and so on. Ask each person to imagine himself or herself in the shoes of someone who might be ostracized. Have students reflect upon the kinds of people who might have the "nerve" to "put down," ostracize, or treat others unfairly. Ask if aggression might be one of the traits of these kinds of people. Explain to students that aggression and bullying are choices made by individuals or groups. In this context, help students relate to the ongoing aggressiveness of bullies, neighborhood gangs, terrorist groups, and warring nations. Ask students if aggression is ever fair, when it results in taking away someone's freedom. Draw an analogy between fairness in sports and fairness and equality in the "game of life." *Give each student a copy of Activity 3-5, A Question of Fair Play.*

3–6 PEOPLE ARE DIFFERENT: INTERVIEW A CLASSMATE

Many people react the same way to certain situations. Ask students to share things that have made them very happy, very sad, hopeful, and so on. Note the similarities and differences in their responses. (Examples: How people of various backgrounds react to broken promises, gifts, success, educational progress, or surprises.) Elicit responses to the idea of "labeling" on job applications or legal documents. On many official papers, citizens may have to identify racial background. Individuals of mixed racial heritage often do not see a box to check for their specific racial combination. Are such directions to label racial background valid? Hold a brief discussion, and have students observe that people sometimes agree and sometimes they do not agree. Have them consider every person's right to his or her own opinion. *Give each student a copy of Activity 3-6, People Are Different: Interview a Classmate.*

3–7 REKINDLING MULTIRACIAL FRIENDSHIPS

Elicit from students their friendship experience with people of diverse races, cultures, religions, or ethnic groups. Inquire as to whether these friendships continue through the years or fizzle out. Discuss the reasons for the changes and the extent to which individuals, peers, or society impacts on the relationships. *Give each student a copy of Activity 3-7, Rekindling Multiracial Friendships.*

3–8 IDEAS OF YOUNG PEOPLE CAN HELP EVERYONE!

Write the saying "Necessity is the mother of invention" on the chalkboard, and ask students to explain it. Have them start a list of things they use in everyday life that they feel are completely necessary—that life would be miserable without. (Suggestions: refrigerators, computers, running water, cars, traffic lights, paper, paved roads, books, tables and chairs, dishes). Elicit from them ideas that might make life even better for members of society. Discuss how a few years ago a 14-year-old girl suggested ways to improve toys for a toy manufacturer—and they listened to her. Should adults take the advice of young people? Does the race, color, gender, or age of the person have anything to do with the value of his or her advice? *Give each student a copy of Activity 3-8, Ideas of Young People Can Help Everyone!*

3–9 FOREIGN LANGUAGES ARE FUN

Have students whose second language is English teach the class words for familiar terms in their native language. (If no one in your class has another first language, you might try to bring in someone from outside the class.) Discuss the fact that some immigrant students are shy in American classrooms because of the language differences. English-speaking students will see how it would be if they were in a foreign country and could not speak the language of the people there. Encourage students to reflect on the richness of the educational environment when students of different backgrounds work together to learn new things. Have students write the word for "Good Morning" or "Hello" in five languages. *Give each student a copy of Activity 3-9, Foreign Languages Are Fun.* Languages spoken in the activity illustration: Bom dia—Portuguese, Mahr hah beh—arabic, Annyong ha se yo—Korean, Kaleemehra—Greek, Habari za asubuhi—Swahili.

3–10 THE HUMAN SENSES

Enhance student comprehension of the commonalties among human beings of all races and cultures by highlighting the five senses. Indicate how all human beings interpret their environments, make choices, and carry out their daily activities as a result of their sensory impressions. Discuss how race, culture, religion, etc., have no bearing on how the senses or other systems of the human body operate. *Give each student a copy of Activity 3-10, The Human Senses.*

3–11 MUSIC IS UNIVERSAL

Elicit from students how sensory responses to music, food, books, and so on, vary from individual to individual, despite racial or ethnic origin. (**Note:** While the origin of some forms of music and art can be attributed to certain races and cultures, the ability to enjoy them transcends these differences and becomes a matter of individual preference.) Have students comment on the extent to which music helps to reduce stress and contributes to mental health. Suggest classical music and play examples for student responses to these questions. Does this music relax you? Is there proof that listening to classical music increases intelligence? Give them opportunities to discuss the effects of some types of lyrics that might cause violence. Ask their opinions regarding the solution to this problem. *Give each student a copy of Activity 3-11, Music Is Universal.*

3–12 THE "YOU" NOBODY KNOWS

Elicit from each student his or her enjoyment of the area in which he or she lives. Have each person describe the places that are interesting for teenagers to visit. To validate each student's self-image and bolster self-confidence, give each student a chance to tell a special story about an experience in his or her community.

Some neighborhoods have special features—a huge rock, a cluster of beautifully shaped trees, a hilly, curving road, a clear, still pond, a vacant lot or a corner store. Ask students to think about their special neighborhood characteristics or experiences and the extent to which they have left an impression upon them. Have them share the positive memories they have about growing up in a certain neighborhood. Have them relate the significance of this area or feature to their maturation process. Ask each student to identify personal attributes or personality traits that might have resulted from this area or neighborhood experience. *Give each student a copy of Activity 3-12, The "You" Nobody Knows.*

3–13 WRITING POETRY CAN BE FUN

Exploring one's neighborhood can be a rewarding experience. Ask students to recall walks or drives they have taken around their communities. List some of the things they describe on the chalkboard. Elicit from them some of their sensory responses to their experiences and ask them to create vivid word pictures to convey their impressions to other people. Read several poems that describe places, and ask students to convey impressions of their neighborhood into poetry or rap song lyrics for others to enjoy. Some examples of poetry that focuses on neighborhoods and interrelationships of diverse groups of people are "Casey at the Bat" by Ernest Thayer, "I Wandered Lonely As a Cloud" by William Wordsworth, and "On the Pulse of Morning," by Maya Angelou. *Give each student a copy of Activity 3-13, Writing Poetry Can Be Fun.*

3–14 WHAT WE HAVE IN COMMON

Have students contribute to a list of similarities and differences between the experiences of people from various ethnic groups. Ask students to think about and distinguish between these and physiological differences among human beings. Emphasize that human beings have more in common with one another than they do with other living species. Elicit from them the thought that individual people must come to this conclusion if racial harmony is to prevail. Write the word HAPPY on the board. Draw ovals and link them to form a chain. Have volunteers write words that represent human reactions to this emotion. Discuss the fact that these reactions transcend gender, racial, cultural, religious, and ethnic lines. *Give each student a copy of Activity 3-14, What We Have in Common.*

3–15 HELPFUL TWISTERS

Emphasize that we are all capable of making contributions to society, especially when our motives are to help our fellow human beings. Students who have difficulty with self-control will benefit from the idea of sweeping their lives clean of destructive tendencies. Present the idea of a tornado—a twister that has the capability of lifting out only the bad traits that are apparent in the lives of some people. Have students suggest what kinds of behaviors would be left that could help in the development of citizens who will contribute to, rather than take away from, society. Give students an opportunity to reflect on their abilities to make a positive difference in their environments. Ask them to share what kinds of negative motives would have undesirable effects on the community. List words such as SELFISH-NESS, DISHONESTY, PITY*, PREJUDICE, and INTOLERANCE on the board, and ask for volunteers to come up to the board, cross out each negative word, and replace it with a positive alternative. (* Offer opportunities for students to think critically about words that have "fuzzy" connotations, i.e., "pity"—discuss the circumstances under which "pity" might be negative or positive.) Elicit from them the importance of being able to recognize when destructive traits exist. Then, discuss how much better individuals would be prepared not only to contribute to society but to reap the benefits of acceptable behaviors. *Give each student a copy of Activity 3-15, Helpful Twisters.*

3–16 MY DESIGN FOR A TEENAGE "HANGOUT"

If there are inappropriate places for teenagers to have fun, let their hair down, and just "act silly," then there must be appropriate places for them to have fun. Ask students to share where young people can go to act their age, have innocent fun, or "hang out" in safety. Also, have them share what they feel are appropriate, non-threatening, safe behaviors for young people to exhibit. In other words, what can young people do and be certain that they will not be accused of breaking laws, destroying their values, or causing trouble for themselves, their families, their peers, or society?

Young people enjoy "hanging out" at various places in their communities. Sometimes it's at the mall, a park, a skating rink, or a restaurant. Elicit from students how members of the community respond to them when they are in groups. Discuss the reasons that authorities sometimes impose curfews for people 18 and under and whether such restrictions are fair. Give each student an opportunity to react to the questions and offer ideas that would be mutually beneficial for adults and young people. How can both teenagers and adults in the neighborhood feel safe when young people want to be together and have innocent fun? Ask students to describe some of the features of an ideal teen "hangout." Have them create a list of the features the "hangout" would need in order to attract teenagers and keep them involved in healthful, productive, and entertaining activities. Give them an opportunity to design such a place with the intent of presenting the best designs to parents, school administrators, school board, community members, and township officials. *Give each student a copy of Activity 3-16, My Design for a Teenage "Hangout."*

3–17 WHAT IS THE PRIZE?

Many people play games, enter contests, and enter the lottery for the prizes they want to win. Usually, the prizes are monetary or material goods. Often, people can get along without these prizes but they just want to add to what they already have. Have students respond to the question, "What are some of the nonmaterial prizes that human beings need and money cannot buy?" Hear all responses. (Suggest: equality, interdependence, patriotism, etc.) Then, ask them to identify those material things that they can do without. Hear all responses. Discuss designer clothes vs. regular clothing and the difference between NEEDS and WANTS. Finally, elicit from students which they think are more important—material goods or nonmaterial values. Also, ask what they think are the ultimate prizes in life (such as freedom, inner peace, or positive self-image). *Give each student a copy of Activity 3-17, What Is the Prize?*

3–18 THE MOST BEAUTIFUL WORDS IN THE WORLD?

Elicit from students the positive effect that compliments can have on people, especially when they are sincerely and freely given. For example, have them make a list of positive things they can say to their peers and others and notice the reactions of the recipients of kind words. Discuss what happens inside a person who has to endure "put-downs." Ask students to contrast these internal feelings with those that occur when people are encouraged. Ask volunteers to share their ideas of beautiful words and how they might be used in developing positive or complimentary comments about someone. Have students name a person who might receive these beautiful words. Caution students against giving false, condescending, or insincere "compliments." Discuss why these could be just as damaging, or even more so, than obvious "put-downs." Write the sentence "If you can't say anything good, don't say anything at all" on the board. Give students an opportunity to explore the meaning and determine the value of this concept in improving human relationships and in formulating more peaceful environments. *Give each student a copy of Activity 3-18, The Most Beautiful Words in the World?*

3–19 BENDING THE RULES

Have students respond to the question "Why do people break rules or defy the laws of society?" Then, ask them to consider whether there are ever times when it's okay for people to bend the rules and do as they please. Write the words STANDARDS, LAWS, and RULES on the board or on a chart, and ask students to give examples of some with which they are familiar. Discuss why they are necessary in a society and what could happen if we did not have them. Have them transfer these considerations to their homes, the school, and various places in the community. For example, it is important to wait in line to be served at a fast-food place or at the motor vehicle agency. Elicit from them the existence of and need for "unwritten" laws and what happens when these are violated. Discuss the importance of individuals' showing basic courtesies when there are no written standards, laws, or rules. Ask students to share their ideas on how people learn these basic courtesies. Discuss, as well, the extent to which people who break rules endanger the lives, health, and well-being of others. *Give each student a copy of Activity 3-19, Bending the Rules.*

3–20 JUST DRIVING AROUND?

Elicit from students their opinions regarding when individuals should begin to assume responsibility for their actions in all of their environments. Give students an opportunity to listen to this scenario and ask for oral responses. "A taxi driver picked up passengers with his meter running. They gave him the address and he proceeded down a busy street while indicating that he was hard of hearing and that he was not sure where to find their location. He said it *might* be up there, pointing in front of him. In the meantime, the passengers were aware that they were paying the initial fee, 30 cents per minute, plus 20 cents for slow traffic or lights. The entire trip took 10 minutes. The turns the driver made, the street signs, and the same buildings that the passengers had seen when they started out showed that the driver had brought them almost back to where they began. *"In the process of doing his job, this taxi driver had cheated his passengers. He drove around aimlessly, killing time, pretending that he didn't know where he was going, and pretending that it was hard to hear the directions. He implied that the passengers needed to be clearer in their directions, even though they had given him the brochure with the street number, name, and cross streets. It was obvious that he had selected streets filled with pedestrians and lots of traffic. His meter never stopped, of course."* Ask students to respond to this scenario by answering the following questions:

1. Do you think this taxi driver really didn't know the way to the passengers' destination or did he deliberately mislead them?

2. How well should people know their jobs?

3. Do you agree or disagree with the conclusions drawn in the last four sentences of the scenario? Explain your position.

Have students think about how people should approach a responsibility, whether it is a simple household chore, a school assignment, or a job. Should they put off responsibilities until another time, procrastinate, or just ignore them altogether? What would be the result of this kind of attitude were it to apply to people in fast-food services, banks, schools, airlines, post offices, doctors' offices, fire stations, gas stations, homes, amusement parks, and so on? When should people begin to take their responsibilities seriously? To what extent should people be able to resist the temptation to "goof off?" To what extent should people be honest in their work? Ask students, "What advice would you give to a person who has difficulty carrying out his or her job responsibilities whether it is at home, in school, in the community, or in the workplace? Would your advice change if this person were volunteering his or her time?" *Give each person a copy of Activity 3-20, Just Driving Around?*

3–21 DRIVING SAFELY

Inquire about the importance of each person's having control over his or her own life. Compare this to the necessity of a drivers' maintaining control of a vehicle. Discuss what happens when a person loses control of a car, and compare this to what can happen when people lose control over certain aspects of their lives. Ask students to offer examples of actions that demonstrate a loss of control. Follow these examples with suggestions about how to resolve the situations. Give students two other specific "loss of control" scenarios:

1. As others are eating, a student jumps on top of a lunch table in the cafeteria and proceeds to leap from one table to another before he finally lands on the floor and runs yelling and screaming down the hallway. Assess the loss of control of this student and the impact he might have on others. Ask students to suggest a way to handle this problem.

2. A teenager comes into the house with an expensive item that the parents did not buy and they begin to ask where the item came from. Instead of giving the teen a chance to explain that he or she is supposed to hide this birthday present for a friend, the parents accuse the teen of shoplifting and ground the youngster for one month. They also threaten to call the police. Assess the loss of control of parents who have misjudged their child.

Have students acknowledge that parents—and other adults—are human and can make mistakes. Emphasize that everyone, young and old, makes mistakes. Ask students the extent to which young people can prove their maturity and sense of responsibility to adults who might underestimate their honesty, positive attitudes, work ethic, and ability to follow the "straight and narrow"—the rules and laws of home, school, community, and the nation. Tell them that good citizens, like good drivers, maintain control at all times. *Give each student a copy of Activity 3-21, Driving Safely.*

3–22 GIVE AN INCH . . . TAKE A MILE

Have students share specific examples of times when they have had to resist the temptation to eat more than they should, spend more than they should, or stay out later than they should. Ask how many have taken advantage of liberties given by adults in the home, school, or community. Discuss the tendency that some people have to go beyond the limits of the laws, rules, or standards, and whether these people make it worse for everyone else. Discuss, as well, why some people feel that they have to break the law. Have students give their opinions regarding the need for curfews, prohibitions, fines and penalties, dress codes, and so on, and give specific examples of their effectiveness or ineffectiveness. Ask them to share times when they have taken liberties with the rules they have to live by, and the extent to which they might have suffered as a result of some indiscretion. (**Note** of **caution:** Teacher awareness of private matters that students should not share with the public is necessary.) *Give each student a copy of Activity 3-22, Give an Inch . . . Take a Mile.*

3–23 SEEING OUR REFLECTIONS IN GLASS HOUSES

Write the sentence, "No one is perfect" on a chart or the chalkboard and ask students to agree or disagree with it and back up their opinions with concrete examples of human frailties. Ask if people tend to judge others more harshly than themselves when it comes to the way human beings behave in society. Have them consider the need to look within themselves before judging another person. Explore the concept of knowing oneself, and ask if we have a right to condemn someone we do not know. Elicit from students the need for self-assessment and self-correction rather than criticism and condemnation of others. Ask them to list ways that individuals can assess themselves beneath each of these headings: ATTITUDE, PUBLIC BEHAVIOR, and MOTIVES. Consider with them whether society would greatly improve if people discovered why they have certain attitudes and behave in certain ways. *Give each student a copy of Activity 3-23, Seeing Our Reflections in Glass Houses.*

3–24 THE TREE: A SYMBOL OF PEACE

Ask students to describe how a tree might symbolize human relationships. For example, inquire as to how the roots might symbolically provide the emotional, and spiritual nourishment that all human beings need. Listen to their responses, and suggest that the human emotion of LOVE can be spread throughout the entire human family by a symbolic root system. Talk about how the human family might share in the benefits of that love that spreads from the roots through the tree trunk and manifests itself through the multiple branches and leaves. Have a student read the poem by Maya Angelou, "On the Pulse of Morning," in which she uses natural elements (a rock, a river, and a tree) to symbolize how all Americans can come to respect each other. Discuss how, despite their diversity, it is possible for many people to come to care about one another's well-being and, in the process, come to appreciate their human commonalties. *Give each student a copy of Activity 3-24, The Tree: A Symbol of Peace.*

3–25 RIGHT SIDE UP!

Elicit from students their opinions as to why so many adults are suffering from social ills such as drinking, violence, illiteracy, depression, rejection, drug abuse, and low self-esteem. Have them focus on the fact that many older people who suffer from these and other social ills made unfortunate lifestyle choices early in their lives. Suggest that now is the time for them and other young people to closely examine their lifestyles and make the necessary changes in attitudes and behaviors to ward off problems later in life. Productive members of society do not turn it upside down, but do everything in their power to reverse negative trends. Give the class an opportunity to hear the following scenarios and respond to them:

1. Craig, an above-average A/B student, shares with his peers that he was not always a good student. He refused to study and thought homework was only for "nerds." Now, he likes the way he feels when he's prepared for class, and he is trying to persuade some of his friends who are like he used to be to change their attitudes.

2. John, a former gang member and drug dealer has given up that lifestyle because he has a little brother whom he wants to protect from violence. Sometimes, he runs into the old crowd and risks their physical attacks, but he lets them know that *he controls* his life now. His air of confidence fends them off, and he has hope that he can lead his brother in the right direction.

3. Petra used to smoke and drink alcohol but has since decided that her health in later life depends on her current lifestyle choices. She knows that she's still young enough to avoid the illnesses that come from abusing tobacco and alcohol.

Inquire of students how these three young people had prepared to contribute to their own progress early in life. Discuss the fact that they were, at first, not using their talents and skills, and developing their potential to better themselves or society. Give students a piece of paper or a card, and ask them to write down one or two negative traits, attitudes, behaviors, or lifestyle choices. Have them indicate how these negative things have hurt them, others, or society in general. Then, ask them to reflect silently on whether they have changed and to write this on the card. In addition, have them suggest what must happen if they are to make progress. Let them know that help or intervention is available if they need it. Indicate that they should always seek help from those who care the most for them and are accessible to them—if not family members, then someone else who is important to them. Ask students to express their ideas as to the risks of not making positive changes. Reinforce the idea that good lies within each person, and that each person needs to be nurtured and should have opportunities to develop emotionally, socially, educationally, and spiritually. Have students agree that in order to get the most out of life, they have to care about doing the right things in life. *Give each student a copy of Activity 3-25, Right Side Up!*

3–26 A Good Report (Card)

Ask students if they would like to have an opportunity to give adults grades. Allow them to express both negative and positive feelings. Then, indicate that adults enjoy giving good reports, especially when students earn them. Also, parents like to compliment their children when they obey, show responsibility, and so forth. Certainly, good reports are preferable to negative reports. Suggest that all students focus on the positive things that at least one adult has done for them; these good report (cards) are a way to reward sincere adult contributions on the behalf of teenagers. While students should not issue bad reports, if an adult is not earning all A's or 5's, students should feel comfortable addressing areas that the adult can strengthen. (For example, if an adult is not a good listener, a young person should be able to address this issue.)

Write the words POINTS/GRADING CRITERIA on the chalkboard or a chart, and indicate that their good reports might help to reinforce strengths and eliminate weaknesses on the part of someone they admire. Give students an opportunity to practice assigning numbers to specific criteria on the chalkboard (Note the rubric for 5–1 on the activity sheet). Have them share how some adults have helped them, and ask them to rate the significance of this contribution using the numbers 1–5, with 5 being the highest. Discuss the extent to which each student's life or outlook on life might be better because of the qualities that one adult was truly happy to share. Ask students to be specific in naming such admirable traits as being supportive, being a good listener, being available and understanding, being able to discipline with love, and being able to exhibit self-control and reason. Discuss the importance of giving good, yet true, reports of adult intervention, encouragement, and support. Ask students to study the broad headings in each category on the report card. Then, have them study the subcategories beneath the broad headings: LISTENING, SUPPORT, COMPREHENSION, KNOWLEDGE, and ATTITUDE. Have them total the numbers for each section and assign a letter grade accordingly: 25–20 = A, 19–15 = B, 14–0 = C, etc. Students may make comments and complete the REPORT SUMMARY at the bottom of the activity sheet. Discuss how students will present these good reports to the recipients. *Give each student a copy of Activity 3-26, A Good Report (Card).*

3–27 It's Time to Shout Out!

Good news and positive experiences should be spread around so that everyone can benefit from at least knowing about them. Ask students to consider their own personal fears about the bad things that are happening in their own environments. Are there fights in school that threaten the safety of others? Do people cheat on exams and brag about their good grades? Are there gangs that promote racism and violence in their communities? Have them suggest ways that they can make a difference. If some students are already making a positive difference in their homes, schools, and communities, ask them to share this with the class. Indicate that it's okay to brag about something good that you are doing to help the world around you to become a better place. Ask for a volunteer to explain what the term "shout out" means. (**Note:** Some listeners like to call their radio stations and ask for certain songs to be played for special people in their lives. They want every other listener to know how much they care, so they take this opportunity to "shout out" their love and caring for strangers to hear.) Ask students to imagine that they have a bullhorn to shout out their good news, and that they can control what comes out of the other end. Have them think about why they want to share; discuss what motivates them in their "shout-outs." Indicate that a great responsibility accompanies the privilege of shout-outs because they want the world to be better—not worse—as a result of what they say; they should have good reasons for their shout-outs. Have them consider the best motives from among the choices listed below:

1. EXCITEMENT
2. FEAR
3. TO PROMOTE TRUTH
4. TO RIDICULE
5. TO PROMOTE UNDERSTANDING

6. CONTENTMENT
7. ENCOURAGEMENT
8. POWER
9. CONFIDENCE
10. IT'S A CHALLENGE

11. ANGER
12. TO BE OFFENSIVE
13. TO GET ATTENTION
14. TO MANIPULATE OTHERS

Give each student a copy of Activity 3-27, It's Time to Shout Out!

3-28 Ouch!!! . . . AHHHHH!!!

Encourage students to consider that each new day in their lives presents an opportunity for constructive behaviors. Ask them to contemplate the alternative of facing each new day with such destructive intentions as violence, cursing, cheating, and so forth. If there is disagreement, discuss the reasons for it. Have students share how they would try to help someone who has suffered some indignity at the hands of another person. For example, what if a peer is upset because someone accused him or her wrongly? What could be said to make the person feel better? Have students consider the fact that each of them can become proficient in soothing hurts. If some people get pleasure from inflicting emotional pain on others, other people can take pleasure in counteracting these negative behaviors. (**Note:** Students can learn to help others by discussing how to react to purposeful insults, how to avoid becoming a victim, and how to view the aggressor as weak, insecure, and in emotional pain. Students must also know when to ask for adult intervention.) *Give each student a copy of Activity 3-28, Ouch!!! . . . AHHHHH!!!*

3-29 Tickets, Please!

Ask students if any assumption can be made about a person who buys season tickets to the games of a certain basketball team. Ask the same about people who buy lottery tickets? Talk about how people can have varied interests and how tickets are purchased to gain access to sports, music, political, and other types of events. Ask students to tell why people spend their money on tickets. (**Note:** Suggest that when they do spend money, people want what they pay for. Elicit from students that audiences expect that what they are paying for will benefit them personally in some way.) Have students look through the newspapers for community events and discuss which events are appealing to them. How many people would prefer entertainment, and buy a ticket to a movie or an amusement park vs. a fund-raiser for a local politician? Ask how many people would buy a ticket to get into the skating rink rather than one to the aquarium or planetarium. Have them develop a sense of what the public wants or needs. Also, discuss the purposes for various types of events, including political, entertainment, educational and informational. (**Note:** Discuss how tickets for fund-raisers provide benefits that go beyond those for individuals.) Elicit from students the idea that the kinds of tickets people buy reflect their priorities and/or interests in life. Ask them to share what they think their ticket-buying reveals about them. *Give each student a copy of Activity 3-29, Tickets, Please!*

3-30 Just Like a Tiger!

Pose this question to students: Is it ever right for people to become aggressively angry about an issue, and to get involved based on anger? Have them indicate instances when someone they know became very angry and acted to make changes in the situation that caused the conflict. Take a poll of the class to find out how many students approve of "righteous indignation." Have them make a distinction between constructive intervention and destructive intervention. Then, discuss the need for every person to gain the confidence to speak out and act on his or her convictions as to what is right and what is wrong. *Give each student a copy of Activity 3-30, Just Like a Tiger!*

NAME _____ DATE _____

MAKING CHOICES IN THE COMMUNITY

People do many things in their neighborhoods. When people have pride in their communities, they participate in activities that contribute to its stability and safety. Think of some of the things that are healthful, educational, and/or fun for families and friends to do. Write ten of these things in the list below:

ACTIVITIES FOR FAMILIES, FRIENDS, AND NEIGHBORS

Families and friends can:

1. _____

   _____

2. _____

   _____

3. _____

   _____

4. _____

   _____

5. _____

   _____

6. _____

   _____

7. _____

   _____

8. _____

   _____

9. _____

   _____

10. _____

    _____

NAME _____ DATE _____

CHECKMATE!

In the games of chess or checkers, opponents seek to take each other's chessmen or checkers by outthinking the other person. There are "safe" places on the board where a player can escape, rethink a survival strategy, and then go for the win.

On the board below, identify the safe places where you can move your pieces. There are very obvious danger spots on the board; however, you must watch out for the subtle places that seem to be safe, yet are deadly traps! You want to win, you want to survive, so be careful and think before you move! Write 1 ON THE GOOD SPOTS TO MOVE TO and write 2 ON THE SPOTS TO SKIP OVER.

YOUR MOVE

ABUSE	VIRTUE	ARROGANCE	EQUALITY	SINCERITY	DISCIPLINE	PRAISE	PEER PRESSURE
TRUTH	SUFFERING	HEALTHFUL	LOVE	VULNERABLE	SELF-CONTROL	FROWNS	OBEDIENCE
POWER	FEAR	DISRESPECT	CRIME	FREEDOM	LYING	MATERIALISM	VOTING
CRUELTY	SMILES	FAITH	MORALITY	COMPASSION	VULGARITY	FRIENDSHIP	PETTINESS
COURAGE	HATRED	GREED	HOSPITABLE	BEAUTY	PRIDE	USING A FAKE ID CARD	INJUSTICE

Discuss your choices with another person. Talk about why you selected some areas of the board and avoided the others. Be specific in your explanations.

NAME _____ DATE _____

ADVICE FROM THE GANG

Success stories are always great to hear because they usually tell how someone has overcome tragedy or misfortune. Many young people who have been in trouble have received help, and are eager to share the pitfalls of their alliances with violence-prone gangs and what they did to turn their lives around. They are being rehabilitated and, as a result, they want to develop skills and talents that were put on hold while they were in gangs.

A racially diverse group of gang members appeared on a recent talk show and displayed their persuasive talents. Each gang member had a loud-and-clear message for young people in the audience. They wanted them to listen!!! Hear what they had to say:

"IF YOU DON'T BELONG TO A GANG, DON'T JOIN ONE!"

"STOP KILLING EACH OTHER!"

"GET YOUR EDUCATION WHILE YOU'RE YOUNG!"

WHAT THEY REVEALED WHEN THEY SPOKE:

- One gang member was married and expecting a child.
- One gang member had recently been shot.
- One gang member had been in jail and never wanted to go back.

Another gang member is in college and regrets that he didn't pay more attention in school when he was younger, but he definitely is determined to finish his college program.

All the gang members agreed that their lives were constantly in danger because of animosity between rival gangs.

All gang members agreed that solutions to their problems could be found in discovering their talents, pursuing them, and finding meaningful work.

All gang members sounded as if they really meant what they said. Their main reason for coming on the talk show was to warn other young people not to make the mistakes they had made. Also, all gang members were working to develop the responsibilities they needed to become full, contributing members of society.

In your opinion, why should society try to help young men and women who have committed crimes? Should the fact that they are trying to turn their lives around cause others to reach out to help them? Check the things you agree with below, and write your reasons for agreeing or disagreeing with these statements on the back of this sheet.

_____ Success can come only when there is opportunity.

_____ Everyone deserves a chance to pursue her or his dreams.

_____ People can be rehabilitated.

Why I Agree _____

Why I Disagree _____

NAME _____ DATE _____

CLAIMING THE CLASS CLOWN

Class clowns or troublemakers are often looking for help, for friends, for understanding, for opportunity, or for recognition. If you're not a class clown or a troublemaker, meet Bill; he is both, except when he is the center of attention. Bill settles down only when he's involved in a group and he can be the leader. Bill becomes excited about discovering new things and asks lots of questions of the teacher and his peers, and is the first one to suggest using references or going outside the class for help. When the teacher is working with the whole class, Bill is always the first one to say he's bored. He looks out of the window, gets out of his seat, talks out of turn, and makes a nuisance of himself. He has also been known to fly paper airplanes in class in order to get his peers to laugh.

Although Bill is bright and wants to learn, he has a problem that infringes upon the rights of his classmates to learn. The teacher has given Bill the benefit of the doubt, but is now ready to call his parents, the principal, and the counselors for help. Everyone knows that Bill is a good kid. He is nonviolent and creative, and many students would like to be his friend. Most kids stay away from him outside of school, however. Bill has a lot to learn about relationships with others, including those who are trying to help him get his education. Do you think you can help Bill?

What does Bill need to do in order to capitalize on his curiosity and desire for leadership? Write a letter of advice to Bill using ideas suggested by the words below. Be certain to reveal that you want to be his friend early in your letter. Include some of his good qualities and things that you might have in common with him. Add other words to this list if you wish.

cooperation	fun	responsibility
generosity	friendship	procrastination
rules	courtesy	self-discipline
politeness	respect	other _____
patience	restraint	other _____
discipline	listening	other _____
concentration	sharing	

Can you or anyone else identify Bill's race, culture, or ethnicity from the written description above? Circle One: YES   NO

Do these things matter in terms of his behavior? Circle One: YES   NO

Follow the format for a friendly letter. Proofread, edit, and share your letter with peers if you like. Use the back of this sheet.

NAME _____ DATE _____

A QUESTION OF FAIR PLAY

Everyone likes to be happy, have fun, smile, laugh, and enjoy life. Playing is a good way to have fun. In American society, both children and adults play. Fairness, following the rules of the game, and good sportsmanship are expected of all players in athletic competition. In professional and nonprofessional sports, you risk injuries if games are played unfairly. Good sportsmanship also gives competitors opportunities to demonstrate their true athletic skills. Think of "play" and "game" as similes and metaphors for LIFE as you read the next statement.

"Life is like a game in which the players have to exhibit fairness and good sportsmanship. This fairness and equality should apply to people of every race, color, religion, and culture so that they can be happy. Some people play the game of life unfairly by not applying the rules that would equalize opportunities to win for everyone. By withholding equality and freedom from certain members of society, some powerful or biased people make the lives of their fellow human beings unhappy. As a result of this unfairness, injustice, and lack of equal opportunity, some people do not have a chance to develop and demonstrate their talents and skills. How can playing games and competitive sports by the rules help us to see the need for granting equality to all members of society, despite their age, race, color, gender, culture, or ethnic origin?"

What can competitive sports teach us about following the "rule of law" as guaranteed to every U.S. citizen by our U.S. Constitution and Bill of Rights?"

EQUAL PROTECTION	RIGHT TO ASSEMBLE	COMPROMISE	LIBERTY
SELF-DISCIPLINE	FAIR PLAY	JUSTICE	FREE SPEECH
OTHER _____	OTHER _____	OTHER _____	

Using some of the words above, react verbally or in writing to the unfairness, injustice, or inequality in each of the situations below:

1. Several young people, good friends, walk in upon a situation in which one of their other friends is beating up a new kid in the neighborhood. The new kid is wearing a turban.

   Your Reaction: _____

   _____

   _____

2. The star quarterback on the school's championship football team did not like the referee's call on his last play. He glared at the referee, cursed at him, and spit at him.

NAME _____   DATE _____

Your Reaction: _____

_____

_____

3. Jim was shopping in the local convenience store and realized that the store manager was following him around. Jim protested.

   Your Reaction: _____

   _____

   _____

4. Gina knew that the dress codes forbade tank tops and short shorts in school. Gina wore them anyway, and told everyone that the assistant principal and her uncle were best friends.

   Your Reaction: _____

   _____

   _____

5. Both Fran and Phillip were winners in a debating competition. Finalists were invited to a banquet at a fancy uptown hotel and the dress was to be formal. Fran's family could not afford to buy her the appropriate attire.

   Your Reaction: _____

   _____

   _____

6. Chris is overweight, unpopular, and depressed. Although very intelligent, people always notice and comment on the size and not the mind of this teenager.

   Your Reaction: _____

   _____

   _____

7. During a flood, some volunteers went to help people who were stranded. One of the members decided not to volunteer his time when he saw that the people who needed help were a race other than his own.

   Your Reaction: _____

   _____

   _____

8. Every day, Dilia ate alone at lunch time. After picking at her food, she sat in her wheelchair and stared into space. It was obvious that she was without friends.

   Your Reaction: _____

   _____

   _____

NAME _____ DATE _____

PEOPLE ARE DIFFERENT: INTERVIEW A CLASSMATE

It will be interesting to learn how you and your classmate react to similar situations. For example, if you tell someone a secret and he or she reveals it to others, how do you react? How would you act if someone were to surprise you? Now you can discover the experiences that people have in life, and discuss their similarities and differences. Conduct a brief interview of one of your classmates. Then, introduce him or her to the rest of the students. Record your interview on video or cassette tape.

Formulate your own questions on the lines below. Use the questions on the Autobiographical Questionnaire in Activity 1-3 and ideas from your teacher to help you decide what kinds of questions to ask:

Question 1 _____

_____

Response _____

_____

Question 2 _____

_____

Response _____

_____

Question 3 _____

_____

Response _____

_____

Question 4 _____

_____

Response _____

_____

NOTE: Compare and contrast your findings of human diversity with those of other students.

NAME _____ DATE _____

REKINDLING MULTIRACIAL FRIENDSHIPS

In the May 3, 1993, issue of *Newsweek* magazine, a 15-year-old student describes his loss of a friend of another race. In the article, he states that there are differences between the way some African-American and European-American students relate to one another in his school. Specifically, the students choose to be with members of their own race in the cafeteria. Most of the white kids all sit on one side and most of the black kids sit on the other side of the lunchroom.

The writer indicated that, despite the laws mandating desegregation, African-Americans and European Americans are still separate, and he feels sad, especially because of his loss of a friendship. He notes that, as young boys, he and his friend "played catch . . . went bike riding . . . slept over . . . went to movies and amusement parks . . . and bunked together at summer camps. Now we are both juniors in the same high school and only exchange a polite Hi or Hey." They never see each other after school.

Obviously, these two young men were good friends at one time and might benefit from renewing their friendship. Is this something that they should try? What are some possible causes of young friends of different races parting ways as they grow older? Imagine that you have had this experience with the loss of a friend because of differences in race, culture, or ethnicity. Think of several reasons why the friendship should be renewed. Support each argument with concrete ideas that reveal mutual benefits of a rekindled friendship. Record your arguments in the boxes below.

ARGUMENT 1	ARGUMENT 2
ARGUMENT 3	ARGUMENT 4

DEVELOP A TALK SHOW ON "REKINDLED FRIENDSHIPS"

NAME _____   DATE _____

IDEAS OF YOUNG PEOPLE CAN HELP EVERYONE!

Have you ever had a great idea and thought it might be possible to invent or create something based upon that idea? An 18-year-old high school student designed a device that would convert water into fuel. As a result of reading the book *2001: A Space Odyssey* by Arthur C. Clarke and working on a scientific concept of using water to produce fuel, he came up with the design. This student won a great deal of recognition for his invention, and a plastics firm is said to be building cylinders and circular plates for the device. Society will benefit from the fact that a young person followed through on an idea.

Do you have an idea that might be useful to society? It does not have to be an idea based on scientific principles. Have you written a poem, story, or song you feel good about and want to share with other people? Most young people are aware of how adults struggle with social, educational and political issues. They don't always have the answers. Do you have ideas about how to fix problems with the economy, law, business, education, politics, medicine, immigration, or civil rights?

Select an idea from those in the previous paragraph, or use one of your own. Narrow the focus and explain the idea or concept on the lines; then, describe its usefulness to society. Or you may wish to do a drawing, cartoon, or comic strip on the back of this page to illustrate your idea.

MY IDEA OR INVENTION

_____

_____

DESCRIPTION OR DETAILS OF HOW IT COULD BENEFIT OTHERS

_____

_____

_____

_____

_____

_____

_____

_____

NAME _____   DATE _____

FOREIGN LANGUAGES ARE FUN

English-speaking students do not always understand how difficult it would be if they were in a foreign country and could not understand the language. This activity sheet can give you an idea of the challenge of learning a new language.

If you were in a foreign country and did not know the language, you would need help. Identify five necessary words for things that you use every day. Then, ask a classmate who knows a language other than English to provide these words in his or her language.

A. 1. _____   4. _____
    2. _____   5. _____
    3. _____   Language _____

Go to a student who speaks another language and ask him or her to help locate the information regarding the days of the week. Make sure that you identify the language.

B. 1. _____   5. _____
    2. _____   6. _____
    3. _____   7. _____
    4. _____   Language _____

C. With help from someone who speaks the language, write the twelve months of the year in a foreign language.

    1. _____   7. _____
    2. _____   8. _____
    3. _____   9. _____
    4. _____   10. _____
    5. _____   11. _____
    6. _____   12. _____

    Language _____

NAME _____ DATE _____

D. Get another person to help you identify five common items and write the foreign language (FL) word for each. Ask classmates who are bilingual to help you pronounce the FL words.

First item: _____ FL word _____

Second item: _____ FL word _____

Third item: _____ FL word _____

Fourth item: _____ FL word _____

Fifth item: _____ FL word _____

E. As an English-speaking student, explain how you think you might feel being in a foreign country without knowing how to speak the language.

_____

_____

_____

_____

_____

_____

_____

_____

_____

_____

_____

_____

_____

_____

NOTE: You can also use foreign-language dictionaries to write the words for these and other items.

NAME _____ DATE _____

THE HUMAN SENSES

All human beings interpret the world around them through their senses. Race, culture, gender, and religion have no bearing on the ability of people to understand, sort, and communicate the information processed in the brain. Often, more than one sense is used to help us to observe, enjoy, and respond to daily experiences. Decide which sense or combination of senses is necessary for people to interpret and respond to the things around them. Write the number or numbers of the correct sense(s) next to each item below:

SENSE(S) NEEDED TO ENJOY OR RESPOND TO:

1.

Books _____   Clouds _____

Food _____   Music _____

Love _____   Driving _____

Flowers _____   Brushing Hair _____

Getting Dressed _____   Cooking _____

Washing Dishes _____   Drinking _____

Movies _____   Frowns _____

Smiles _____   Arguing _____

Swimming _____   Music _____

Perfume _____   Art _____

Shopping _____   Conversation _____

Dancing _____   Playing an instrument _____

Sending E-mail _____   Babysitting _____

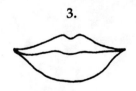

2.

3.

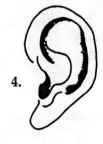

4.

5.

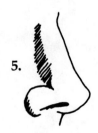

NAME _____   DATE _____

MUSIC IS UNIVERSAL

People all over the world listen to music. Sometimes we dance to music and other times we just listen and enjoy the visual imagery. Some people like soft music. Others like loud music. What kind of music do you like? Listen to different kinds of music and record your individual reaction to what you've heard. Is the music cool, romantic, or just "okay"? Describe each kind of music with vivid details that reveal your reactions.

My reactions to _____
                              (Name of Music)

_____
_____
_____
_____
_____
_____
_____
_____
_____

Now, write something about your favorite kind of music or your favorite song below:

Type of Music:

_____
_____

A Favorite Song:

_____
_____

THINK ABOUT THIS!!!

People listen to music and often find harmony and peace. Would there be more harmony and peace if people listened to each other . . . REALLY LISTENED???

NAME _____ DATE _____

THE "YOU" NOBODY KNOWS

What are your favorite after-school activities? Most neighborhoods have a library, playing fields, video store, bakery, U.S. Post Office, police and fire departments, supermarket, gas stations, and bus and train stations. Where do you hang out in your neighborhood? How much time do you spend talking on the phone with your friends? How often do you go out? Do people in the community know you and like to have you around? Do you have a job? Do you take pride in your neighborhood and try to make it better?

Identify some of the places and people in your neighborhood by drawing a cartoon or comic strip of your activities during ONE DAY in your life. Be certain to include yourself in the drawings, along with other people. Rather than human figures, you can use a symbol to stand for each person. Create dialogue that is entertaining or informative. As you tell your story, reveal some interesting things about yourself that most people do not know.

NAME _____   DATE _____

WRITING POETRY CAN BE FUN

Take a walk around your neighborhood. Look at the people, the buildings, the streets, and the kinds of activities that are happening. Some things in the community are very interesting and unusual. Do you see a grandfather pushing the baby in the stroller? How about the people standing outside the businesses with picket signs that say "ON STRIKE"? Are there wonderful smells coming from a local bakery? How many different languages do you hear?

Look at the sunrise or view the sunset. Visit the mall, recall a character in a story, or focus on your feelings as you walk around your neighborhood. Try to capture your emotions as you interact with friends or family members. People can express themselves in many ways. Why not write a poem or rap song lyrics about some of your real or imaginary experiences? It does not have to rhyme, but it should bring pictures to the reader's mind so that he or she can identify with your experiences. Begin by making a list of topics you might want to consider for writing a poem.

Topic: _____

Topic: _____

Topic: _____ (Choose One)

Topic: _____

Title: _____

_____

_____

_____

_____

_____

_____

_____

_____

_____

_____

Written by: _____

Copyright Date: _____

NAME _____ DATE _____

WHAT WE HAVE IN COMMON

Racially, ethnically, and culturally diverse groups share common traits. Because of this, people ought to be able to form CHAINS OF COMMONALTIES that link us together. Connect the chain links by writing words that relate to each category. Select one idea from each category for the two other chains. This will show how people respond similarly to various life experiences. The complete chain will depict how people are more alike than they are different. The last one, HAPPY, is started for you.

CATEGORY 1—WHAT DO PEOPLE USE WHEN THEY ARE:

- COOKING A MEAL

- CLEANING A HOUSE

- HAVING A CONVERSATION

- TRAVELING

- SHOPPING

CATEGORY 2—WHAT DO PEOPLE DO WHEN THEY ARE:

- SLEEPY

- HUNGRY

- UPSET

- VOTING

- HAPPY

© 1999 by John Wiley & Sons, Inc.

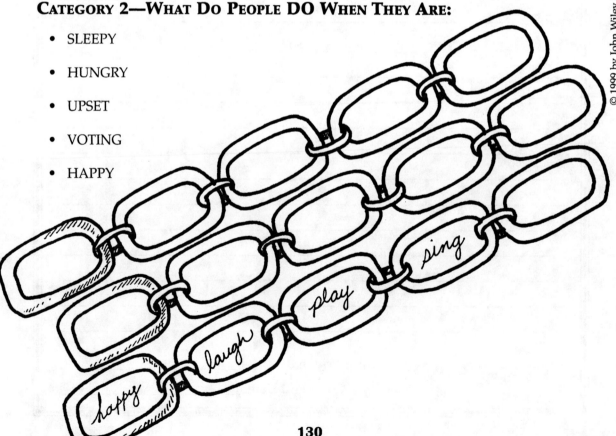

NAME _____   DATE _____

HELPFUL TWISTERS

Because you want to become a positive, contributing member of society, you want to get rid of negative things in your daily life. You know how destructive some things can be and you want to get rid of them . . . QUICKLY! A special tornado—designed to extract only garbage, trash, and useless debris from human nature—is visible, and you're looking forward to its powerful cleansing action. What things will this tornado destroy? What powerful, positive ideas will be left—things so powerful that all negativism will be washed away forever?

    Identify and check off the dozen or so negative words on the next page and write them on the HELPFUL TWISTER. Then discuss with your peers how the powerful, positive things that are left can build rather than destroy your ability to become a good citizen. You might have differences of opinion regarding the connotations of some words, i.e., pity.

NAME _____   DATE _____

____ wisdom	____ compassion	____ envy
____ anger	____ love	____ dishonesty
____ hope	____ creativity	____ power
____ bullying	____ listening	____ perseverance
____ pride	____ arrogance	____ curiosity
____ violence	____ playing	____ trustworthiness
____ intelligence	____ studying	____ responsibility
____ patriotism	____ intimidation	____ open-mindedness
____ pity	____ friendliness	____ complaining
____ volunteerism	____ abuse	____ initiative
____ hatred	____ frowning	____ obedience

NAME _____ DATE _____

MY DESIGN FOR A TEENAGE "HANGOUT"

Where do you and your friends go to have fun? Are there safe places for you to get together and not cause suspicion among the adults in the area? If you could design a place where you and your friends could meet—a really "cool" place—what would it look like? What would it have in it? Where would it be located?

In the space below, design such a building, a park, a mall, or a club for teenagers. After sketching and describing your "hangout," make a list of behaviors and actions that you don't think should be part of your meeting place. How would you try to get other kids not to misuse your new space?

BASIC DESIGN

DEVELOPING APPROPRIATE BEHAVIORS FOR TEEN CLUB MEMBERS

(**NOTE:** Brainstorm with your peers about how you could get such a list without "turning off" the other kids.)

1. _____   5. _____

2. _____   6. _____

3. _____   7. _____

4. _____   8. _____

NAME _____ DATE _____

WHAT IS THE PRIZE?

EQUAL OPPORTUNITY TO EXPERIENCE "LIFE, LIBERTY AND THE PURSUIT OF HAPPINESS"

In a recent survey, teenagers who were questioned about their life desires responded that they want and need HAPPINESS more than material things. Look at the list of material goods below and identify those that are necessary. Put an X on those things that you can totally do without. Then, of the items that are left, indicate those you would give up if you could have happiness instead.

MATERIAL GOODS	I WOULD GIVE THESE UP FOR TRUE HAPPINESS AND JOY
Designer clothes	
Compact discs	
Video games	
Computer	
Favorite magazines	
Favorite books	
Regular clothes	
Toys	
Telephone	
Private bedroom	
Unlimited food	
Money	
Jewelry	
Perfume/cologne	
Car	
Bike	
Roller blades or snow boards	
Tickets to concerts, amusement parks, or movies	

NAME _____ DATE _____

THE MOST BEAUTIFUL WORDS
IN THE WORLD?

The most beautiful words in the world are those that are thought of and then uttered to encourage and uplift another person. Conversely, the ugliest words are those that are thought of and then uttered to hurt, put-down, or destroy the self-esteem or heart of someone. Giving voice, therefore, to beautiful, kind, or encouraging words can change negative relationships and/or environments. When a person thinks of negative, insulting, or discouraging words and does not SAY or give voice to them, he or she has contributed to processes of peace. Moreover, contributions to pleasant, safe, and productive environments can be rapidly multiplied when people are conscious of the power they have to jump-start the peace process just with words.

Words are combined to make sentences. Sentences are combined to make paragraphs. Some words sound beautiful while others have wonderful meanings that make the speaker and listener feel happy, safe, hopeful, loved, excited, and ready to take on any task. On the list below, locate only the beautiful words and begin to think of and give voice to kind, pleasant, encouraging, and peaceful sentences or paragraphs to compliment others. On the following activity sheet, direct your compliments to five specific people and identify their relationships and roles. Select your favorite words and use them to formulate comments that will compliment and encourage these special people. You may add words from your own vocabulary as needed. Place the letter N on Neutral words and the letter X on negative words. Remember, add other words and use various forms of words as needed, for example (progress—progressive, hope—hopeful).

WORD LIST

serene • darkness • light • blessed • velvet • crystal • evil • enchanting capable • evil • peace • circle • star • fact • friend • life • productive • dream promise • zoo • refreshing • liar • progress • bunion • understanding • music cry • mustard • factory • two • dear • tunnel • melody • crisis • future statement • nightmare • hot • surprise • smile • birthday • prayer • secret taste • baby • admire • creative • wish • heartburn • cozy • tire • pill • ugly one • pale • love • gamble • forgive • appreciate • tremble • dance • comfort effort • honest • shock • sweet • money • against • harmony • drag • join exercise • fear • weep • virtue • jealousy • sunshine • liberty • fever • marvelous rock • humble • water • yesterday • itch

NAME _____ DATE _____

YOUR OWN BEAUTIFUL WORD LIST

(In addition to your own, you may use words from the list on the previous page.)

_____   _____
_____   _____
_____   _____
_____   _____
_____   _____
_____   _____
_____   _____

BEAUTIFUL COMPLIMENTS FOR SPECIAL PEOPLE

Identify the name, relationship, and function of each person

1. Name _____ Role/Function _____
   Compliment: _____
   _____

2. Name _____ Role/Function _____
   Compliment: _____
   _____

3. Name _____ Role/Function _____
   Compliment: _____
   _____

4. Name _____ Role/Function _____
   Compliment: _____
   _____

5. Name _____ Role/Function _____
   Compliment: _____
   _____

NAME _____ DATE _____

BENDING THE RULES

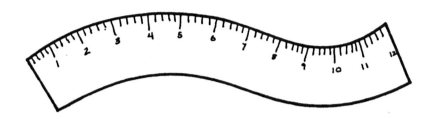

Are there times when rules should be altered, changed, or broken? Should people who say that they are using common sense be allowed to do as they please, even though they are not following the rules? When traditions or laws are not followed, should they be done away with? Read the situations below, examine the last sentence of each one, and check whether you AGREE or DISAGREE with the outcome. Then, discuss the results with others.

1. In the past, professional athletes were not allowed to participate in the Olympic Games. The Olympics were only for amateur athletes. Today, amateur and professional athletes can compete in the Olympic Games; the tradition has been forsaken.

    _____ AGREE   _____ DISAGREE

2. Olympians who have won medals have been told to wear certain approved outfits for the award ceremonies. One medal winner decided to choose her own outfit.

    _____ AGREE   _____ DISAGREE

3. Lifeguards are told to prevent swimmers and surfers from going into the water when there are strong undercurrents and dangerous waves. Surfers love the strong, high waves and some would risk their lives for the thrill of a "great ride."

    _____ AGREE   _____ DISAGREE

4. The school dress code prohibits the wearing of hats in the school building. Boys and girls like baseball caps and often use them to complete an outfit or to achieve a certain look. Only girls are allowed to wear hats that go with their outfits.

    _____ AGREE   _____ DISAGREE

5. The United States Constitution indicates that all human beings are created equal and should have equal rights. Because of this, people of all races and colors have the right to freedom, love, and lives of joy. People from different races, religions, cultures, and countries have experienced hateful attacks from fellow citizens.

    _____ AGREE   _____ DISAGREE

3–19 *Continued*

6. You're the captain of a ship and you have orders to return to port without delay. On the way to port, you and the crew spot a small vessel in distress. Four people cry out for help, and you decide to delay your return to port to help, despite orders.

    _____ AGREE   _____ DISAGREE

7. Everyone in society should be able to make up his or her own rules regarding life and how to relate to others. Standards of behavior are up to each person.

    _____ AGREE   _____ DISAGREE

THINK AND WRITE ABOUT IT!!!

What would be the effect on society if rules and laws that people continuously ignore or break are done away with? Does breaking or ignoring the laws mean that we don't need them? Write your response to this question below:

_____

_____

_____

_____

_____

_____

_____

_____

_____

_____

_____

_____

_____

_____

_____

_____

_____

_____

_____

NAME _____ DATE _____

JUST DRIVING AROUND?

So you think that it's okay to goof off sometime? Well, you are young and you do have the right to play around and do nothing every once in a while if you want to. But, you're growing up! Soon, you will be an adult and you'll have less and less time to play, goof off, or just sit and do nothing—not that you shouldn't relax or have fun. Everyone must have time for recreation. However, when some people are not focused on something productive, trouble often brews in their minds, and too often they act on these nonproductive ideas. Even when planning recreational activities, people need purpose and direction and the ability to discern between those "downtime" activities that are obviously beneficial and those that obviously invite trouble. Good times do not always have to be planned; and yet, many people have gotten into trouble because of aimlessness, idleness, and purposeless "downtime."

People who spend the bulk of their time goofing off, hanging out, or just driving around with little or no focus are, essentially, goalless. Often when people have this kind of life style, they purposely take advantage of others. Think about the many activities that are available for individuals and groups in our society. Some activities are productive and some are subtlety or overtly dangerous. Some are like treasures and others are like hidden land mines. Read the following accounts of people who are involved in different kinds of activities. Write serious words of advice and direction to those who are headed for danger or trouble.

A. Your parents trust you to take care of the car for the day. You are to wash it, take it to the gas station for an oil change, and park it in the garage. Several of your friends have asked you to drive to the mall in the next town. The trip is twenty miles away and you have to take a major highway to get there.

ADVICE: _____

B. "Hey, it's Mischief Night! So what if we go out and wrap toilet paper around a few trees, break a few windows, and chop some mailboxes off their posts? Who's going to stop us?"

ADVICE: _____

C. Angry because her parents grounded her for two weeks, Angela snatched the car keys from the hook in the back room, stormed into the garage, opened the car door and started the engine. With tires screeching, she backed out into the street and headed toward the hangout where she knew her friends would be waiting.

ADVICE: _____

139

NAME _____ DATE _____

D. Frank picked Jen up for a date in his red convertible. She had told her parents that they were going to a movie and then out for pizza. This was not the truth.

ADVICE: _____

E. Jerry's coach has promised not to tell his parents about a report that he was with a group of kids who were caught shoplifting at a clothing store in the mall. He has been in trouble before and is trying to get his life together. He'd already made up his mind to tell his parents before he talked to the coach. He doesn't want to keep any more secrets from them.

ADVICE: _____

F. While driving past a local deli, Harry sees two boys picking the lock on a bike that is chained to a post. The police station is in the next block, but he thinks that by the time he gets there and notifies the police the boys will be gone.

ADVICE: _____

EVALUATE YOUR ADVICE TO OTHERS

Read all of your ADVICE to those who are behaving irresponsibly, heading for trouble, or are trying to make a positive decision. Have you helped these people set realistic goals, focus on positive behaviors, or lay a foundation for success: Have you assisted those who are less fortunate or encouraged others to think and act rationally? Comment on your advice verbally or in writing, and explain if these people are in less danger because of your advice?

_____
_____
_____
_____
_____
_____
_____
_____
_____
_____
_____
_____

NAME _____ DATE _____

DRIVING SAFELY

Knowing when to put on the brakes or step on the accelerator is an important driving skill. When drivers are inexperienced, distracted, or speeding, they can easily lose control of the vehicle. Driving a car, motorcycle, bus, or truck carefully can be compared to living your life carefully. Your goal in driving a vehicle is to get to your destination safely. Use the following criteria to identify the safe choices for a person who wants to control his or her life and create opportunities for others to survive, as well.

A. Out of Control   **D.** Proceed with Caution

B. Brake Carefully   **E.** Safe to Go Ahead

C. Stop

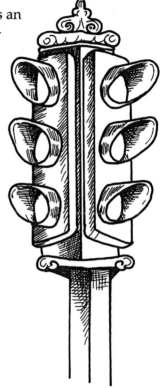

Place the correct letter on the line next to each choice:

_____ 1. Yo-yo or crash dieting

_____ 2. Gossip

_____ 3. Premarital sex

_____ 4. Fighting

_____ 5. Smoking cigarettes

_____ 6. Taking drugs

_____ 7. Giving in to peer pressure

_____ 8. Overeating

_____ 9. Taking vitamins

_____10. Not doing homework

_____11. Studying frequently

_____12. Listening to others

_____13. Interracial dating

_____14. Asking for advice

_____15. Avoiding destructive behavior

_____16. Other _____

_____17. Other _____

NAME _____ DATE _____

GIVE AN INCH . . . TAKE A MILE

?   ?   ?

People in American society have ongoing debates on many issues. Among them are whether to legalize drugs, raise the speed limit on the highways, reinstate capital punishment, or have curfews for teenagers. Even when decisions are made, some people still do exactly as they please, despite the law. Write your response to each of the following hypotheses.

WHAT WOULD HAPPEN IF . . .

1. drugs were legalized? _____

_____

_____

_____

2. every state enforced capital punishment? _____

_____

_____

_____

3. students never had to do homework? _____

_____

_____

_____

4. people could decide their own speed limits? _____

_____

_____

_____

NAME _____ DATE _____

5. young people were shielded from all sex and violence? _____

_____

_____

_____

6. school uniforms were required in all schools? _____

_____

_____

_____

7. students could give adults report cards? _____

_____

_____

_____

8. young people could get jobs at age 12? _____

_____

_____

_____

9. parents were punished for their children's crimes? _____

_____

_____

_____

10. young people were allowed to run the government? _____

_____

_____

_____

NAME _____   DATE _____

SEEING OUR REFLECTIONS
IN GLASS HOUSES

Some talk shows and tabloids often show the worst of human characteristics. We may or may not be able to identify with or understand the misery of many of the people featured. However, it is true that there are no perfect people and that we have all made mistakes. Therefore, we have no right to put others down or think that we are better than they. The phrase "People who live in glass houses shouldn't throw stones" is an important reminder that all of us can improve our attitudes and show more respect for one another. Identify some of the "glass houses" that are hidden in the lives of the people below. Assume the role of an advice columnist, and suggest ways that each person can improve his or her attitude, lifestyle, or outlook.

1. Scarlet hates the way her mother searches her room and has threatened to lock her door.

    ADVICE: _____

2. Jill's best friend is considering sleeping with her boyfriend. Jill thinks it's a good idea because "it's the 90's."

    ADVICE: _____

3. Matt's father abandoned his family several years ago. Now, Matt is a star athlete at a leading university and is expected to be drafted by a professional team. Matt's father is proud of his son and wants to communicate with him. Matt is not sure what he should do.

    ADVICE: _____

4. Alma works at a fast-food restaurant and has seen some of her co-workers slip money into their pockets. She knows it's wrong, but she's afraid to tell.

    ADVICE: _____

5. Fred's grandmother is very attractive, but he thinks that she dresses too young for her age. He doesn't bring his friends around because he's embarrassed that his youngish grandmother does not fit into society's image for her.

    ADVICE: _____

NAME _____ DATE _____

6. Tisha's mother doesn't approve of the clothes her daughter wears to school, she picks out the clothes for her to wear each day. Tisha resents this, but wears what her mother wants her to wear. However, when she gets to school, she changes into her choice of clothes.

   ADVICE: _____

7. John likes Shelley, but he knows that she's seeing another boy. He still wants to ask her out.

   ADVICE: _____

8. Nobody in the neighborhood wanted the new family to move in. They spray-painted racial slurs on the house and made prank calls to try to scare them away.

   ADVICE: _____

9. A senior citizen who has been living in the community for many years insists on watering her lawn every day. Sometimes, she forgets that the water is on.

   ADVICE: _____

10. Jason insists on playing his radio very loudly. Some of the people in the neighborhood are very annoyed.

    ADVICE: _____

11. Car thefts are increasing, and a certain group of kids has been blamed. These kids say that they are innocent.

    ADVICE: _____

12. A new pool has been built for the entire community. However, some people don't want a certain ethnic group to use the pool.

    ADVICE: _____

THINK ABOUT THIS!!!

What mistakes or imperfections in your life symbolize your "glass house?" To what extent do these things keep you from "throwing stones at" or judging others? To what extent do these imperfections help you to empathize with or be more tolerant of others?

NAME _____ DATE _____

THE TREE: A SYMBOL OF PEACE

In Maya Angelou's inaugural poem, "On the Pulse of Morning," natural elements symbolize how diverse groups of Americans can come together and make this a better country. The symbols are a rock, a river, and a tree. Use the words beneath the tree to highlight both the diversity and the commonalties within the human family. Then, write your own poem, slogan, or statement expressing your hopes for peace and indicating the role you can play in achieving peace. To help plan your composition, think of the functions of the roots, trunk, branches, and leaves. Then, think about the many concerns people have regarding the need for better human relationships.

Based upon your understanding of Maya Angelou's poem, develop your own description of how peace can be spread throughout society. Use some of the symbols and words that convey human concern to create your composition.

A. Read or listen to Maya Angelou's poem.

B. Focus on the real functions of a tree, and what each part of the tree symbolizes in human relationships.

TREE ROOTS _____

_____

TREE TRUNKS _____

_____

TREE BRANCHES _____

_____

TREE LEAVES _____

_____

C. Think of why the following facts should lead all human beings to work together to achieve peace.

1. Many different races and cultures in society

2. Many different places of birth

3. Common needs, hopes, and dreams

4. Common earthly home and related dependence upon it

5. Desire to leave a legacy for future generations

Now, write your own composition. Try to use elements of nature as symbols (birds, trees, water, land, etc.).

NAME _____ DATE _____

SYMBOLS AND WORDS OF HUMAN CONCERN

frowns • fear • anger • courage • smiles • compassion • love • tolerance
right • wrong • caring • feelings • hope • attitude • acceptance • listening
bias • violence • joy • rejection • heart • human • despair • pride • equality
humiliation • life • change • conflict • peace • diversity • dreams • promise
commonalties • morality • forgiveness • availability • jealousy • goals • peer
pressure • truth • privilege

MY IDEAS FOR SPREADING TOLERANCE, RESPECT, EQUALITY, AND PEACE

_____
_____
_____
_____
_____
_____
_____
_____
_____
_____
_____

RIGHT SIDE UP!

As you read the newspapers, listen to the news, watch television, and read the latest magazines, you can discern that the lives of many people are being turned **upside down!** Even though many citizens do the right things every day, some people spend their time doing the **wrong things.** We cannot always see or enjoy the good things because the bad things get in the way like a tiny, lethal cancerous growth in an otherwise healthy body. What does it take to locate, destroy, or change the ugly, cancerous, lethal behaviors in our society? How can upstanding citizens work with and help to change the attitudes and behaviors of people who are a drain upon society? How can people who do the **right things** help turn society **right side up?** In other words, how can we help those who do wrong things **want to do right things?**

Think of yourself as **a surgeon**, equipped to cut away deadly cancers in the human body. Think of society as the human body and crime, drugs, rapes, injustice, racism, prejudice, and poverty as cancers that have to be cut out of the body if it is to regain its health. As a surgeon, you must preserve the good cells and either regenerate, retain, or destroy the bad cells by helping people to change their negative outlook. People who behave badly can be rehabilitated; their bad cells (bad attitudes and behaviors) can be destroyed or replaced by good attitudes and behaviors.

Think of yourself as **an interior decorator** who must coordinate the colors, shapes, fabrics, and furnishings into an overall, pleasurable environment. What must you get rid of? What must you bring into the environment? Think about toxic waste that's ruining our forests, rivers, air, and land. What can you do to preserve our physical environment?

Think of yourself as a **lawyer**—an expert in the laws of the land. You must ferret out the criminals who insist on breaking the laws and provide freedom for the upstanding citizens of the society. What laws are designed to protect those who don't cause trouble? How are you going to punish (with justice) those who infringe upon the freedom of others?

Think of yourself as a **teacher**—one who is responsible for teaching the citizens of the nation. What can you do to make sure that everyone receives a good education and, in the process, emerges with a good work ethic, mutual respect, and the ability to contribute?

You are **a future adult citizen** of this country. How can you prepare yourself to eliminate the bad things in your own environment and multiply the good things that are going on? How can you become an inspiration to your peers and others who want to do the right thing—who want to turn the lives of people right side up?

For the occupations listed above and below, devise a few specific actions that the people who choose these fields can take in order to get rid of societal cancers and improve the social health of this country. Share your assessment with peers, family, and members of the community.

NAME _____ DATE _____

1. Postal worker _____

   _____

2. Engineer _____

   _____

3. Chef _____

   _____

4. Teacher _____

   _____

5. Parent _____

   _____

6. Rabbi, priest, pastor or other spiritual leader _____

   _____

7. Garbage collector _____

   _____

8. Artist _____

   _____

9. Bus driver _____

   _____

10. Airline pilot _____

    _____

11. Computer programmer _____

    _____

12. A taxi driver _____

    _____

NAME _____ DATE _____

A GOOD REPORT (CARD)

Report cards are given out to show progress and accomplishment. Think of how hard you work for good grades in the various courses you take in high school. Fortunately, there are adults in your life who are making an effort to help you prepare for your future. Why not issue good reports to those who try to help you and other young people? To whom could you issue good reports? Consider your parents, counselors, mentors, teachers, and spiritual leaders—and the roles they assume as you interact with them. Think of how they model behaviors, react to challenges, and set the tone for how you should pursue success and satisfaction in your educational, social, and spiritual environments. You can count on these adults to be there for you when you need them. With this report, you can show your appreciation for their efforts on your behalf.

Use the grading criteria listed to rate one person who has had a positive influence on you. Add the total number of points for each section on the report card and write appropriate comments to accompany the grades. Convert the numerical scores to letter grades in each category. Then, end your evaluation with a summary of this person's impact on your life.

POINTS/GRADING CRITERIA

5 – Highest level of effort
4 – Above-average effort
3 – Average effort
2 – Below-average effort
1 – Little or no effort

CATEGORIES OF PROGRESS AND ACCOMPLISHMENT

- Listens to problems
- Concerned for physical well-being
- Supportive of goals
- Accepts choice of friends
- Guides emotionally/spiritually
- Knows his/her role/area of expertise

- Exhibits both firmness and flexibility
- Maintains high standards and expectations
- Shows reason and self-control
- Has empathy (remembers what it's like to be young)

NAME _____ DATE _____

REPORT CARD

Name _____ Role _____

(Parent, Counselor, etc.)

POINTS	SKILL AREAS	COMMENTS	LETTER GRADE

_____ **LISTENING**

____ Listens to my problems

____ Gives appropriate advice

____ Speaks when necessary

____ Values my opinions

____ Other _____   _____

Total Pts. _____

_____ **SUPPORT**

____ Cares for my physical needs

____ Provides for my mental and physical health

____ Uses love, not ridicule, in discipline

____ Helps me to make wise choices

____ Protects me from harm

____ Other _____   _____

Total Pts. _____

_____ **COMPREHENSION**

____ Remembers being young

____ Understands my needs

____ Shares his/her experiences

____ Avoids comparing me with other people

____ Other _____   _____

Total Pts. _____

_____ **KNOWLEDGE**

____ Helps me with my schoolwork

____ Knows how to get information

____ Sees that I'm trying my best

____ Values a good education

____ Other _____   _____

Total Pts. _____

_____ **ATTITUDE**

____ Presents positive viewpoints

____ Justifies anger/disappointment

____ Models "Never Give Up" position

____ Goes the "last mile" for me

____ Other _____   _____

Total Pts. _____

REPORT SUMMARY (Check One or Two)   Final Letter Grade _____

____ EXCELLENT PROGRESS   ____ NEEDS IMPROVEMENT

____ MAKING AN EFFORT   ____ CONFERENCE REQUESTED

NAME _____ DATE _____

IT'S TIME TO SHOUT OUT!

© 1999 by John Wiley & Sons, Inc.

The world should never suffer because of the presence of any one person. In fact, the world should be a better place, because each ONE of us has many opportunities to contribute and to build rather than destroy the quality of life. How do you rate? Are you making society suffer, or are you one of the reasons for hope that the world can become a better place? If you are a reason for hope . . . CHEER ABOUT IT!!!

Identify specific contributions that YOU can make to the environment in which you live each day. SHOUT OUT your CONTRIBUTIONS. From the list below, select positive actions with which you can identify, and write the identifying numbers on or near the bullhorn. Then, list the reasons that are important to you on the back of this sheet.

1. I spend time with my family.
2. The world is better because I'm in it.
3. I treat others as I want to be treated.
4. I'm honest.
5. God is/is not important to me.
6. I made the honor roll.
7. I respect myself.
8. I create pleasant surroundings.
9. I'm responsible.
10. I have a positive attitude.
11. I compete hard, but I'm fair.
12. I'll warn another person of danger.
13. My words have power, so I watch what I say.

14. I can succeed.
15. I'm a good listener.
16. I have fun, but not at another person's expense.
17. I know that I need others to help me as I grow and learn.
18. Other _____
   _____
   _____
19. Other _____
   _____
   _____
20. Other _____
   _____
   _____

NAME _____   DATE _____

OUCH!!! . . . AHHHHH!!!

For every comment that is likely to hurt your feelings—or another person's—write a response that will counteract, erase, or soothe ruffled feathers and make you or another injured person feel better. If the statement is not likely to hurt, write OK next to the number.

1. YOU'RE A FAT PIG . . . I HATE YOU!

2. I KNEW I WOULD GET A BETTER GRADE ON THAT TEST THAN YOU.

3. I'M TELLING! I SAW YOU HIT SUE!

4. YOU'RE EXPECTING ME TO PROTECT YOU AFTER WHAT YOU DID TO ME? WELL, I'M NOT ONE TO SEEK REVENGE.

5. I KNEW YOU DIDN'T WANT TO SEE AN X-RATED MOVIE, BUT I WANTED TO SEE IT ANYWAY.

6. AT FIRST I THOUGHT YOU WERE OUT OF CONTROL! NOW, I SEE THAT YOU ARE AN ENTHUSIASTIC PERSON.

7. I THOUGHT I HAD HEARD ALL THE EXCUSES. THIS ONE IS A NEW ONE ON ME.

8. MY FAMILY IS FROM THIS COUNTRY. WHAT ARE YOU DOING HERE?

YOUR RESPONSES

1. _____
2. _____
3. _____
4. _____
5. _____
6. _____
7. _____
8. _____

NAME _____ DATE _____

TICKETS, PLEASE!

Tickets to various events are sold in communities throughout America. People buy tickets because they want to see events that meet their need or desire to be entertained, persuaded, or informed. From the set of tickets displayed below, decide how they will benefit the buyers by classifying them according to their purposes. Write the numbers of the tickets beneath the appropriate heading.

| TICKET | 1 Political, Educational, and Religious Fund-Raisers | TICKET | | TICKET | 2 Art Institute | TICKET | | TICKET | 3 Museum or Aquarium | TICKET |

| TICKET | 4 Amusement Park/ National Park | TICKET | | TICKET | 5 Casino/ Dance Club | TICKET | | TICKET | 6 Sports Events | TICKET |

| TICKET | 7 State Fair/ Rodeo | TICKET | | TICKET | 8 Circus or Zoo | TICKET | | TICKET | 9 Theater/Movies | TICKET |

ENTERTAIN	INFORM	PERSUADE
_____	_____	_____
_____	_____	_____
_____	_____	_____
_____	_____	_____

Indicate those tickets that are most beneficial to the improvement of human relationships by writing a comment on the back of this sheet. Which events are most beneficial to teens? Explain.

NAME _____ DATE _____

JUST LIKE A TIGER!

When people treat others badly or unfair situations cause problems, responses can range from little or no reaction to anger, aggression, or violence. Using the scale below, indicate the extent to which you might react to each of the situations described. Record the number on the appropriate lines.

3   VERY STRONG, ANGRY,
     VIOLENT REACTION

2   STRONG REACTION (JUSTIFIED)

1   MILD-TO-MODERATE REACTION

0   NO REACTION

_____ Someone takes your lunch money from your book bag.

_____ Your opinion is ignored during a discussion.

_____ A friend promised not to reveal some very personal information about you. Now, everyone knows your business.

_____ Your parents require you to babysit when you've made plans to go out with your friends.

_____ A telemarketing employee interrupts your phone conversation.

_____ A new student becomes more popular than you.

_____ Some students cheat on exams, while you and others study.

_____ Adults write and produce the scripts for violent and sexually explicit movies and television shows. Yet, they complain when some young people imitate what they see.

_____ Some news articles and television news reports give the impression that teenagers are hooked on drugs, involved with gangs, disobedient to parents, and are generally "up to no good."

_____ Because you are _____ people make fun of you. (Fill in your race, religion, culture, etc.)

Based on your reactions, what might you do to change some of these situations? Which ones can YOU control? Which ones need adult or institutional intervention?

_____

_____

_____

_____

_____

_____

"IT TAKES A WHOLE VILLAGE TO RAISE A CHILD"

INTRODUCTION

Parents and guardians who tend to children from their earliest years depend upon adults in public and private medical, religious, recreational, social, and educational institutions to reinforce what they have taught in the home. In these cases, members of the proverbial "village" are expected to work in concert with children's immediate families to help prepare them for their roles in society. Because most children will eventually leave the security of their homes, they must be guided towards discretion until they are mature enough to control the inevitable demands and pressures of adulthood. The seeds that are planted by the family during the formative years produce self-perceptions and social awareness that are important entities in the maturation process. The activities in "It Takes a Whole Village to Raise a Child" allow young people to explore their needs in a variety of contexts with individuals outside their immediate families. As a result of their interactions with others, young people find that there are few linear relationships but many complex, multi-layered interactions with people from diverse and similar backgrounds. Within these community or "village" settings of schools, business, recreational, and religious institutions, adults provide young people with mentoring, educational, economic, physical, and spiritual needs.

It becomes apparent to most young people that they will eventually have to assume adult roles in society and that self-confidence, self-esteem, and a set of functional moral principles are necessary for survival in the "village." As students interact with other village/community members, they develop caring attitudes, a healthy respect for work, compassion and respect for diverse races and cultures, a sense of right and wrong, and the ability to think and act independently. Moreover, students' awareness of their own emerging responsibilities becomes clearer as a result of working on concepts such as disabilities, leadership, materialism, individuality and teamwork in this section. With the strength of the family and caring members of the community working together to help each young person learn, assume, and carry out his or her responsibilities in the "village," each young person's self-confidence will grow. The lessons in "It Takes a Whole Village to Raise a Child," therefore, are designed to ensure the development of high levels of confidence, positive self-esteem, mutual respect, and other survival skills that will make successful lives in any community possible for every child.

===================== **ACTIVITIES** =====================

TEACHER DIRECTIONS
FOR SECTION 4 ACTIVITIES

4–1 "IT TAKES A WHOLE VILLAGE TO RAISE A CHILD"

Find out how much responsibility young people place on the adults in their lives for their well-being. Ask them to offer specific examples of the kinds of information, guidance, and behaviors adults should pass along to the young people who will someday be in charge of society. Have them indicate which adults they look to for guidance, advice, and caring. Elicit from students, as well, the environments in which they interact with these adults and what they want in terms of advice on how to prepare for life in the larger society. Indicate that there are certain standards of behavior, laws and regulations, and societal expectations regarding extending access to civil rights, equal employment and educational opportunities, and freedom and equality. Remind them that, as citizens, they are entitled to their freedoms; only if they break the laws of society are they subject to the loss of their rights, freedoms, and equal educational and employment opportunities. Talk about how families and members of educational, religious, political, and medical institutions work in concert on behalf of children. Write the word INTERDEPENDENCE on the chalkboard and ask for a definition. Have students agree that in our global society interdependence is unavoidable; that all human beings must learn to work together if we are to survive. Write the African proverb IT TAKES A WHOLE VILLAGE TO RAISE A CHILD on the chalkboard or a chart. Ask students to indicate who makes up the "village" and what they would need, as young people, from village members. Suggest that as maturing young people, they are responsible for helping adults to raise them—that they are part of a village. *Give each student a copy of Activity 4-1, "It Takes a Whole Village to Raise a Child."*

4–2 THE NEEDS OF THE CHILDREN WITHIN THE "VILLAGE"

Extend the concept of the "village" as crucial in the training of young people to assume their adult roles. However, it is only to the extent that young people understand and accept what adults have to offer them that the training takes. Students must understand that the government is not the family and does not overrule anyone's parents as the major caregivers and teachers. The inference in promoting the concept of the "village" is that it only serves to reinforce those values, truths, virtues, and standards that emanate from the home and the parents or guardians of each child. Have students look at the various members of the "village" and prepare to approach them with specific needs. What are these needs? Young people, no matter what their racial, ethnic, or cultural backgrounds need the gifts of: love, discipline, identity, acceptance, recognition, moral support, and opportunity. Ask each student to indicate from among these "gifts" which are most necessary. Elicit from students how what they learn as young people can help them develop into good citizens of the community. Ask them to share why it is necessary for each person in the "village" or community to assume a responsible role. Have students share their visions of roles they might assume in a village of the future. Explain to them that they are laying the foundation for these roles even now. Encourage them to set high goals and to make education their first priority. *Give each student a copy of Activity 4-2, The Needs of the Children Within the "Village."*

4–3 ASSESSMENT CHART FOR "VILLAGE" READINESS

Elicit from students how they can really evaluate and assess the readiness of "village" members to give them what they need. Define each of the things that all young people need, and proceed with plans for interviews to establish "village" readiness. (**Note:** Consider allowing some of the students to interview you, as a way to validate the process. Of course, the information is useful for the final evaluation.) The activity sheet asks students to follow STAGES I, II, and III. These are to assist students with organization and scheduling of their interviews. For each stage, suggest other people who are accessible, including family members, other relatives, and friends. School staff might also be considered. Make certain that students extend appreciation to those who have granted interviews. Have students evaluate their individual experiences and compile the results. Lines of communication that were established during the interviews can be kept open by disseminating the results. Ask students to decide which methods of distribution they wish to use, and really share their information. Some suggestions are videotapes, E-mail, letters, booklets, and brochures.* Send the results of the survey about the readiness of the "village" to meet the needs of the children to other schools, students' homes, social agencies, businesses, recreational centers, and religious organizations. Follow up with a community/village meeting of areas that need to be improved and strategies for making certain that the job gets done. Enlist the help of local newspaper, radio, and television reporters. (* **Note:** The ideas for sharing are optional. Teachers and students should discuss what is possible in their situations.) *Give each student a copy of Activity 4-3, Assessment Chart for "Village" Readiness.*

4–4 A YOUNG PERSON'S PLEDGE TO THE "VILLAGE"

Elicit from students the fact that, as young people, they can make a commitment to their own progress as developing adults. Obedience to parents and following their rules and regulations are good for maturing young people to consider as "cool," appropriate, and safe. Certainly, this will help in laying the foundation for their following the rules and regulations in the larger society. Obedience and cooperation are key elements in learning to take control of personal lives before trying to take control of society in their adult lives. Have students define the words, "pledge" and "promise," and to discuss what they mean in their lives. *Give each student a copy of Activity 4-4, A Young Person's Pledge to the "Village."*

SURVIVAL IN THE "VILLAGE"

A RATIONALE FOR "FAMILY FIRST" MOTTO

Rules of home, school, government, religion, and businesses often reinforce each other. People who frequent these environments find that there are specific standards of behavior, dress, work, and so on that are necessary in order for things to function correctly. In a perfect world, young people would go from home to any of these other institutions and find that "the left hand knows what the right hand is doing." Since the world is not perfect, there are differences in standards in many of the environments that students frequent. Checks and balances are, therefore, necessary so that there is reinforcement of values that emanate from the child's first teachers, his or her parents or guardians, to those institutions that receive the young person for further training. Children's chances of survival and developing have much to do with the extent to which their earliest training is validated in the larger environments and, most importantly, to the extent that they can trust people outside their families. Young people must learn to discern those members of the "village" who have their best interest at heart; who can be trusted to reinforce and not sever positive familial values, relationships, or bring physical or emotional harm. There must also be high levels of trust on the part of young people for members of their families. (**CAUTION:** Teachers need to be aware of dangers within the home of some children and how to use the "Family First" motto in this and other lessons.)

4–5 SURVIVAL IN THE "VILLAGE"

Elicit from students their opinions regarding the adults from whom they should receive advice when making important decisions in their lives. Ask them to compare the personal attention that they receive from family versus the kind of attention they receive from members of various institutions, including school, business, and religious institutions. Have them indicate if there are ever times when young people should go to another person BEFORE they go to a member of their immediate family. Write the words: **Family First** on the board and take a vote as to how many people would adhere to this motto. Discuss the fact that there are social, government, religious, and health agencies in which the members may offer help when a young person is desperate, confused, or frightened. Other organizations have employment, health, or entertainment as important services for young people. Elicit from students the fact that while early instructions, values, and positive self-concepts emanate from family members, many of these values are reinforced by adults in schools and other community settings. The student's job is to think about, internalize, and demonstrate an understanding of the advice and/or instruction received. His or her survival during the training process depends upon keeping the lines of communication open among parents, young people, and the community "village" in the interest of developing strong citizens for leadership roles. Elicit from students the importance of recognizing and staying away from people who do not have their best interest at heart. Discuss ways to recognize and avoid people who might cause physical or emotional harm to them. *Give each student a copy of Activity 4-5, Survival in the "Village."*

4–6 DEVELOPING A DEEP SENSE OF RESPONSIBILITY

To get the most out of life as an adult, one has to be able to function independently and with a sense of responsibility that does not subtract from another human being's quality of life. Elicit from students how the individual's sense of responsibilities change as he or she grows into adulthood. Indicate the need for individual citizens to set high goals and expectations and work to realize them. Ask students how a sense of responsibility would qualify a person for membership in future "villages" who will have the job of raising the next generation. Have students finish this statement: If, as an adult member of the village/community, I oppress or abuse others, then _____. (Possible response to the hypothesis: I must change my attitude and behavior. I must seek to do right rather than wrong and to develop high personal standards that will become a part of my life as a citizen.)

Remind students that neither adults nor young people should, in the process of developing positive self-esteem, destroy that of other human beings. Extending mutual respect and equality should be a way of life for all self-confident individuals. (Have a class discussion based on these statements.) *Give each student a copy of Activity 4-6, Developing a Deep Sense of Responsibility.*

4–7 WHAT IS A SQUARE?

Ask students to interpret the connotations of the phrase "following the crowd," and to think about experiences they have had regarding it. Inquire as to the qualities a person has to have to be a leader, and take a poll as to what kind of leadership position individual students prefer. Discuss names that young people apply to certain students such as "nerd" and whether this is a compliment or an insult. Encourage each student to consider his or her own goals, aspirations, and individual rights. *Give each student a copy of Activity 4-7, What Is a Square?*

4–8 QUESTIONNAIRE FOR PEER COUNSELORS

Elicit from students how prepared they are to help classmates who might have problems. Indicate that individuals often make commitments based on their past experiences with certain problems and want to share the way that they overcame these situations. (**Note:** These concepts are not designed to separate "goody-goody" students from those who have problems. Rather, the idea is to help individual students learn that no one is perfect, but people can reverse negative behaviors and choose a positive lifestyle.) Discuss how positive choices are self-rewarding and of great benefit to the individual and to those with whom he or she interacts. (**Teacher Caution:** Ask students to make up fictional "mistakes" to reduce embarrassment or prevent revealing private matters.) *Give each student a copy of Activity 4-8, Questionnaire for Peer Counselors.*

4–9 HELPING OUT . . . FOR FREE

Have students share personal experiences with helping a person in need. Elicit from them the value of serving others by volunteering in society. Bring out the fact that providing a service for someone without asking for anything in return benefits the giver, as well as the receiver of the service. Discuss the reasons for the mutual rewards. *Give each student a copy of Activity 4-9, Helping Out . . . For Free.*

4–10 WHAT? VOLUNTEER FOR MY OWN GOOD? . . . HOW? . . . WHY?

Reinforce the idea of volunteerism in the various settings in which young people find themselves. Have each student suggest ways that he or she can help other people without expecting anything in return. Elicit from individual students the mutual benefits of giving. For example, challenge students to consider the words **compassion, empathy, identify with, understand,** and other words that convey human kindness, sympathy, and generosity. Elicit from students the origin of these feelings. Suggest, if they don't, the **heart** as the place where the **desire** to help fellow human beings originates. Also, indicate that it's an individual reaction to want to extend a helping hand. The benefits for the **giver** are in the actual **giving;** the joy comes from within and does not have to have the reinforcement of a "thank you" or a "reward" from the receiver. Challenge students to place themselves in a situation in which they might need help. Have them describe how they might react to offers of help. (**Teacher Caution:** Be sensitive to students who might suffer from economic hardships, family dysfunction, etc.) Discuss the fact that people who receive help are not inferior to other human beings and do not want to be treated in condescending, arrogant ways. Explain to students, or elicit from them, the fact that the intent of extending dignity to others is the crucial approach in offering help, and the key to personal fulfillment for the volunteer—the giver. *Give each student a copy of Activity 4-10, What? Volunteer for My Own Good? . . . How? . . . Why?*

4–11 GET REAL!

Inquire of students about the *reasons* for polluted air, water, and land in America and around the world. Have them list the *results* of unclean air, water, and land. Replace the words *reasons* with *causes* and the word *results* with *effects*. Indicate that they have revealed *cause-and-effect relationships* regarding the topic of pollution. Discuss the need to identify cause-and-effect relationships when considering controversial issues in our society. Elicit from students several controversial issues that prevail in society and are reflected in the lifestyle choices that people make. For example, there is the controversy surrounding the "right to choose" vs. the "right to life" abortion issue. Also, there are different opinions regarding the issues of prayer in public schools, the passing out of condoms in schools, sexual abstinence, AIDS, doctor-assisted suicide, legalization of drugs, and so on. Without risking infringement on parental authority, discuss some of these or other controversies. (Teacher Caution: Alert administrative staff and parents of your plans to hold class discussions on controversial topics. Ask for their participation and advice prior to initiating these activities.) Inform students of this important effort to get parental and administrative input and support. Indicate to students the necessity of having valid and factual support for their opinions, and the possible need to do some research. Talk about the "gray" areas that make it difficult to draw conclusions on some issues. Students should differentiate between fact and opinion as they discuss controversial issues. Encourage them to consider the "big picture" and their future roles as adult members of society as they discuss these issues. *Give each student a copy of Activity 4-11, Get Real!*

4–12 HEROES WHO ARE NOT "HANDICAPPED"

Have students share their knowledge of how society generally treats citizens who are physically challenged, and how this often hampers the progress of many capable people. Discuss various disabilities that people might have that prevent their full participation in life's experiences. Have students focus on the fact that everyone is entitled to equal opportunity in employment, education, and housing, despite their challenges. Elicit from students the fact that individuals who are physically challenged want the same things that able-bodied people want. Specifically, they want equality in terms of access to places in the community, equal educational and employment opportunities, self-reliance, independence, joy, love, respect, justice, challenges, and so on. Pose this thought for students to ponder: "All of us are disabled in one way or another." Discuss the fact that physically-challenged citizens have disabilities that they cannot necessarily hide, while the rest of humanity can often hide various kinds of emotional, psychological, medical, social, and other weaknesses. Ask students to locate and report information on people who have made contributions to society, despite their disabilities. *Give each student a copy of Activity 4-12, Heroes Who Are Not "Handicapped."*

4–13 PLANNING AN INTERVIEW WITH A HERO

Extend the impact of the previous activity by focusing on the self-esteem that physically and emotionally challenged people may have. Elicit from students what actions it takes to instill confidence in human beings who've not always been considered capable, intelligent, and worthy of recognition and opportunity. Ask students their opinions regarding the need for more positive reports about disabled people in the media. *Give each student a copy of Activity 4-13, Planning an Interview With a Hero.*

4–14 JUST A LITTLE RESPECT

Giving and receiving are complete when they occur in concert with each other. The exchange does not have to be concrete, or tangible, in nature. Giving and receiving respect must take place frequently in our society and between adversaries in order to advance civility, tolerance, and justice. Have students focus on mutual respect as a goal that they can reach by recognizing positive attributes and internalizing them. Discuss the fact that when they as individuals live by these attributes, they are more aware of them in others. When people have these in common, there is more of an opportunity for harmony. *Give each student a copy of Activity 4-14, Just a Little Respect.*

4–15 DISCIPLINING OTHER PEOPLE'S CHILDREN: YOUR VIEW

Ask students to give their opinions regarding the need for young people to have rules and regulations to live by. Discuss the consequences of the absence of laws—how society would become chaotic without rules. Have students make up a list of adults in society who should be responsible for seeing to it that young people adhere to the rules. Elicit from them whether anyone outside their own parents or guardians has the authority to force them to obey rules, laws, and curfews. Discuss their reactions to having someone other than their parents or guardians tell them what to do. Discuss the feelings that occur whenever authority figures make us follow rules. Why do some people find it difficult to obey, or have an aversion to adhering to laws? How can a person learn to be at ease with authority figures, even if the authorities are not his or her parents or guardians? *Give each student a copy of Activity 4-15, Disciplining Other People's Children: Your View.*

4–16 JUDGE THIS!!!

Write the words, LAW, JUSTICE, FAIRNESS, and INTEGRITY on the chalkboard. Ask students to define each word and explain why they are all important in a democratic society. Elicit from students their opinions as to the need for the existence of more love than hate or more right than wrong in the world. Have them compare and contrast the benefits of positive experiences over the consequences of negative experiences. Discuss the role of the justice system in helping to ensure that reasonable conflict-resolution strategies exist to prevent senseless violence when people have disputes. Ask students to share incidents that needed a mediator or a judge to help resolve the conflicts. Have students acknowledge the significance of the laws as standards so that justice, fairness, respect, and integrity can be extended to the parties involved in the dispute. Have them internalize the concepts and begin to act as judges on controversial issues. *Give each student a copy of Activity 4-16, Judge This!!!* (**Note:** Inform students that incidents of a personal or sensitive nature should not be made public.)

4-17 No Joke!

Ask students to share their views as teenagers on the importance of completing their education. List as many responses on the chalkboard as possible. Write the word SERIOUS on the board, and elicit how and why this is one of the most important attitudes that students can have. Have them compare and contrast various attitudes that are demonstrated by students who don't take education seriously. What happens when students play around or act inappropriately? Ask for personal observations of people who treat educational opportunity lightly, as if it were a lark or some kind of a joke. Have individual students offer examples of people who really wanted an education but were prevented from getting it. Discuss the laws in early America that made it illegal to teach slaves to read. Elicit from students the fact that education is freedom and, therefore, needs to be taken seriously. *Give each student a copy of Activity 4-17, No Joke!*

4-18 Twins, Triplets, Quadruplets, Anyone?

Invite students to share their experiences with twins, triplets, quadruplets, or other multiple-birth siblings, relatives, or acquaintances. Ask students specific reasons for the pleasure these multiple births often bring. Discuss, as well, some of the hardships that might come about as the result of multiple births. (For example, the births of sextuplets and septuplets—have students share what they know about pressures on the families and/or community support.) Have students consider fraternal and identical siblings, and ask them to share what they know about a multiple-birth child's struggle to gain his or her own identity. Use humor to point out how multiple-birth siblings appreciate it when others recognize them as individuals by reading the poem "The Twins" by Henry S. Leigh. Discuss various concepts from the poem, and have students draw inferences about the themes and apply them to real life. (**Teacher Caution:** Be sensitive regarding the feelings of multiple-birth siblings in the class.) Ask them to share only if they wish to. *Give each student a copy of Activity 4-18, Twins, Triplets, Quadruplets, Anyone?*

4-19 Carrying the Torch

Ask students how they think Olympic torch bearers are chosen. Discuss the fact that this very special honor is given to people who have made some kind of contribution or have overcome some great personal difficulty. Elicit from students how they think the world would be if great numbers of people displayed the qualities and lived by the kinds of values symbolized by the torch bearers. Have them develop a list of criteria they would consider using to select Olympic torch bearers. Remind them to include Americans from the many different racial, ethnic, and cultural groups. Ask students to give their opinions regarding the inclusion of immigrants who are attempting to gain their citizenship in various countries around the world. Also, what would be some of the societal conditions that would make it necessary to exclude anyone from carrying the Olympic Torch? (**Teacher Caution:** It is important for students to grasp the concept of mutual respect and consideration of diverse groups of people who might not ordinarily be considered for this honor.) *Give each student a copy of Activity 4-19, Carrying the Torch.*

4–20 TOGETHER WE STAND . . . DIVIDED WE FALL

Write the word INTERDEPENDENCE on the chalkboard, and ask the class to define and give examples that verify the meaning. Discuss the fact that partnerships are an integral part of being interdependent, and that each separate entity is made better or becomes whole as a consequence of joining together. Have students consider a chain and the extent to which the chain is strong until one of its links is broken or damaged. Ask them to provide the partner for each of the following: Male, Student, Hammer, Lock. (Male-Female, Student-Teacher, Hammer-Nail, Lock-Key) Talk about how each item or person has a logical counterpart and certain functions are achievable when they operate interdependently. *Give each student a copy of Activity 4-20, Together We Stand . . . Divided We Fall.*

4–21 WWW.README.EDU

In our technology-driven information age, how can teenagers be motivated to read printed text in books? Ask students to share scenes from a favorite book with the class and explain why the book is so memorable. Share your own experiences with books, and indicate the need for independent motivation to read. Discuss the problems with illiteracy in America, and ask students to give their opinions as to how they can help combat this problem. Suggest the need for each person to make a personal decision to read books on a regular basis. Once this personal commitment has been made, ask students to come up with ideas for encouraging their peers and members of their families to read. Have them consider the extent to which the Internet can be used to promote the reading of printed text in books. Ask students to make up slogans such as "Read for Your Life." *Give each student a copy of Activity 4-21, www.readme.edu.*

4–22 a. IT'S A HUMAN THING . . .

b. IT'S A FEMALE THING . . .

c. IT'S A MALE THING . . .

Ask students how their views of things in the world are influenced by gender, age, values, culture, and ethnicity. Indicate that it is normal for people to have varying viewpoints based on their upbringing and experiences. Have them consider how so much of what we do is the result of our being human, and nothing more, but encourage their awareness of other things that are definitely the result of our culture, age, gender, and so on. Ask them to provide experiences in which their views might be gender-specific, age-specific, or culture-specific and to indicate the extent to which these various perspectives are valid. (**Note:** Emphasize that people do not have a right to judge the viewpoints of others. Each person has a right to his or her opinion.) Elicit from students their varying opinions on the following controversial issues: enforcing teenage curfews at shopping malls, reducing the number of immigrants who are allowed to enter the United States, requiring that English only be used in public places, airing negative political advertisements, dating rules that allow girls to ask boys out and pay all or part of the cost, or risking being alone and without friends rather than joining in destructive behaviors. Observe students as they discuss these issues, and give them feedback on how considerate they were of each other. Ask them if they were aware of the need to give every person an equal opportunity to share viewpoints. Elicit from them the fact that human beings need to be affirmed—to feel accepted, valued, and reaffirmed during the discussion. *Give each student a copy of Activity 4-22a, It's a Human Thing.*

Extend the impact of this activity by having students comment on the beauty of cultural differences and the right that individuals have to express their uniqueness. Inquire of students as to whether there are different societal expectations for specific races or cultures. Examine all responses in depth. Challenge students to consider areas of their lives that can and should be changed. Pose this question: Have you ever done anything really "stupid" and later asked yourself—"What Was I Thinking?" (**Caution:** Do not have students share private, personal, or embarrassing situations.) Follow with an inquiry regarding whether society has different expectations for males and females (i.e., it's alright for girls and women to cry but boys and men are expected to hold back the tears). *Distribute copies of Activity 4-22b, It's a Female Thing, and Activity 4-22c, It's a Male Thing.*

Have male and female group discussions. Then, bring the two groups together to share their responses. Discuss, as well, how girls might have answered the responses from the male perspective and how boys might have answered the responses from the female perspective. Clarify the similarities and the differences.

4–23 ID Card-Carrying Members Only!!!

Discuss the fact that everyone belongs to groups in human society. Have them offer examples of several kinds of groups such as: families, choirs, bands, the U.S. Senate, clubs, Boy Scouts, Girl Scouts, gangs, unions, sports teams, the U.S. Army, Navy, Marines, and so forth. Ask students to explain why some groups are viewed as positive and others as negative. Elicit from them the fact that society benefits from groups that contribute to its well-being but suffers from groups that have negative purposes. Have them bring out controversies surrounding certain groups, and suggest ways that these conflicts might be resolved. For example, certain military schools have been traditionally all male, and have resisted enrolling females. There are also political issues that separate people into warring factions. (**Teacher Caution:** Some students might want to discuss groups that sympathize with volatile issues such as prayer in schools, abortion, gays in the military, gun control, the rise in violence and incidents of racism, etc. Teacher discretion is crucial in the use of parents, administrators, or counselors to help students work out personal anxieties connected with these or other issues.) Encourage students in their understanding that all groups should be productive, positive, and beneficial to the mental, spiritual, and physical health and well-being of their members as well as to society. Discuss the need for everyone to be careful of the kinds of groups they choose to be members of. *Give each student a copy of Activity 4-23, ID Card-Carrying Members Only!!!*

4–24 HEADLINES FOR GOOD

Take a poll of the number of students who read newspapers on a regular basis. Ask these students to share their opinions regarding the tone of many of the articles as seen in the headlines. Indicate that print journalism is a business and that the goal is to sell as many newspapers as possible. Ask if the need to increase circulation has anything to do with attention-grabbing headlines, the types and tone of the articles, and the extent to which newspapers compete with each other in getting a "scoop" on a story. Discuss the impact on society of sensational stories that highlight murders, rapes, gang activity, embezzlement, terrorism, tragedy, and natural disasters. Ask students to respond to these questions: How does this type of reporting increase the appetite for human pain, disappointment, and tragedy? Do people feed off the misfortunes of other human beings? Do people have the opportunity to improve themselves when they are bombarded with negativism? Are some people influenced to do certain things from negative stories in print and visual media? Can students give examples of this? Do citizens have the right or the responsibility to criticize the news media? Discuss the pros and cons of this question. Have students offer suggestions as to how the headlines of newspaper articles can be changed to accentuate the positive, tell the truth, and help create more positive feelings and reactions from consumers of the news. *Give each student a copy of Activity 4-24, Headlines for Good.*

4–25 911, I NEED YOU!

Ask students to explain why we have emergency telephone numbers and emergency services. have them list some of those they are familiar with. Ask if people who are in need of emergency services are ever concerned about the race, ethnicity, gender, or culture of those who are coming to the rescue. The answer to this question should be NO! Discuss how most people show *tolerance* and extend *human dignity*, without regard to superficial differences of skin color or accent, when their lives are in danger. Discuss why this type of information is not important in an emergency. Ask students if such information should be important in nonemergency situations, and have them explain their positions. Have them suggest the type of information that *is* important to both the victim and the rescuer. For example, rescuers need to know: name, address, the nature of the problem or emergency, and so on. *Give each student a copy of Activity 4-25, 911, I NEED YOU!*

4–26 NO ANCHOVIES—PLEASE!

Ask students to share some of their favorite choices of toppings for pizza. Discuss their personal preferences. Ask each student to relate his or her choices of pepperoni, olives, extra cheese, and so on, metaphorically, to some of the values all people should display. Have students define the following:

LOVE • UNDERSTANDING • FUN • COMMUNICATION • VALUES
DISCIPLINE • FRIENDSHIP • TRUTH • CONSIDERATION

Have students use their understanding of these and other concepts to decide which toppings reflect values that should exist in society. Individual preferences reveal that answers do not have to be the same. One person might choose CHEESE as a wonderful metaphor for LOVE, whereas another person might feel that LOVE is better reflected in PEPPERONI. *Give each student a copy of Activity 4-26, No Anchovies—Please!*

4–27 a. SUCCESS IS SERVICE

b. SUCCESS IS SELF-SATISFACTION

Write the word SERVICE on the board, and ask students to define it. Elicit from them their opinion regarding the connotation that people usually attach to the word. Have them focus on the idea that many people "look down" on those who work in service industries, are servants, or choose to serve others. Ask them what value Princess Diana must have placed on the meaning of the word. She served the poor and powerless because she knew that she shared with them the same human qualities, and that material wealth means little in a world of human interdependence—a world where people must care about and help each other in order to survive. Ask students to share what they know about two other women who cared about the poor and the powerless—Mother Hale and Mother Teresa. They also placed human beings of varied races, cultures, and physical capabilities on an equal plane. The premise upon which these women carried on their work was their belief that all human beings are created equal. In addition, they all found that their *success* was in the *satisfaction* they felt from *serving* their fellow human beings.

Discuss what these women had in common within their hearts and minds that made them *sacrifice* personal gain for what they considered a privilege—helping others. Have students begin to focus on what they have within their hearts and minds that might help them to want to serve their fellow human beings. Ask them to compare and contrast their feelings about the work of these women and their own potential for emulation—or lack of it. Discuss the work of men who serve, too. Challenge students to make up slogans, poetry, and songs using the four italicized "s" words. *Give each student a copy of Activity 4-27a, Success Is Service, and Activity 4-27b, Success Is Self-Satisfaction.*

4–28 AN OPEN LETTER OF COMPLAINT

Gambling is a serious problem in America and students' awareness of its destructive nature is important. Have students define the word gambling and indicate the extent to which participating in it can cause personal problems. Discuss the lottery and how some winners have had their lives turned upside down because of their wealth. Ask students whether people can have "too much money." Based on their experiences in reading about lottery winners, ask students to write an open letter to the Lottery Commission. Students whose experiences lead them to believe that society is better because of the lottery can choose to write letters of approval. Students whose experiences lead them to believe that society is worse because of the lottery should write letters of complaint. Ask students to use correct business letter format and specific evidence to support their main points. *Give each student a copy of Activity 4-28, An Open Letter of Complaint.*

4–29 PROMISES, PROMISES, PROMISES

Write the word PROMISES in large letters on the chalkboard. Then, ask students if anyone has ever promised them something and not delivered. Clarify the fact that promises are meant to be kept. Have students share experiences and compare and contrast their feelings when promises are fulfilled and when they are not. Draw an analogy between promises made by family members and friends and those made by advertisements. Discuss their feelings regarding the reliability of products when compared with their descriptions in commercials. Next, elicit from students their opinions regarding promises made by the government to citizens. Have students list some promises from The U.S. Constitution, The Bill of Rights, and civil rights legislation on the board beneath the word PROMISES. Examples of promises might include Freedom of Speech, Freedom of Religion, Equal Educational Opportunity, Equal Employment Opportunity, and Protection Against Unreasonable Search or Seizure. Allow students to add other rights or promises that citizens are supposed to benefit from in the United States. Inquire as to whether these promises have been kept by the U.S. government, and whether all citizens uphold them when interacting with others. Have students give specific examples of when these promises work and when they don't. Elicit from students whether there are only certain groups of people who enjoy the fulfillment of government promises. Follow with an inquiry as to whether there are certain groups of people who have to fight and struggle for their rights. Have students identify specific groups (e.g., women's groups, racial groups, cultural groups, and human rights groups) and evidence to support their claims. Discuss the injustices that exist. Ask students to give their opinions as to how every citizen can begin to enjoy receiving the rights and promises guaranteed by the laws of the land. *Give each student a copy of Activity 4-29, Promises, Promises, Promises.*

4–30 A Unique Design!

Show students pictures of scientists, writers, musicians, bankers, athletes, parents, realtors, doctors, lawyers, pastors, priests, rabbis, artists, and so on. Indicate that these people have accomplished goals and that they are also capable of doing so if they put their minds to it. Encourage students to focus on their multiple intelligences (talents and skills) and to imagine the possibilities for success in whatever vocation they choose. Build the self-confidence of students by informing them that they all have unique gifts. Indicate that many young people have already used their abilities at home, at school, and in the larger society. As a motivating force, share this scenario:

> Shannon, a very stylish teenager, loved to wear the latest designer clothes that she purchased from the mall. However, she sometimes wore decorated jeans that she had designed using her artistic talents. She was surprised when other teens noticed her jeans and asked where she'd bought them. They were surprised when she told them that she hand-painted the flowers, faces, letter, geometric shapes, landscapes, and skylines. Each flower, face, letter, shape, garden, and building had its own unique design because of Shannon's skill in selecting her paints and her creativity with the brushes. Before she knew it, Shannon was hand-painting personalized jeans for other kids as well as for herself. Every individual wanted items that reflected his or her personality painted on the jeans. Pretty soon, Shannon stopped shopping for designer clothes that other people created, realized that she could develop her skills by practicing, and discussed with her parents the possibility of starting a small business. They were

only too happy to help Shannon develop a business plan, along with some specific goals—including going to college to major in art and minor in business administration.

Discuss the fact that Shannon first used her creative abilities in her own wardrobe. Second, she was not afraid of what other people would think of her hand-decorated clothes; she had lots of self-confidence. Third, she was willing to share her knowledge and abilities with her peers by volunteering to decorate their jeans, as well. Fourth, Shannon knew that she could not venture out on her own without her parents' permission and encouragement. Finally, this artistic young woman did not forget that she had to plan for her future, and she worked with her parents and her school counselors to set goals for her education.

Elicit from students the idea that Shannon's uniqueness was not lost when she brought other people into the picture. Ask them to indicate the extent to which Shannon used her creative talents to help other people, and if this is something everyone should strive to do with her or his abilities. Have students react to the idea that the girl in this scenario stopped buying designer clothes at the mall and began to appreciate her abilities and rights to create her own unique designs. Have students spend a few minutes thinking about how they can use their own unique abilities to make their own lives better—and those of their peers and the larger society, as well. *Give each student a copy of Activity 4-30, A Unique Design!*

"IT TAKES A WHOLE VILLAGE TO RAISE A CHILD"

Adults must take care of, teach, and protect their children until they are able to live independently. The adults in society, and the institutions that service their needs, make up the "village." They work together in the interest of training the young to take over society when they reach maturity. Human beings live in families and depend on adults who run stores, schools, religious institutions, and government agencies to help them provide for the needs of family members. Therefore, there is much interdependence and a great need for cooperation among adults in domestic, economic, social, educational, and political areas. Because today's children will be tomorrow's adults, quality time and effort must be devoted to their training. Respond to the title of this activity and the statement beneath it by explaining what the words actually mean in an interdependent society.

EXPLANATION OF THE TITLE:
"It takes a whole village to raise a child."

_____
_____
_____
_____
_____

EXPLANATION OF THE STATEMENT:
"Children and young people are the hope of society."

_____
_____
_____
_____
_____

NAME _____   DATE _____

What values or standards do young people need to inherit from adults in the "village" or society? In that parents or guardians are the first caregivers—or teachers—select some of the words from the WORD BANK below, and consider the extent to which families should prepare their young people for participation for life in the larger society. Then, prepare to make comments about the role that other members of the "village" might have to assume in helping to reinforce the teachings of the family. For example, how might the village members extend the positive home training and offer more opportunities of independence for the maturing child? Complete the chart to reveal the necessity of adult interdependence in the raising of children.

WORD BANK

identity • recognition • trust • hope • faith • peace • service • discipline
opportunity • self-esteem • belonging • truth • safety • love • standards
creativity • courtesy • generosity • honesty • compassion • justice

FAMILY AND SOCIETY WORKING TOGETHER FOR THE CHILD

Select at least five words and place them in the left-hand column. Explain how both the nuclear family and the "village" will make certain that the child learns and uses these concepts in his or her life. The first one is done for you.

WORD	ROLE OF THE FAMILY	ROLE OF THE "VILLAGE"
1. TRUTH	Model the telling of truth. Immediate and consistent consequences for lying and lessons on the self-satisfaction that accompanies telling the truth (avoid material rewards).	Make valid laws and stand by them. Support truth in print and visual media. Create opportunities for the young to see honest members of society in politics, education, and so forth.
2.		
3.		
4.		
5.		
6.		

NAME _____ DATE _____

Which of these concepts can you, as a young person, help someone else with?

_____

_____

_____

_____

Explain how you will accomplish this. Also, compare your responses with your peers and develop responses for other words from the word list.

_____

_____

_____

_____

_____

_____

_____

_____

_____

_____

_____

© 1999 by John Wiley & Sons, Inc.

NAME _____ DATE _____

THE NEEDS OF THE CHILDREN WITHIN THE "VILLAGE"

"It takes a whole village to raise a child" is an old African proverb that many people are talking about today. But what does this proverb mean to you?

Adults want to raise children who can be independent and take care of themselves in the world. They want young people to be contributors to the good of all in society. Certainly, you want the same positive things out of life. What do adult members of the village have to offer to you and other young people? How can you take advantage of the experiences of older people who have knowledge about how the world functions? How can you match your needs with resources that are available in the village?

Most adults realize that young people need the gifts of LOVE, DISCIPLINE, BELONGING, MORAL SUPPORT, RECOGNITION, IDENTITY, and OPPORTUNITY. These gifts are necessary for encouraging you to set high goals and work to achieve them. From the gifts listed above, select the ones you most want or need from yourself, your family, your peers, and your community. Explain why each of these gifts is important to you.

Complete the chart according to YOUR PERSONAL NEEDS and the GIFTS that are available in your village.

WHAT I NEED FROM THE VILLAGE

	My Needs	The Reasons	What's Available
MYSELF			
FAMILY			

NAME _____ DATE _____

WHAT I NEED FROM THE VILLAGE *(Cont'd)*

	My Needs	The Reasons	What's Available
PEERS			
COMMUNITY			

Complete this sentence:

I need _____ more than anything else in order to prepare myself for making a contribution to my community (village).

NAME _____ DATE _____

ASSESSMENT CHART FOR "VILLAGE" READINESS

Following the three stages in this lesson, discuss your needs as a future adult member of society with teenagers and adults in your family, community, and class. In your discussions, you are trying to find out how "village" members can help to prepare you and your peers to take over their responsibilities when they leave. First, identify your personal needs. Second, identify "village" members who can fulfill those needs. Plan meetings with members in each category on the chart and ask them what they will contribute to your growth in each PERSONAL NEEDS area. Then, based on their responses, complete the chart. There are some suggestions in each category. (**Note:** If meetings are not possible, complete categories based on your own assessments of what you need, expect, or want from each member.)

YOUR PERSONAL NEEDS	STAGE I FAMILY/ RELATIVES	STAGE II COMMUNITY MEMBERS	STAGE III CLASSMATES
1 LOVE		Acceptance	Affection
2 SELF-CONTROL	Discipline	Laws/Curfews	
3 IDENTITY	Bonding Security		
4 BELONGING		Friendship	
5 RECOGNITION	Sharing Family Heritage		
6 OPPORTUNITY		Education Employment	

NAME _____ DATE _____

A YOUNG PERSON'S PLEDGE
TO THE "VILLAGE"

You can make positive decisions that will benefit you, your family, and other members of society (the "village"). What values, standards, and behaviors should you want to follow as an earnest, well-meaning member of our society? To the main ideas in the boxes, add crucial details that can be used for developing A PLEDGE for young "village" members.

Work with a partner to add important details to each theme. Be certain that you are willing to use these specific ideas as guidelines for success in your own personal life.

LAYING A FOUNDATION FOR SUCCESS IN LIFE

MAKING ACADEMIC PROGRESS
INTERDEPENDENCE AND COOPERATION
SELF-ANALYSIS AND SELF-CORRECTION
DEVELOPING LEADERSHIP SKILLS
VALUING THE RACIAL AND CULTURAL HERITAGE OF OTHERS
SPIRITUAL AND CHARACTER DEVELOPMENT

Now, based on the details you have used to describe the meaning of each theme above, write a pledge or a promise that you can live by. Use the back of this sheet, a notebook, or a computer.

NAME _____   DATE _____

SURVIVAL IN THE "VILLAGE"

If you were drowning, you would definitely want someone to dive in and save you or throw a line and pull you out! Think of the many dangers that exist in the world and the extent to which those who care about you will go to protect you from harm. Many harmful activities occur throughout the day in society; however, many more dangers occur at night. Most adults feel that it is best for young people to be in the house at a reasonable time instead of "hanging out" until the wee hours of the morning, so curfews exist for young people in many communities. Being safely inside is a matter of survival.

Similarly, most adults believe that it is best for young people to take the advice of older people when it comes to getting an education and preparing for the future, but many young people think that they can make their own decisions. Do you need the advice of older people in society or can you make it on your own? Do you know your personal needs and the members of your village who can help you fulfill your needs? Here's how to learn the "village" survival strategies:

SURVIVAL STRATEGY 1—
KNOW YOUR PERSONAL NEEDS

What do you, _____, need from the members of the village?
(Your Name)

In a hypothetical "village" that is responsible for your development, what should the adult members give every young person? Place the letter "A" (AGREE) by those items you need. Place the letter "D" (DISAGREE) by those you do not need or want.

____ LOVE	____ ACCEPTANCE	____ DRUGS
____ HATE	____ LONELINESS	____ EDUCATION
____ DISCIPLINE	____ RECOGNITION	____ EMPLOYMENT
____ LAWS/RULES	____ BEING IGNORED	____ SELF-DISCIPLINE
____ VIOLENCE	____ OPPORTUNITY	____ HOPE
____ IDENTITY	____ JAIL	
____ OBLIVION	____ SAFETY	

Once you know your own personal needs and realize that there are times when you need help fulfilling them, open the lines of communication with people who can provide protection, caring, and knowledge. The survival strategies that adults in the "village" give you will equip you with the tools you need for a life of self-sufficiency in the larger, outside world. Remember, human beings are interdependent; they need one another.

SURVIVAL STRATEGY 2—
GET TO KNOW THE MEMBERS OF THE VILLAGE

In his Newsweek article, "I Wasn't Left to Myself," General Colin Powell discusses the safety net of family, church, school, and community members who kept him from giving in to the "temptations of the street." He implies that social structures that can protect all kids from becoming involved in juvenile crime, gangs, teenage pregnancy, and dropping out of school should be strengthened and/or reconstructed. He calls them "safe places." Some "safe places" are listed on the chart. Who might be in these places to help you? Name specific members of this "village"; adults who can give guidance to you and other young people. Identify the members of the village by writing the names, roles, occupations, or professions in appropriate categories on the chart. You do not have to fill all categories.

WHO IN THE VILLAGE WILL HELP YOU?

	Family	Trusted Neighbors	School	Youth Clubs
1.				
2.				
3.				
4.				

	Volunteers	Social/Religious/Health Agencies	Businesses
1.			
2.			
3.			
4.			

Discuss specific members, locations, and responsibilities of your entries with peers and adults. Extend your chart to include categories you know of that are not listed here.

NAME _____ DATE _____

DEVELOPING A DEEP SENSE
OF RESPONSIBILITY

Every person has a conscience that helps him or her to discern the difference between right and wrong. What are your personal standards of behavior? To what extent does your conscience guide you in making decisions to follow responsible courses of action? What roles do your heart and mind play in the decisions you make to uphold or not to uphold the laws of the environments of home, school, and community? At a certain time in your life, you become capable of making individual decisions. Having a deep sense of responsibility about one's life as a contributing member of society is very important. What are some of the most important issues that you, as an individual, need to be responsible about? As an adult, you have to do the right thing on your own. Now is the time to begin to develop a sense of personal responsibility. Then, when you have to make important decisions, you will choose the right things to do.

When you were very small, someone taught you how to be responsible about simpler things. Some of these were:

- combing and brushing your hair
- brushing your teeth
- hanging up your clothes
- cleaning your room
- bathing
- feeding yourself
- obeying house rules
- cooperating

Now you are older. You're a teenager preparing to move into the adult world—into the larger society. Your larger society includes your neighborhood, state, country, and world. The things you have to be responsible about are more difficult than when you were a toddler. You must be able to identify, internalize, and make a commitment to act positively regarding important issues. For each item below, write I for IMPORTANT or NI for NOT IMPORTANT on the lines.

_____ Being able to adapt to changes in situations without violence, pouting, or exasperation

_____ Ability to respect diverse races, cultures, and ethnic groups—tolerance of the rights of other people

_____ Being self-reliant, decisive, and independent

_____ Ability to follow rules, laws, or adhere to limits

_____ Ability to set goals and pursue them

_____ Maintaining a positive attitude

_____ Ability to take directions from authority

_____ Knowing when to seek help when being treated unfairly

_____ Following through on responsibilities

NAME _____ DATE _____

____ Having personal standards of behavior that reflect my spiritual upbringing

____ Speaking up for my rights without infringing upon the rights and freedoms of other citizens

____ Setting priorities to accomplish all of my tasks at home, at school, and in the community

____ Realizing that cheating, stealing, and lying, are all forms of dishonesty that I must avoid

____ Choosing my friends wisely and not giving in to peer pressure; avoiding anyone who would "bring me down"

____ Knowing that the "crowd mentality" is a dangerous course—that to act individually on the side of right is safer and wiser for me—that I can dare to be different

____ Being able to take the responsibility for my own actions and decisions—never blaming others for my decisions

____ The ability to rise only to those challenges that propel me toward success or offer opportunities for me to help someone else succeed

____ Creating a lifestyle that reflects "who I am" spiritually, educationally, politically, socially

____ Having a sense of humor regarding myself—avoiding laughing at and ridiculing others

____ Seeking peace with my fellow human beings—choosing nonviolence

____ Other _____

_____

Set high expectations for yourself as you approach adulthood by finding a "deep sense of responsibility" regarding your spiritual, social, traditional, family, and personal values.

Compare and contrast your checklist with those of your peers. Identify the commonalties that transcend race, gender, culture, and ethnicity.

NAME _____ DATE _____

WHAT IS A SQUARE?

Is it okay to be different from everyone else? Is it a positive or a negative situation when a parent sets a curfew for a son or daughter? What if all the other teenagers can stay out after dark and you have to be in before dark?

Some years ago, people were called "square" or "uncool" if they did not go along with the "in crowd." People who were "not with it" were ostracized or ignored by those who were considered "cool." Think of words for each category to define what traits individuals must have to be "cool" or "with it" or "square" or "uncool" in today's society. Then, decide what category you fit into, if any. Can people change from one category to another? Which state is preferred for a person who wants to be successful—to be his or her own person?

Study the configuration of each geometric shape and discuss with your classmates how they can be used to describe the various actions, behaviors, and personalities of people. List class-generated words and phrases beneath each category on the chart.

SQUARE/UNCOOL	COOL/WITH IT
1.	1.
2.	2.
3.	3.
4.	4.
5.	5.

THINK ABOUT IT!

Is it important to know who YOU are and what YOU want out of life? How important is it to be different?

How is it possible for others to define or place labels on people who are self-confident? For example, do the meanings given to shapes hold true for people with high self-esteem?

- ☞ Straight lines are rigid and ungiving
- ☞ Circular lines are flexible
- ☞ Spaces provides security
- ☞ Apexes suggest finality

If you had to select a geometric shape that describes you, which one would you choose? Explain.

NAME _____ DATE _____

QUESTIONNAIRE FOR PEER COUNSELORS

Tessie wanted to help her classmates and her school by volunteering to be a peer counselor. One of the requirements was to respond to a questionnaire so that the adult staff could evaluate her ability to work as a peer counselor. At first, Tessie was reluctant to apply because she had not always been a model student. In fact, she admitted that she still made mistakes or unwise decisions. But, Tessie knows that she is a good person and that her past mistakes and the way she corrected them could be of help to her peers. So, she applied and was accepted as a peer counselor.

Pretend that you are applying for the position of peer counselor and that you have not always been a model student. Complete each of the ten items below by creating fictional but realistic responses that show personal growth in the life of a teenager. In your responses you must admit past "mistakes or errors in judgement," explaining how you corrected them and became a stronger person as a result. Your responses should discuss BEFORE and AFTER perspectives and highlight learning on the part of the potential peer counselor.

Be creative and insightful as you complete each item. (See sample response for item #1)

HOW QUALIFIED ARE YOU TO BECOME A PEER COUNSELOR?

1. School policies prohibiting the use of drugs, alcohol, and tobacco products

   Sample Response: *At one time I believed that drinking and smoking were harmless. I've seen too many kids end up in trouble or dead because of these negative choices. Now, I have other ways of calming my nerves or showing my power. I concentrate on things that will make me happy naturally and there is no risk of becoming addicted or dependent upon dangerous substances. I feel better about myself because I'm in control of my life.*

1. School policies prohibiting the use of drugs, alcohol, and tobacco products

   _____

   _____

   _____

2. Attendance and punctuality to classes _____

   _____

   _____

3. Discipline referrals _____

   _____

   _____

4. Behavior in school or out in the community _____

   _____

   _____

NAME _____ DATE _____

5. Role model for others _____

_____

_____

6. Study habits _____

_____

_____

7. Relationships with people who are from different racial, ethnic, or cultural back-grounds _____

_____

_____

8. How attitudes of students influence the atmosphere of the school

_____

_____

9. Parental involvement in relationships with students and teachers

_____

_____

10. School as training ground for students' adult roles in society

_____

_____

Compare your responses with those of your classmates. Then, develop a set of rules for the entire class or school to follow. Include demonstrations of how peers should treat each other and how young people should relate to the adults in a school/community setting. Include specific ways that peers can resolve personal and interpersonal conflicts in school and in the community.

Take a poll of all students regarding the need for creating a positive atmosphere in the school. Ask each student to suggest the MOST IMPORTANT CHARACTER TRAITS that all students should exhibit to maintain a positive environment wherever they are.

WHAT ARE IMPORTANT CHARACTER TRAITS FOR TEENAGERS TO EXHIBIT?

1. _____ 2. _____ 3. _____

4. _____ 5. _____ 6. _____

NAME _____ DATE _____

HELPING OUT . . . FOR FREE

In a day when teenagers are thought to be uncaring, there are many who volunteer their time and energy to make life easier for other people. Think about instances that you are aware of when young people have reached out to older people to help or just enjoy their company. Also, think about times you know of when teenagers have worked in various areas of the community—not for money—but to create bonds between diverse groups of people, then write your story. Here is one example:

TWO YOUNG MEN TO THE RESCUE

The teacher emerged from the school building ready to go home after a full day of teaching. Upon arriving at her car, she found that the rear tire was flat. With a look of despair, she turned to go back into the building when a young man driving out of the parking lot saw the situation. He turned his car around, jumped out and asked, "Would you like some help?" He opened the trunk and began to look for the jack when another young man came out of the building. He inquired as to whether he could help. The appreciative teacher watched as the two young men, one African American and the other European American, worked together to change the flat tire. Their racial heritage was not important to the task they performed or the pleasure they shared in being of help. Only their human concern was important at that moment. The teacher thanked both young men and offered them sizable tips but they refused these and left smiling. She left smiling, as well, and told the story to all who would listen.

YOUR STORY OF A CARING PERSON

_____

_____

_____

_____

_____

_____

_____

_____

NAME _____   DATE _____

WHAT? VOLUNTEER FOR MY OWN GOOD?
. . . HOW? . . . WHY?

Helping someone without expecting anything in return is a great gift you can give to yourself, because the giver benefits along with the receiver. A smile, words of thank you, and other examples of appreciation satisfy, encourage, and affirm the giver. Often, people who extend kindness to others do not even want verbal or written expressions of gratitude. It is enough for these people to know that someone is better because of their involvement.

Help is on the way!

Read the scenarios and decide what you would do in each case. Needy people exist in every sector of society, and there are many young people who can help to relieve pain and suffering. Then, develop a scenario based on an imaginary or a real-life experience in which volunteers can decide to make life better for others.

SCENARIO 1

Imagine that you are an "A" student in math who happens to be confined to a wheel chair. A friend has informed you that he knows someone who needs extra help in math. He asks you to spend some time after school helping this student prepare for the next math test. What will you do? Explain your decision.

_____

_____

_____

_____

SCENARIO 2

A member of the community has had trouble with his car and you're taking auto mechanics at school. He's willing to pay you to correct minor problems with his car, but you know that he is on a fixed income. You're really good at this kind of work; in fact you have a job at a garage on weekends. What will you do? Explain your decision.

_____

_____

_____

_____

NAME _____ DATE _____

SCENARIO 3

A group of homes in a nearby community has been badly damaged by a hurricane. The residents have no storm insurance and are without basic needs of food, clothing, and shelter. Some of your friends want to help, but there is no organized plan. What can YOU do to help convert their good intentions into concrete help? Explain your decision.

_____

_____

_____

_____

_____

_____

_____

SCENARIO 4

(Make up a scenario in which young people are challenged to make contributions to society. This could involve serving those who need to be encouraged, are homeless, disabled, shut-in, and so on.)

_____

_____

_____

_____

_____

_____

_____

Present your idea to the class. Also, listen to their ideas and devise a strategy for an actual volunteer program. Remember to solicit adult support and advice for assessing community needs and developing a plan for helping to serve them.

NAME _____ DATE _____

CLASS OR INDIVIDUAL PLANS FOR HELPING OTHERS

Assess needs in your community through programs in your school, religious, or social institutions. Then, identify specific plans that you, your peers, and adult members of the community can meet these needs. **Never volunteer alone or without adult supervision.** Always serve others with respect and genuine concern.

VOLUNTEERING FOR GOOD

Community Needs	Plans for Meeting Needs
1. _____	_____
_____	_____
2. _____	_____
_____	_____
3. _____	_____
_____	_____
4. _____	_____
_____	_____
5. _____	_____
_____	_____
6. _____	_____
_____	_____

Implement or act on these plans by identifying a specific need to fulfill. Identify person(s) and place. Then, set dates and times. (**Note:** Remember to add the name of an adult)

NEED: _____ PERSON(S): _____

_____

PLACE: _____ DATE: _____

TIME: _____ VOLUNTEERS: _____

ADULT SUPERVISOR(S): _____

NAME _____ DATE _____

GET REAL!

The term "Get real!" conveys the idea that someone is not facing reality. Think of the position you hold on several controversial issues in our society. If you had the opportunity to bring certain issues up for discussion among your peers, how would you defend your opinions? Facts are based upon reality and can be verified. Your position or opinion on these issues would have more credibility if you were able to support them with specific evidence or facts. Try to gather enough factual information to back up your opinions on controversial issues. Consider conducting a survey of your peers, looking up statistics from various sources, finding current articles on these issues, and so on.

Write the basis for your arguments for or against the controversial issues listed below. Remember to strengthen each response with reality in the form of FACTS, EXAMPLES, and CAUSE-EFFECT RELATIONSHIPS to help clarify your position and to help persuade others to agree with you. The first one is done for you.

ISSUE 1—MANDATORY SCHOOL UNIFORMS

Cause—A. Too much competition among students for designer clothes.
B. Putting down peers who can't afford expensive clothes.
C. Students are more interested in their clothes than in their studies.

Effect—A. Uniforms would reduce competition for fancy or expensive clothes.
B. Parents would save money and their children wouldn't be teased.
C. Students could concentrate on their school work.

Your position on this issue: _____

_____

_____

ISSUE 2—TEENAGE SMOKING

Cause—A. _____

B. _____

C. _____

Effect—A. _____

B. _____

C. _____

Your position on this issue: _____

_____

_____

NAME _____ DATE _____

ISSUE 3—YEAR-ROUND SCHOOL

Cause—A. _____

B. _____

C. _____

Effect—A. _____

B. _____

C. _____

Your position on this issue: _____

_____

_____

ISSUE 4—SEXUAL ABSTINENCE

Cause—A. _____

B. _____

C. _____

Effect—A. _____

B. _____

C. _____

Your position on this issue: _____

_____

_____

ISSUE 5—CLEAN NEEDLE PROGRAM FOR DRUG ABUSERS

Cause—A. _____

B. _____

C. _____

Effect—A. _____

B. _____

C. _____

Your position on this issue: _____

_____

_____

NAME _____ DATE _____

ISSUE 6—PRAYER IN PUBLIC SCHOOLS

Cause—A. _____

B. _____

C. _____

Effect—A. _____

B. _____

C. _____

Your position on this issue: _____

_____

_____

_____

HEROES WHO ARE NOT "HANDICAPPED"

Heroes exist among diverse groups of human beings, including those whom many would consider disabled. In reality, physical and emotional challenges exist for all human beings, but some people are challenged more in one area than others.

Christopher Reeve, an actor who played Superman, is a hero in real life. Recently, he sustained serious injuries to his neck and spine and is struggling to regain some of his normal bodily functions. The reports indicate that he is making progress beyond what was originally thought possible. Doctors thought that he would be completely paralyzed for the rest of his life, but Christopher Reeve is making heroic efforts to walk again. In the process of his struggling to regain control of his own life, he is working to make life better for other people who have sustained neck and spinal cord injuries. He is most interested in research that would give greater mobility to people who are now wheelchair-bound. Certainly, his efforts and resumption of his movie career demonstrate his positive outlook and prove that Christopher Reeve is not handicapped.

Another hero is a young man who is a great runner, despite the fact that he lost both legs below the knees in a train accident. Milton Franklin's story is one of recovery and triumph, for he not only learned to walk again, but he learned to run. Determined not to let this accident ruin his life, Milton Franklin decided to work to regain his former skills. Doctors fitted him with artificial legs and he began his program. It took many months of physical therapy for him to learn skills that had come naturally before he lost his legs. First, he practiced learning how to stand up and stay balanced on his new artificial legs and feet. Then he practiced walking. Finally, Milton Franklin began to practice his running techniques. To increase his strength and perfect his techniques, he started jogging with members of a New York-based running club for amputees. Mentally, he was in control because he made the decision that to succeed he had to treat his prostheses as if they were his real legs. He knew he had to work hard, and he did. Because of his confidence, practice, and high personal goals, Milton Franklin succeeded in his wish to become a great runner. He has won three gold medals for running. Milton Franklin is not handicapped; he is a mentally and physically capable contributor to his own quality of life, and an encouragement to others who are physically challenged.

Many people feel sorry for—and even reject—those they consider "weak" or "handicapped." What advice would you have for able-bodied people, regarding the need to extend human dignity to those who are physically challenged? You can record your comments on the next page.

What specific things can be said to increase acceptance and tolerance of people who are physically challenged? Have a discussion with a classmate on the contributions of people like Milton Franklin and Christopher Reeve to all of society. Record ideas from your discussion and use points from the stories of Christopher Reeve and Milton Franklin to support arguments that all human beings are created equal.

© 1999 by John Wiley & Sons, Inc.

NAME _____ DATE _____

ALL HUMAN BEINGS ARE CREATED EQUAL

_____
_____
_____
_____
_____
_____
_____
_____
_____
_____
_____
_____
_____

NAME _____ DATE _____

PLANNING AN INTERVIEW WITH A HERO

People are challenged in many ways. There are those who are challenged because of differences in physical abilities, language, culture, race, or ethnicity. Have you ever been teased because you are too tall, too short, too big, too little, or for any number of other reasons? Then you might have some idea of how a person who is disabled feels when he or she is teased.

Some famous people who are disabled have lots of support from doctors, family, and friends. There are other people who are not well known. Many of them are young people who have medical and family support but little or none from their peers. Identify a person in your own life who is challenged, and make an effort to get to know him or her.

How can you open the lines of communication with someone who is not used to having friends and support from peers? Begin your relationship with this new friend by introducing yourself and then asking some very sincere questions. Plan your brief introduction and interview questions below and on the back of this sheet. Suggestion #1 will help you to get started.

YOUR INTRODUCTION _____

_____

YOUR QUESTIONS FOR AN INTERVIEW WITH _____

1. Suggestion #1: What are some of your talents? _____

   _____

   _____

2. _____

   _____

   _____

3. _____

   _____

   _____

4. _____

   _____

   _____

NAME _____   DATE _____

JUST A LITTLE RESPECT

Most people want respect from their fellow human beings. Too often, it is difficult to achieve because of biases based on race, culture, ethnicity, and other kinds of prejudices. In order to receive respect, you have to give respect. When the giving and receiving of respect is MUTUAL, human beings can live together peacefully.

Where do you stand on the issue of giving respect to people? Which human attributes are MOST IMPORTANT in the development of caring and concern for others? In ascending order, place the letter of the attributes on the staircase, from the least important to the most important. Then place an (*) by those attributes that you have already internalized and use in your relationships with others. You do not have to use all of the letters.

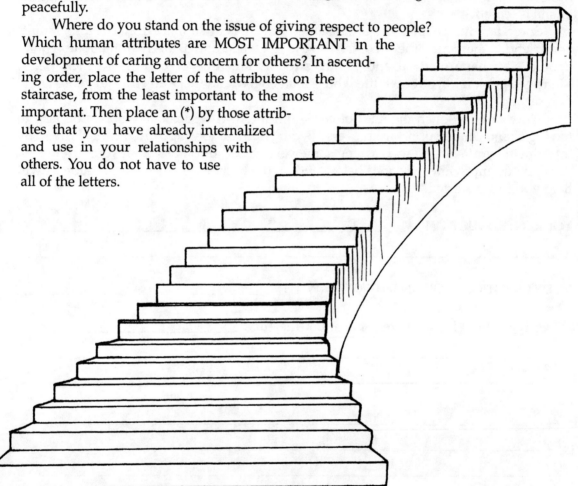

HUMAN ATTRIBUTES

a. kindness
b. singing
c. hopefulness
d. fear
e. power
f. alienation
g. good work ethic

h. tolerance
i. love
j. money
k. beauty
l. good listener
m. religious beliefs
n. acceptance

o. strong ego
p. friendship
q. rioting
r. conversation
s. maturity
t. self-confidence
u. education

v. responsibility
w. truthfulness
x. belief in equality
y. respect for authority
z. appreciation of others

NAME _____ DATE _____

DISCIPLINING OTHER PEOPLE'S CHILDREN: YOUR VIEW

If it takes a whole village to raise a child, what would keep adults from correcting the children of their friends and neighbors? How would you react if one of your neighbors yelled at you for doing something that was obviously wrong? Do you agree or disagree with the idea of someone other than your own parents or relatives disciplining you?

Read each scenario below and place yourself in the position of an adult who is unrelated to the child in the passage. In the absence of his or her parents, provide this child with nurturing, corrective advice—or consider going to the parents with the information you think will help the child. Hold discussions with your peers on responses to each of the scenarios and on the follow-up questions.

SCENARIO 1

Margo had a 9 P.M. curfew on weekdays and a 10 P.M. curfew on weekends. Without fail, she was in the house before the deadlines. However, without her parent's knowledge, she would frequently sneak out of her bedroom window. While her parents were asleep, Margo would hang out with her friends long past her curfew and come home at the crack of dawn on occasion. Knowing the dangers that Margo faces in disobeying her parents, how would you help her? (Remember, you are assuming the role of an adult.)

1. Will you advise Margo? Why or why not?

   _____
   _____
   _____

2. What advice will you give to her? Explain.

   _____
   _____
   _____

3. In the interest of parental control, what, if anything, would you say to her parents?

   _____
   _____
   _____

NAME _____ DATE _____

SCENARIO 2

Jim is only 15 years old, but he drives a car—even though he does not have a license. There are several adults in the neighborhood who have seen him driving but, because they don't know his parents very well, they have not told them. Jim is a friend of yours and you want to protect him from getting into trouble with the police, or worse. Also, you have met his mother. How would you handle this situation?

1. Would you assume that Jim's parents already know that he drives and that they don't care, and why should you?

   _____

   _____

   _____

2. What might you say to Jim about his breaking the law?

   _____

   _____

   _____

3. How might your informing Jim's parents impact on your relationship with them as neighbors?

   _____

   _____

   _____

FOLLOW-UP QUESTIONS

☞ How did you feel correcting someone else's child? What is the difference between being "nosy" and "caring"?

☞ In what circumstances is correcting the son or daughter of others a valid action?

☞ What message does a person send when he or she intervenes in the actions of children other than his or her own?

☞ Are there people already taking the place of parents in your life? Who are they, and do they have a right to discipline you?

☞ Do you think that most parents appreciate sincere support from other parents? Explain.

☞ If you were a parent, under what circumstances would you want another adult to correct your child?

NAME _____ DATE _____

JUDGE THIS!!!

Based on the laws of society, which are designed to maintain reasonable order among the citizenry, which individual behaviors listed below are NOT ACCEPTABLE? You are the judge who must see that JUSTICE is carried out. For each act of INJUSTICE, assign an appropriate corrective action. Make certain that the punishment fits the crime!

Select at least five examples of unacceptable behavior from the list beneath the chart. Then, judge the severity of the example, put yourself in the place of the person who has committed the infraction, and think of a consequence of negative behavior and write it in the CONSEQUENCES box.

Unacceptable Behavior	Consequences
1. _____	1. _____
2. _____	2. _____
3. _____	3. _____
4. _____	4. _____
5. _____	5. _____

HUMAN BEHAVIORS

peer pressure • racism • human rights • dealing drugs • justice • ridicule mutual respect • personal integrity • courage • police brutality • vandalism self-control   ridicule • greed • avoiding fighting • tolerance • cheating on tests • courage • bomb-making • protecting the environment • carrying guns or other weapons

NO JOKE!

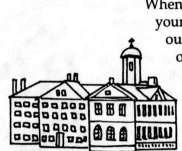

When you're thinking about your future, you want to seriously consider all of the opportunities that come your way. Several questions will help you to focus on the important things: What are your talents and skills? What educational and career goals will help you to develop these talents and skills? Who are some of the people you need to speak with about your plans? What things do you really need to be serious about right now? What are some things that might distract you from successfully pursuing your goals? What things must you remain aware of that are good or not good for you as you plan for your future?

Based on your goals, how can you eliminate things that will distract you from your plans for success? How can you focus on those things that will help you to achieve your goals? Read and respond to the statements below by writing the numbers beneath the appropriate heading—DO or DON'T.

DO	DON'T
_____ _____	_____ _____
_____ _____	_____ _____
_____ _____	_____ _____
_____ _____	_____ _____

1. dare to dream of success

2. surround yourself with people who share your highest goals

3. spend five to ten hours in front of the television daily

4. create a network of dependable, interested adults

5. listen to instruction in class and do your homework

6. avoid stepping on others to get what you want

7. develop a reputation as a "giver" rather than a "taker"

8. develop your own set of rules and follow them rather than those of society

9. let others know that you can do everything and that you don't need anyone else

10. laugh at other people's mistakes

11. investigate colleges and their programs, and identify those that will meet your needs

12. do something constructive each day

Develop more DO'S and DON'TS and categorize them on the chart above. (Example: 13. join a gang, 14. think for yourself)

NAME _____   DATE _____

TWINS, TRIPLETS, QUADRUPLETS, ANYONE?

While they are infrequent, multiple births are a fact of life. The relationships emerging in the lives of twins, triplets, quadruplets, or quintuplets can be lots of fun, yet we've all heard of times when these siblings want to establish their own individual identities. Read the humorous poem "The Twins" by Henry S. Leigh. Explain what you think

the poet is saying about the quality of life for multiple-birth siblings. If you are a multiple-birth sibling, share some of your experiences in an original poem or story.

THE TWINS

by Henry S. Leigh

In form and feature, face and limb,
I grew so like my brother
That folks got taking me for him
And each for one another.
It puzzled all our kith and kin,
It reached an awful pitch
For one of us was born a twin
And not a soul knew which.

One day (to make the matter worse),
Before our names were fixed,
As we were being washed by nurse,
We got completely mixed.
And thus, you see, by Fate's decree,
(Or rather nurse's whim)
My brother John got christened *me*,
And I got christened *him*.

This fatal likeness even dogged
My footsteps when at school,
And I was always getting flogged
For John turned out a fool.
I put this question hopelessly
To everyone I knew,
What *would* you do, if you were *me*,
To prove that you were *you?*

Our close resemblance turned the tide
Of my domestic life;
For somehow my intended bride
Became my brother's wife.
In short, year after year the same
Absurd mistakes went on;
And when I died, the neighbors came
And buried brother John.

POET'S VIEWPOINT

_____

_____

_____

_____

NAME _____ DATE _____

CARRYING THE TORCH

Olympic Games torch bearers are chosen for the wonderful things they do in their communities. Some have overcome difficult emotional or physical challenges, and still others have become famous because of their unusual athletic abilities. The torch is a symbol of all that is best within the human spirit. Think of why you, your peers, and members of your family should be considered for the honor of carrying the Olympic torch. What are you doing to improve your life and that of those around you?

Within each category below, state in your own words the standards or the qualities that Olympic torch bearers can use to improve how people get along in our society. Use the word(s) at the beginning of each item to help you to set realistic GOALS or plan ACTIVITIES that can improve human relationships in America, your school, or your neighborhood.

STATE A GOAL OR PLAN AN ACTIVITY

1. Spirit of Volunteerism _____

    _____

2. Personal Talents or Skills _____

    _____

3. Cultural Heritage (race, language, ethnicity) _____

    _____

4. Value System _____

    _____

5. Political Views _____

    _____

6. Work Ethic _____

    _____

7. Educational Background _____

    _____

8. Religion _____

    _____

NAME _____ DATE _____

TOGETHER WE STAND . . .
DIVIDED WE FALL

Identify the parts on the chart that can be combined to create a whole. Write the reason that the whole is necessary. One combination is done for you.

PARTS		WHOLE	NEED FOR THE ITEM
H_2 Teachers		$H_2 + 0 =$ Water	Life-saving liquid
Videotape Employees			
Children Respect for Others			
Hopes & VCR Dreams			
Students 0			
Self-respect A Sense of Responsibility			
Politicians Parents			
Employers Voters			

Mutual Respect • Education • Family • Good Government • Productivity
Water • Moving Picture • Success/Accomplishment • Oxygen • Hydrogen

Discuss your responses with your peers.

NAME _____ DATE _____

WWW.README.EDU

READ FOR YOUR LIFE

Parents and teachers try to motivate young people to increase the time they spend reading for pleasure. Since more and more homes have computers, there are increased opportunities to inform young people about exciting and enjoyable books. If each person who has read a good book would briefly describe it and place the description on the World Wide Web or the Internet, reading for pleasure could skyrocket among teenagers. Identify at least two books that you have read. Write vivid descriptions that would make someone else want to rush out and get these books. Be sure not to reveal entire plots as you develop descriptions that can be placed on the Internet.

DESCRIPTION 1

1. Title of book _____

2. Author _____

3. Publisher _____

4. Description _____

_____

_____

_____

_____

DESCRIPTION 2

1. Title of book _____

2. Author _____

3. Publisher _____

4. Description _____

_____

_____

NAME _____ DATE _____

IT'S A HUMAN THING

Culture and gender often play a big part in how human beings conduct their lives. Pretend that you are discussing your views with someone you've met only recently. Carry on an imaginary conversation with this person by answering the questions below:

1. Based upon your culture and gender, how do you see the world around you?

2. How do your views impact on the way you live and interact with other people?

3. What do people expect of you based upon the values you have been taught? Are their expectations tied to your gender?

4. To what extent does the world change your point of view, your attitude, and your behavior?

5. Does being human outweigh age, race, culture, gender, or ethnicity in how people should treat each other? Explain.

6. Are you prone to imitating negative behaviors and destructive images for the sake of popularity or acceptance? Or do you think for yourself?

7. Does the fact that all human beings experience the same kinds of emotional responses to violence, illness, joy, embarrassment, peace, and so on provide a basis for interracial harmony?

Complete one of the related worksheets, "It's a Female Thing" or "It's a Male Thing." In each category, write at least four specific things that are EXPECTED of YOU as a female or male in society.

205

NAME _____ DATE _____

IT'S A FEMALE THING

EXPECTATIONS OF SOCIETY

1. _____
2. _____
3. _____
4. _____

EXPECTATIONS OF FAMILY/FRIENDS

1. _____
2. _____
3. _____
4. _____

EXPECTATIONS OF SELF

1. _____
2. _____
3. _____
4. _____

PERSONAL REFLECTIONS

(Check those statements that apply to you.)

____ I LISTEN

____ I TAKE WHAT I CAN USE

____ I MAKE AND PAY ATTENTION TO MY OWN DECISIONS

____ IT'S A FEMALE THING

____ WHAT WAS I THINKING?!
(Times of mistakes in judgement or embarrassment)

____ I FEEL POWERFUL

____ I CONFRONT ISSUES THAT I FEEL STRONGLY ABOUT

____ I GIVE

____ I'M ALL THAT . . . AND MORE!

____ OTHER _____

NAME _____ DATE _____

IT'S A MALE THING

EXPECTATIONS OF SOCIETY

1. _____
2. _____
3. _____
4. _____

EXPECTATIONS OF FAMILY/FRIENDS

1. _____
2. _____
3. _____
4. _____

EXPECTATIONS OF SELF

1. _____
2. _____
3. _____
4. _____

PERSONAL REFLECTIONS

(Check those statements that apply to you.)

____ I GIVE

____ I TAKE

____ I SEEK OPPORTUNITIES TO GROW

____ MY CHOICES ARE MY OWN ALTHOUGH I'M WILLING TO LISTEN

____ WHAT WAS I THINKING?
(Times of mistakes in judgement or embarrassment)

____ IT'S A MALE THING

____ I REFUSE TO GIVE UP MY POWER

____ I AM CONNECTED TO OTHERS YET I WON'T YIELD TO NONSENSE

____ I'M THE MAN!!!

____ OTHER _____

NAME _____ DATE _____

ID CARD-CARRYING MEMBERS ONLY!!!

Many people belong to groups, clubs, gangs, and so on. America is filled with organizations to meet the needs and desires of those who join them. Some groups are political, others are educational, and still others are recreational. Some groups are known to cause trouble, while others are recognized for the good that they do. From the categories of various groups listed below, use the letter X to identify those groups whose actions are unwise and could cause problems for you, then select the groups you would most want to join. To the right of the identification cards (IDs), write the reason that you want to be a member and how you can contribute to the group.

Reasons why I would like to belong to each of the following groups:

Group 1: _____

Reason: _____

_____

_____

Group 2: _____

Reason: _____

_____

_____

Group 3: _____

Reason: _____

_____

_____

Other: _____

Reason: _____

_____

_____

Name _____ Date _____

HEADLINES FOR GOOD

Read each negative headline below and think of the impact it might have on readers. If that much of our news is negative, how might the news media lessen the negative effects? Find positive words to replace the negative moods in the headlines below. Then, discuss with peers the extent to which readers might be influenced by the positive statements! What might be the impact on society if headlines, news articles, and television reports change the attitudes of the members of society for the better?

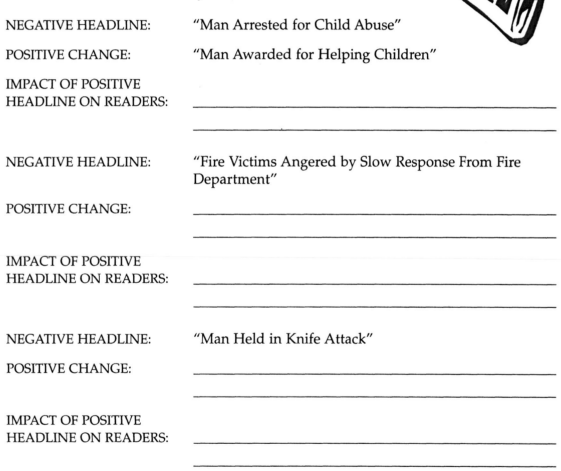

NEGATIVE HEADLINE: "Man Arrested for Child Abuse"

POSITIVE CHANGE: "Man Awarded for Helping Children"

IMPACT OF POSITIVE
HEADLINE ON READERS: _____

_____

NEGATIVE HEADLINE: "Fire Victims Angered by Slow Response From Fire Department"

POSITIVE CHANGE: _____

_____

IMPACT OF POSITIVE
HEADLINE ON READERS: _____

_____

NEGATIVE HEADLINE: "Man Held in Knife Attack"

POSITIVE CHANGE: _____

_____

IMPACT OF POSITIVE
HEADLINE ON READERS: _____

_____

What should your role be in making society safer, kinder, saner, and more tolerable? How can we begin to change the public appetite for negative news? We do not want to avoid the truth in reporting news; however, when is the negative side of a news story sensationalized in order to increase sales? From the NEGATIVE headlines on the following page, select ONE and make it POSITIVE. Then, on the lines, describe how your positive change will influence those who read it.

NAME _____ DATE _____

MORE NEGATIVE HEADLINES

- Number of Prisoners Doubles
- Tensions Heighten Between Rival Gangs
- Accountant Arrested for Embezzlement
- Illicit Drug Use Soars Among Teenagers
- Alcohol & Tobacco Advertisers Get Richer

- Women File Charges Against Abusers
- Test Scores Lower Among Inner-City High School Students
- Five People Killed in Drunk Driving Accident
- Husband Charged With Bigamy
- Ten Orphans Rejected by Families

MY POSITIVE CHANGE OF ONE HEADLINE

NEGATIVE HEADLINE SELECTED: _____

_____

POSITIVE CHANGE: _____

_____

MOTIVES/REASONS FOR MY CHOICE: _____

_____

_____

EXPECTED IMPACT OF POSITIVE CHANGE ON READERS:

_____

_____

_____

_____

_____

_____

_____

_____

_____

_____

NAME _____ DATE _____

911, I NEED YOU!

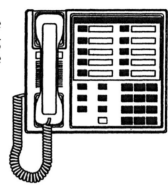

Calls for help come in from various locations when people have emergencies. Preparations for emergencies range from knowing when to call **911** to just yelling **"HELP!"** in hopes that someone will hear and come to the rescue. In times of emergency, people tend to look beyond physical, racial, and cultural differences and concentrate on the human needs in the situation. Human commonalties mean more than differences in race, religion, gender, ethnicity, and so on. In fact, courageous volunteers or teams of trained emergency personnel reach out to help those in need without regard to these differences. Likewise, persons who need help do not worry about the race, color, culture, gender, or ethnic background of their rescuers; they just want assistance.

In each category below, think of a situation in which a person might need help and indicate a person, a group, or an institution that might rescue him or her from danger. Then, write a sentence indicating the extent to which TRAINING, CONCERN, and COURAGE, are more important than race, culture, color, religion, or gender in trying to meet the needs of those who are helpless. Develop interesting stories for each environment. The first one is done for you.

KITCHEN ACCIDENT	ON THE HIGHWAY
1. EMERGENCY:	2. EMERGENCY:
A woman is standing too close to the stove and her long-sleeved robe catches on fire. She screams for help many times as the fire jumps from her sleeve around to her back.	
SENTENCE:	SENTENCE:
A family member finally hears her calls for help. CONCERN for the victim caused this family member to rush and snuff out the fire.	

NAME _____ DATE _____

SPORTS EVENT	AIRPORT
3. EMERGENCY:	4. EMERGENCY:
SENTENCE:	SENTENCE:
HIGH-RISE BUILDING	**SCHOOL ENVIRONMENT**
5. EMERGENCY:	6. EMERGENCY:
SENTENCE:	SENTENCE:

THINK ABOUT THIS!!!

Do people really care about the racial, cultural, or ethnic heritage of their rescuers? Should they? Explain.

_____

_____

_____

_____

_____

NAME _____ DATE _____

NO ANCHOVIES—PLEASE!

Each pizza has the basic ingredients of crust, cheese, and tomato sauce. You can add various toppings to make it even more delicious. Imagine that you are making a PEACE PIZZA. What would you add to make an award-winning pizza pie to increase the chances that the people who eat it will have hearts filled with love, trust, values, and so on? The basic crust is provided for you. Create your toppings by completing the phrases below. One is done for you.

SELECT ONE FOR EACH TOPPING:

HOPE

UNDERSTANDING

TRUST

VALUES

KINDNESS

TRUTH

COURAGE

PEACE

FRIENDSHIP

OTHER _____

OTHER _____

EXAMPLE: Cheese of <u>Love</u>

Green peppers of _____

Tomato sauce of _____

Sausage of _____

Olives of _____

Pepperoni of _____

Mushrooms of _____

NAME _____ DATE _____

SUCCESS IS SERVICE

The human heart is the accurate conveyer of one's deepest emotions. Feelings of love, courage, contentment, concern, and compassion all emanate from within the human spirit. Mother Hale, Mother Teresa, and Princess Diana knew this, as was seen in their unselfish, heartfelt service to the most needy of earth's inhabitants. The success of these remarkable women was in their waiting on their neighbors in the "global village." Not one of them expected anything in return.

Mother Hale, Mother Teresa, and Princess Diana rejected temptation to ignore the needs of those who are less fortunate. Even though Diana had the benefits of wealth, she, like Mother Teresa and Mother Hale, reached out to touch the "poorest of the poor." As with Mother Hale of Hale House in New York, Princess Diana and Mother Teresa had no aversion to touching people with AIDS. Mother Hale brought AIDS babies and their drug-addicted mothers into her home and nursed them back to health. Diana placed herself in danger by visiting victims of land mines in Angola. Mother Teresa reached down to pick up a dying man and chose to tend to his needs rather than attend an affair in her honor. Giving hope to the sick and dying brought joy to these women. Of course, there are many, many other people who have given of their time, skills, and mostly of their hearts, to the service of their fellow human beings. As they give to their fellow human beings, volunteers find that the rewards of the heart are greater than money or fame.

If it is true that the heart convey one's innermost desires, hopes, and dreams, is there evidence that a compassionate spirit lies within your own heart? Moreover, isn't it true that what is inside a person's heart manifests itself in outward behaviors? What are you able to observe within the hearts of a majority of people in today's society? Do you see the kind of heartfelt concern that it takes to find success in service to others, or are most people only concerned about themselves? Does the kind of compassion that Princess Diana, Mother Hale, and Mother Teresa exhibited before their deaths still exist?

For each item on the following page, write the letter **Y** for **YES** and the letter **N** for **NO**. Then, respond to at least two of the items with specific evidence that you have heard about, read about, or experienced personally. Use the results of this survey to decide how you will serve others.

NAME _____   DATE _____

HEARTS FOR SERVICE

PEOPLE WHO WANT TO HELP OTHERS HAVE:

____ a sense of community

____ materialistic attitudes

____ a desire to give rather than to receive

____ airs of superiority toward those who are less fortunate

____ shared purposes

____ a sense of satisfaction

____ a spirit of advocacy

____ combined efforts

____ ongoing spirits of volunteerism

____ compassion that transcends race, color, religion, etc.

____ a warm and compassionate heart

____ willingness to donate time and money

____ limits on their concern for others

____ a need to make other people feel worthy of recognition

____ questionable results

____ a great need for recognition

____ sad, burdened countenances

____ limited resources

____ knowledge about needs

____ money-driven motives

MY PLANS FOR SUCCESS THROUGH SERVICE/VOLUNTEERING

WHO?
WHAT?
WHEN?
WHERE?
HOW?
NOTE: Parental approval/accompaniment is crucial for you!!!

NAME _____ DATE _____

SUCCESS IS SELF-SATISFACTION

"Helping the poorest of the poor" was the creed by which Mother Teresa lived. She saw the problems of the homeless, the sick, and the destitute and decided to volunteer her time and effort to help people who could not help themselves. This tiny woman who owned only three saris (dresses) when she died had a passionate drive to relieve human suffering.

Use the diagram areas below to identify a societal problem and plan your solutions for it. Conclude this exercise by projecting a date and a time that you might be able to help solve one of these problems. You might want to work with a partner or in small groups to identify specific problems and develop valid suggestions for resolving them. One example is done partially for you.

PROBLEM: Who?   A Family living in a car.

                      What?   Both the mother and father are unemployed.

                      Why?   Their employers laid them off and they do not
                                      have the money to pay rent or to buy a house.

YOUR
SOLUTION: _____

_____

_____

_____

PROBLEM: Who? _____

                      What? _____

                      Why? _____

YOUR
SOLUTION: _____

_____

_____

_____

NAME _____ DATE _____

AN OPEN LETTER OF COMPLAINT

People often dream of becoming rich or famous and many spend hundreds of dollars playing the lottery, betting on horses, or participating in other "get rich quick" activities. Recent reports on lottery winners indicate that greed, envy, and distrust change what was supposed to be happiness to misery and pain. Marriages have broken up, plots of murder have been uncovered, and bankruptcies have been reported among instant millionaires. Based on these reports and the statement below, write a letter of complaint to the Lottery Commission of a city that encourages people to engage in this and other types of gambling.

NOTE: If you do not agree with this perspective, write a letter from the opposite point of view.

Your Name _____

Address _____

Date _____

Lottery Commission

C/O _____

Address _____

Dear Commissioner:

_____

_____

_____

_____

_____

_____

_____

_____

_____

_____

Sincerely,

(Your signature)

Think about this: Do people ever really "get something for nothing"?

NAME _____ DATE _____

PROMISES, PROMISES, PROMISES

The United States Constitution, including the Bill of Rights, guarantees all citizens equal treatment under the law. Citizens of diverse racial, ethnic, and cultural heritage have fought in wars and in civil rights movements to make freedom and equality a reality for every citizen. Yet, many of them have not experienced real justice.

What happens when a certain racial, ethnic, or cultural group is denied equality, whether in textbooks, the media, or in relationships in society? Basically, their freedom and that of everyone else is compromised. We are only as free as our willingness to fight for and support the freedom of our fellow citizens. Because a few have denied full equality to certain racial, cultural, and ethnic groups, too many people have yet to experience "freedom and justice for all." Aren't promises meant to be kept?

Equal educational and employment opportunities have been promised to all citizens and yet, too often, African Americans, Native Americans, Hispanic Americans, Asian Americans, and those of mixed racial or ethnic origin have been purposely ignored or pushed aside. Also, minorities are often portrayed negatively in visual and print media. What can you do to advance equality in America—to fulfill the promises made to all citizens by the U.S. Constitution and the Bill of Rights?

Using the categories below, formulate a strategy for presenting the truth, correcting inequities and, as a result, creating harmony, freedom, and equality among citizens of diverse backgrounds. Your task is to find ways to raise the levels of AWARENESS as to the NEED FOR TRUTH and to find ways to CORRECT INEQUITIES. Discuss the PROMISES below or indicate others based upon your experiences or ideas for erasing racism, stereotyping, and prejudice. Complete the chart and discuss ways to implement your ideas.

FULFILLING PROMISES OF EQUALITY

How to Raise Awareness of the Need to Uphold Our Nation's Promises	Specific Tasks to Be Conducted to Find Truth and Correct Inequities
PROMISE 1 _____	
Freedom of speech _____	
_____	
_____	

NAME _____ DATE _____

FULFILLING PROMISES OF EQUALITY *(Cont'd)*

How to Raise Awareness of the Need to Uphold Our Nation's Promises	Specific Tasks to Be Conducted to Find Truth and Correct Inequities

PROMISE 2 _____

Equal educational opportunities _____

_____

_____

PROMISE 3 _____

Equal employment opportunities _____

_____

_____

PROMISE 4 _____

Protection against unreasonable _____

search or seizure _____

_____

_____

PROMISE 5 _____

Other _____

_____

_____

Discuss your ideas for educating young people and adults about the need to ensure that all citizens benefit from the promises or rights guaranteed by the U.S. Constitution and the Bill of Rights.

NAME _____ DATE _____

A UNIQUE DESIGN!

You are a unique person. There is no one on earth quite like you, and this is a wonderful, natural occurrence in human nature. Even identical twins have some differences that make them unique. The individual characteristics of human beings cause a sense of wonder as people observe and relate to each other in various environments. Some people are humorous and provide entertainment for others. Some people are intellectuals and help civilization advance technologically, medically, socially, and so on. Still others are creative with words, music, or dance. There are people whose athletic abilities astound their fellow human beings and artists whose paintings, sculptures, pottery and so on leave the rest of society in awe. Many people enjoy and benefit from expressing their own individuality. On the other hand, some people never get to express their unique talents because they are caught up in fads that make them want to take on the identity of others.

For example, people who make designer clothes count on your wanting to be like everyone else. They promote the desirable characteristics of their products and convince you that, to be in style, you must wear their labels. You don't even know these people, and they count on you to spend lots of money to display their names and labels. Where are YOU in this picture? Why are you not wearing your own name? Think of the money you would save if you wore your own name. Better yet, think of the way you would be able to share your own individual traits, ideas, and values with others if you made your own designer labels.

Read the following ideas and use them to help you express your uniqueness as you go through life. Identify the ones you can use IMMEDIATELY by writing the letter I next to the idea and the letter L next to the ones you might want to use LATER in life. Remember, your unique, individual traits, talents, skills, and values should emerge as you work on your designs. Develop a rough design for at least one idea in the space at the bottom of this activity sheet.

1. Design a sign for the public that describes your most admirable traits, your value system, or some of your favorite teachings (home training).

2. Design a symbol of peace that would persuade people to extend human dignity to each other. Plan to make labels of this for other people to use.

3. Design an identification bracelet or necklace that spells out your name. Each letter should convey a special meaning. (Pat—Peaceful, Active, Tall)

4. Make up a slogan that could be shouted out after the Pledge of Allegiance at all athletic events in your school. Use words that convey UNITY.

5. Decorate a pair of jeans or a jacket with your own name. (If you are artistic, paint flowers, geometric shapes, or other designs on these clothing items.)

6. Design a T-shirt that would promote a spirit of volunteerism in your school or community. Remember to use your traits and values to bring people together. Make cer-

NAME _____ DATE _____

tain that the recipients of service are made to feel good about themselves when they see your design on the shirt.

7. Just to make sure that your designs are positive and would not break societal/school/family rules or codes, make a list of negative ideas or traits that might creep into your work. Then, draw a big X on these ideas with the words NEVER USE THESE.

8. Develop a slogan that tells others who you are and what your future goals are. Plan to display this slogan on your notebook, at the top of letters that you write to family and friends, on ribbons, on T-shirts, on the refrigerator at home, on bulletin boards along with those of peers, or on poster boards that can be used at school and community events.

MY UNIQUE DESIGN

A ROUGH DRAFT

CHOICES, CHANGES, AND CHALLENGES

INTRODUCTION

Young people who observe many of the negative realities of life such as neglect, abuse, poverty, greed, racism, and injustice must be aware of the choices they have to either contribute to or become disengaged from society. The activities in the *Choices, Changes, and Challenges* section encourage students to act, to do something to reverse negative situations in their environments, and to work for improved societal changes for themselves and future generations. First, they are led to look within themselves for negative traits and to find ways to eliminate them. Only then will they be sufficiently prepared to go out into the larger society and help to reduce or eliminate destructive tendencies. Specifically, students are challenged to become the very best that they can be by working on self-improvement via family and societal relationships, pursuing educational excellence, and planning for meaningful employment opportunities. In these lessons, students learn that changing negative thoughts and actions to positive ones results not only in increased self-determination and hope, but also in fewer conflicts with those with whom they interact. Furthermore, they learn that confident, self-assured, and forward-thinking individuals with intact value systems, specific goals, standards of behavior, and a strong work ethic have an excellent chance of realizing their dreams. Therefore, exposure to the concepts in this section helps students to pursue their own goals, prepare for their adult roles, and contribute to and work for positive changes in their community and the world.

Other activities in *Choices, Changes, and Challenges* encourage students to interact with and develop respect for diverse groups of people in order to improve society and eradicate intolerance, violence and racism. They discern the significance of being givers and not takers; they want to be recognized as competent young men and women whose concern for their fellow human beings manifests itself in high levels of positive self-esteem and a sense of accomplishment and well-being for everyone. Moreover, through self-confidence building and mutual respect activities, students learn how to think and respond appropriately to situations that might ordinarily cause conflict, feelings of low self-esteem, or powerlessness. These activities make feasible students' efforts to "fine-tune" their lives. By recognizing self-esteem without arrogance and social awareness with responsibility, students will be poised and ready to help make the world a place where everyone can enjoy peaceful, productive, and meaningful lives.

=================== **ACTIVITIES** ===================

5–1   Choices

5–2   Breaking Bad Habits

5–3   Making Choices for My Life

5–4   Diamonds in the Rough . . . Need Polishing

5–5   Absolute Truths to Live By

5–6   Overcoming Shyness

5–7   I'm Too Young to Be Stressed Out!!!

5–8   Getting Rid of the "Big Bad Wolves"

5–9   Resolving a Personal Conflict

5–10   Check Yourself

5–11   This Far and No Farther

5–12   Living the Golden Rule

5–13   When Hate Prevails . . . Love Must Enter

5–14   Garage Sale in the Year 2020

5–15   I Can Reduce Racism, Hatred, Prejudice, and Violence???

5–16   Pro or Con—Where Do You Stand?

5–17   Follow the Leader? Why?

5–18   Not Me!

5–19   Protecting My Self-Esteem—and Yours

5–20   Success According to _____

5–21   The Best That I Can Be

5–22   Twenty Minutes to Pack

5–23   What's Hot? What's Not?

5–24   Who Are You in Your School?

5–25   I Plan to Work as a . . .

5–26   Reasonable Paths

5–27   Success Is Within Your Reach

5–28   The Keys to Your Success

5–29   I Think I Can, I Think I Can, I *Know* I Can!

5–30   The Expert

TEACHER DIRECTIONS FOR SECTION 5 ACTIVITIES

5-1 CHOICES

Young people are the hope of the future and teachers have the grave responsibility of helping to prepare them for their adult roles in society. On this premise, elicit from students what it would take for adults to instill a sense of responsibility in young people. Also, ask their opinions regarding the age at which young people should start accepting responsibility for their actions and what kinds of techniques can be used to help individuals become responsible. Allow students to respond to these questions and offer other comments. Then, ask them what adults would have to do to teach young people the importance of hard work, patience, kindness, and caring attitudes. Ask them to share individually their ideas for ensuring that they will be rational citizens as they reach maturity. (**Note:** Take notes as students speak, and plan to share these student ideas with fellow educators.) Perhaps schoolwide programs can be developed to help reinforce students' individual commitment to choosing reasonable ways to take care of themselves, each other, the aging population, and the earth. *Give each student a copy of Activity 5-1, Choices.*

5-2 BREAKING BAD HABITS

Ask students their opinions regarding where teenagers should seek help when they are in trouble. Ask them to be specific about the reasons that a young person would go to a friend, a parent, a teacher, or a counselor. Discuss the concept of trust as a factor as people share their problems with others. Elicit from students the value of consulting parents first (but be sensitive to students for whom this may not be true). Ask students their opinions regarding the sharing of problems with their peers. What would be the most convincing argument? Can young people be persuasive in their efforts to help their peers? Discuss some of the consequences that are apparent when people have bad habits and refuse to give them up. Have pupils share their feelings regarding warnings—do they work? Have them share their experiences. Warnings regarding the need to take care of one's health—the need to eat properly, exercise, and avoid drugs—abound in the print and visual media. Discuss with students the consequences of ignoring these warnings. Ask about student awareness of the fact that cigarette smokers risk contracting cancer, emphysema, and other diseases as a result of their smoking habit. Have them share their experiences and inquire as to other kinds of substances that make people ill. Reinforce the need for young people to make early lifestyle decisions. Elicit from students some of the other consequences of negative lifestyle choices. *Give each student a copy of Activity 5-2, Breaking Bad Habits.*

5-3 MAKING CHOICES FOR MY LIFE

Elicit from students the value of individual decision making and the extent to which the quality of life can be improved when people hold themselves accountable for choices. In other words, "I can only blame myself" is a great way to reduce the stress that comes with trying to find someone else to blame for consequences suffered as a result of poor decisions. Ask students to share what they recognize as *absolutes* or *standards* of behavior that prevent trouble, offer some level of comfort, and create high self-esteem. Have them identify some of the choices they are confronted with in their various environments such as obeying or breaking rules, lying or truthfulness, stealing or paying, and so on. Ask them to consider the extent to which their decisions impact on other people and whether an individual who breaks a rule or law and causes another person to falter should bear some of the responsibility for the other person's pain. Have students consider "gray areas" and draw inferences regarding the positive or negative effect of the following: choosing to empathize or have compassion, choosing to place blame, choosing to give in to pride or ego, choosing to extend generosity, choosing to bear grudges, choosing to seek revenge, choosing to gossip, and so on. Discuss the rewards (positive effects) or consequences (negative effects) of some of these choices. Give opportunities for students to personalize and to compare and contrast the results of their lifestyle choices in these and other situations. *Give each student a copy of Activity 5-3, Making Choices for My Life.*

(**Note:** To raise students' level of awareness regarding their propensity for negative or positive lifestyle choices, have them write a short composition on the back of the activity sheet. Ask them to write a paragraph that describes specific rewards or consequences for some of their current lifestyle choices. Have them indicate how these current decisions point to the kind of future they will have, using some of the words from the charts in their compositions. Then, ask them to read their compositions and reflect on the kinds of changes they might have to make in their lifestyle choices.)

5–4 DIAMONDS IN THE ROUGH . . . NEED POLISHING

Students need to know that teachers and other adults are human and capable of making mistakes. However, as adults, we must demonstrate that somewhere along life's way we have learned not to repeat mistakes or errors in judgment. (**Note:** Share only personal incidents that will teach positive lessons to young people. Couch such incidents or situations in humor. Don't use sad, oppressive stories that might demoralize at-risk students.) Elicit from students the need for people to learn from their mistakes and errors in judgment. Indicate that everyone can and has the right to start over. Write the words SELF-CONTROL, DISCIPLINE, TEMPTATIONS, I'VE GOT TO HAVE IT NOW!! and MY WORD IS MY VOW on the board. Have students define these words and agree that these words reflect possible goals for all of us—that some goals are good for us and others are not. Have students select those words that indicate the need for improvement in attitude and positive changes in the way people relate to each other. Discuss the meaning of "putting your best foot forward" and what it says about individual responsibility in human relationships. Ask how they can share what they know about self-improvement as they interact with one another and children who are even younger. *Give each student a copy of Activity 5-4, Diamonds in the Rough . . . Need Polishing.*

5–5 ABSOLUTE TRUTHS TO LIVE BY

Elicit from students some of the most important values they have been taught by their parents, guardians, and close family members. List some of these on the board and discuss them in terms of their personal religious, social, and cultural perspectives. Discuss the similarities and the differences in what students hold as values for living good, moral lives. (**Note:** Be aware of the need to refrain from teaching specific religious viewpoints.) Let students share the extent to which their religion influences their value systems. *Give each student a copy of Activity 5-5, Absolute Truths to Live By.*

5–6 OVERCOMING SHYNESS

Note students in the class who might be shy and unable to express their feelings freely. Plan to take time with these individuals and explore ways in which they might overcome anxieties that prevent their participation in discussions. The self-esteem of shy students can be bolstered by having them confront their fears head-on. Discuss the need for confrontation, rather than avoidance of the anxieties that cause shyness, with individual students who suffer from this internal conflict. Elicit from the entire class ways in which they can become "partners" with their less vocal classmates. Challenge students to refrain from teasing, mocking, or intimidating shy classmates and to create concrete "bonding" options. (**Note:** Teachers need to use caution when involving an entire class in this process. By drawing too much attention to the shy child, these discussions may have the opposite effect.) As shy students begin to gain self-confidence, give them many opportunities to open up and share their opinions on issues that are pertinent to improved human relationships. *Give each student a copy of Activity 5-6, Overcoming Shyness.*

5–7 I'M TOO YOUNG TO BE STRESSED OUT!!!

Unfortunately, too many young people suffer internal anxieties that manifest themselves in external aggression, depression, and other physical ailments that drain their joy. Without getting into personal family problems that would be better handled by their parents and counselors, ask students to consider ways to release tensions that might cause them to be unhappy, frustrated, depressed, aggressive, and so forth. Discuss how individuals in the class might handle peer pressure, academic failure, values crises, lack of respect, divorce, grief, unemployment, and other concerns. Have students share successful interventions that have given or can give them relief. *Give each student a copy of Activity 5-7, I'm Too Young to be Stressed Out!!!*

5–8 GETTING RID OF THE "BIG BAD WOLVES"

Elicit from students the fact that most people harbor some fears that they keep private. Indicate that this activity is designed not to have them share their own private fears with other people, but rather to help each person to face fear and identify ways of reducing or getting rid of some of the things that prevent their being able to make personal progress. Draw analogies between real-life fears of human beings and those experienced by characters in fictional works. In that fiction often mirrors fact, ask students to identify fictional characters who overcame their fears. Have them specify certain attributes such as courage, perseverance, wisdom, intelligence, honesty, and the need for intervention in overcoming traumatic situations in fiction. Give examples such as Odysseus the main character in Homer's *Odyssey*, and talk about how he was able to overcome obstacles and reach his goal . . . home. Discuss how young people in our contemporary society can adopt such attributes as hard work, honesty, and sincerity, and begin to rid themselves of personal fears. Without asking for specific examples of student fears, ask them to think of characteristics they need to develop in order to conquer their problems. Challenge students to explore literary themes such as characters' motives and goals. Ask, "Why did Odysseus strive against all odds to go HOME? What is good about HOME?" *Give each student a copy of Activity 5-8, Getting Rid of the "Big Bad Wolves."*

5–9 RESOLVING A PERSONAL CONFLICT

Ask members of the class to volunteer to share their experiences with personal conflicts, problems, or confrontations. Elicit from volunteers how they handled or resolved these conflicts and whether they were temporary or permanent solutions. Suggest that parties who are involved in a disagreement have to assume various degrees of responsibility for conflict resolution and that there are several specific things that they can or should do in order to resolve the conflict. Looking at the "big picture" is a first step; how much damage could these parties do to each other if the confrontation were to continue? They surely do not want to destroy each other, and would first want to TALK. Second, parties in conflict can LISTEN to each other's point of view on whatever the issue might be. Third, they can help each other to SAVE FACE, especially if they meet privately in a neutral environment. Ultimately, both parties can PREVENT FUTURE CONFLICTS and even FORM POSITIVE RELATIONSHIPS if they approach solving their problems in a logical way. Human beings need to learn to resolve their conflicts by practicing several techniques that work. Select one of the real-life situations students have shared, and ask how some of the steps above could have been used to resolve the conflict. Write the highlighted words on the board or on cards and discuss the fact that using past experiences to prevent future problems is a good conflict-resolution strategy. Have students define each word and explain the extent to which it might be used to resolve conflicts. Bring up other real-life conflicts, and try these words out. For example, how might the words *mutual respect* work in a situation where two people are arguing over a parking space? Ask students to suggest other words, as well. Define and practice using:

• cooperation	• mediation	• rights	• conciliation
• negotiation	• understanding	• temporary	• responsibility
• intervention	• friendship	• permanent	• other words:
• mutual respect	• agreements	• justice	_____
• neutral territory	• confidentiality	• shared power	_____

Have students indicate their plans to really try some of these strategies or make up some of their own, if necessary, to fit a particular situation. *Give each student a copy of Activity 5-9, Resolving a Personal Conflict.*

5–10 CHECK YOURSELF

Ask students to share whether they have violated any kind of law—and the extent to which they had to pay fines, serve detention, provide community service, or do chores at home. Elicit from them the fact that people should always obey the law on their own rather than having someone else tell them when they are wrong. Have them agree that the idea of holding oneself accountable for personal actions is crucial to good citizenship. *Give each student a copy of Activity 5-10, Check Yourself.*

5–11 THIS FAR AND NO FARTHER

Have students share when parents or other adults in their lives have set curfews or other kinds of limitations on them. Inquire as to how close they have come to violating the expectations, rules, and regulations. Discuss, as well, the reasons for rules, laws, codes of dress or behavior, and policies in various areas of society. Increase student comprehension through extensive questioning and responding. The following questions can be placed on a transparency, charts, or the chalkboard.

1. Why do schools have dress codes and codes of behavior for students?

2. Why does society have laws for its citizens regarding drinking and driving, paying taxes, going to school, carrying weapons, equal rights, and so on?

3. Why do parents make their children clean their rooms or come home at certain times of night?

4. When does the power of parents or public authority end, and at what point does the individual become totally responsible for following the rules and laws?

5. Which limitations are effective in the environments of home, school, community, and government?

6. Who is responsible when there are breakdowns in the rules, and what corrective measures need to be taken?

7. Why is it okay to go all the way in some things but not in others?

8. How should a person handle the "gray areas"?

Student discussions on these and other questions help to increase their understanding of the issues, clarify their personal values, see the many benefits of rules and laws, and develop the motivation to do what is right for themselves and others. Elicit from students the importance of "red flags" that go up and warn the individual that he or she *must go this far and no farther.* Discuss the consequences of not heeding warnings. Have them respond to the question: "Why is it okay to go all the way in some things but not in others?" (**Note:** Caution is necessary when considering issues of premarital sex, sexual preferences, child abuse, etc. For these and other sensitive issues, the need for parental involvement is indicated. Also, student privacy is *paramount*, and no individual should be asked to share his or her personal business. Some sensitive issues might be addressed through references to news items or fictional works.) Have students consider this scenario:

Bob and Michael have been best friends since they were in fourth grade. They are both in high school now, and their friendship is about to end because of a girl. Michael has been dating Marcy for six months, and has recently discovered that Bob is attracted to her. They've argued about this, and Bob thinks that he has a perfect right to "talk to" Marcy because she and Michael are not married. Marcy knows about the conflict between the two friends, and has done nothing to encourage Bob.

Ask students to give their opinions on how this problem should be settled. Whose internal warnings or "red flags" should go up? Pose several more issues where students have to make a choice between doing something risky or dangerous or putting on the brakes. (**Note:** Chatting with strangers on the Internet or in person is risky behavior. See Activity 5-3 for more ideas.) *Give each student a copy of Activity 5-11, This Far and No Farther.*

5–12 LIVING THE GOLDEN RULE

The idea that individuals must hold themselves accountable for their behavior speaks to the need to have them become aware of the criteria for good citizenship. Then, based on this knowledge, they should make choices that are beneficial to themselves and other members of society. Have students contemplate their roles as **givers** rather than **takers** in their various environments. Internal motivation has much to do with the extent to which each person can give of herself or himself and avoid causing discomfort to others. Discuss the meaning of the **golden rule, limits,** and **accountability.** Ask students to share how their beliefs, values, and lifestyles help them as they relate to other people and make choices in their lives. Elicit from them some of the mottoes, creeds, values, and belief systems that they use in their daily lives, and the extent to which these ideas can help improve the way people relate to each other. *Give each student a copy of Activity 5-12, Living the Golden Rule.*

5–13 WHEN HATE PREVAILS . . . LOVE MUST ENTER

Elicit from students when it is appropriate to react to provocation, and what it takes to be able to discern the severity of conflicts. Although some conflicts have nothing to do with racial, cultural, or ethnic origin, knowing how to rate the severity of them can help in responding to and resolving a variety of problems in human relationships. Discuss some of the experiences that have prevented harmonious relationships in diverse racial, cultural, and ethnic environments. Give each student an opportunity to share his or her opinion regarding how to resolve a situation without violence. Have the class vote on the most reasonable solutions to **one problem.** Talk about how hatred can take root and burrow into the minds and hearts of some people. Discuss the cause-and-effect relationships—the reasons and results of hatred that would dictate the actions, thoughts, words, and deeds of many people. When this happens, hatred does not stop, it keeps going . . . it lasts a long time . . . it prevails . . . unless . . . ! Draw a heart, a universal symbol of love on the board. Say: "If HATRED can be taught, LOVE can be taught." Discuss the need for people who harbor hatred to have a change of heart—the need for love (concern, compassion, empathy, kindness, etc.) to prevail in the relationships of people. Discuss the idea that only love and genuine awareness of our commonalties as human beings will help to eradicate hatred. *Give each student a copy of Activity 5-13, When Hate Prevails . . . Love Must Enter.* Have students read the ten problems and/or human conflicts. Discuss key words from each that can be placed on the "Breaking Down the Problem" chart.

5–14 GARAGE SALE IN THE YEAR 2020

Most people have a tendency to collect material goods. Infrequently, some consciously get rid of unnecessary items before their homes are cluttered with them.

More people allow unhealthy accumulations until they have to throw away or sell the "junk." Ask students to imagine themselves as adults who must get rid of material goods, and have them suggest the kinds of things that might be on the market in the twenty-first century. Ask them to state reasons why owners of these goods might want to sell them. Have students also think of values as nonmaterial but necessary for life. Discuss the idea of negative value systems that are nonproductive, and the need to get rid of those that take away from the quality of life. *Give each student a copy of Activity 5-14, Garage Sale in the Year 2020.*

5–15 I Can Reduce Racism, Hatred, Prejudice, and Violence???

Elicit from students how they, as individuals, might begin to change racist attitudes in society. Have them give their opinions as to the types of positive and negative images that are given about the various races, cultures, and ethnic groups in the media: television, radio, newspapers, magazines, and billboards. Which racial groups always come across as good, intelligent, beautiful, and powerful? Which racial groups always come across as bad, unintelligent, homely, and weak? Who in the media has the authority to change or correct the negative images and give authentic representations of every race? Have students define the word **generalization,** and discuss the fact that **no one race** has a monopoly on all the good or all the bad characteristics. Discuss the need for specific information that portrays the positive and negative about every group. Pose the following question for individual consideration: Can I, as an individual, do at least **one positive thing** to reduce or eliminate racism, hatred, prejudice, and violence? *Give each student a copy of Activity 5-15, I Can Reduce Racism, Hatred, Prejudice, and Violence???*

5–16 Pro or Con—Where Do You Stand?

Place the words: CONTROVERSIAL ISSUES on a chart or on the chalkboard. Ask students to define the words and indicate topics that are important to them as teenagers. Take a poll as to where students stand on some of the issues, and ask them to give reasons to support their opinions. Indicate the need for students to clearly state their positions. "Sitting on the fence" results in confusion. Indicate the need for facts to back up opinions, especially when one desires support from other people. Write PRO and CON, and have them identify a controversial school or community issue and express individual positions on it. **Example:** How do you feel about extending class periods from 45 to 90 minutes? Assess the position of members of the class. Should schools have metal detectors? Discuss how such issues are brought to the attention of adults in society and how decisions are made. *Give each student a copy of Activity 5-16, Pro or Con—Where Do You Stand?*

5–17 Follow the Leader? Why?

Ask students to give examples of when they have followed someone else's lead without regard to this person's value system, reputation, or motives. Suggest that many people in society wish to follow, emulate, or get close to the "rich and famous." On the other hand, some people think it's fine to follow and imitate the behavior of questionable people. Elicit from students if it is wise to imitate, admire, or follow the lifestyles of people they don't know personally. Have students compare and contrast the options they have for admiring and following the lead of parents and close family rather than their favorite athletes, singers, television and movie stars. Have them consider the apparent misery of some of those who are in the limelight and cannot live private lives. (**Note:** Without going off topic, talk about money as the reason that ordinary people admire and want to follow the rich and famous or people in power. Ask students this question, "Should power or money be the driving force in one's search for a leader?") For maturing young people, role models and leaders are important, and followers have to be aware of the qualities of their chosen leaders. Have students define the roles of both the leader and the follower, and determine which is more important. Discuss the benefits in having a leader and the responsibilities involved in leadership. Conversely, have students identify what benefits and responsibilities exist for the follower. Elicit from students whether there are ever times when followers should question the motives, behaviors, goals, and actions of the leader, break ranks, and go their own way. Have them consider, for example, violence-prone gangs and the consequences of joining them and living by their codes. Also, have students consider the possibility that they can become leaders in their environments, and that they must be sure that they have the attributes that are necessary in a good leader.

Have students work in cooperative groups to develop lists of **qualities**, **responsibilities**, and **benefits** for both leaders and followers. Ask them to consider the cause-and-effect relationships of certain behaviors in developing their lists. Have students isolate the causes (reasons) and effects (results) of behaviors and attitudes, and point out redeeming or leadership qualities. Explore ways in which violence, name-calling, mixed messages, lies, vengeance, sadness, aggression, and despair can be replaced with peace, respect, honesty, truth, reconciliation, joy, tolerance and hope. Comparing and contrasting behaviors of these and other highly visible people will help students to discern valid leadership qualities and learn how to convert negative behaviors to positive ones. Talk about how good leaders can encourage and inspire their followers and propel them toward satisfaction, self-confidence, and freedom. Point out how leaders who have a negative impact on others often discourage free thinking and squelch creativity and joy. When the groups have completed their lists, have them discuss the positive traits that they as individuals can use and, as a result, be part of the solution to a more peaceful, tolerant, and sane society. *Give each student a copy of Activity 5-17, Follow the Leader? Why?*

5–18 NOT ME!

Ask students to share how individual standards of morality often dictate the choices that people make. Even when others seem to be enjoying themselves in behaviors that might prove destructive, individuals who might be tempted to join in these behaviors see a red light go on and decide to live by the principles they have adopted. "Not me!" can be the rallying cry for people who live by their principles or values. Have students select partners or arrange themselves in small groups. Ask them to come up with comprehensive responses that consider all aspects of the following questions: (Discuss why YES or NO responses are not sufficient.)

1. Can standards of morality help in decision making?
2. Can standards of morality boost self-esteem?

3. Does violence, as portrayed in the media, always win?

4. Is bigger or stronger better?

5. Does mean-spirited behavior cause even more meanness in the world?

6. Does kindness beget kindness?

7. To what extent can kindness or meanness be related to race, ethnicity, or culture?

8. Is there anything wrong with adopting high standards of morality? What is right about having high morals?

9. What personal warning signals can be devised to help young people make quick decisions?

10. What rewards are there in living up to one's principles?

Ask all students to offer explanations for each question as they share their responses with the larger group. Finally, elicit from students the need for individual awareness of how behavior is a direct outgrowth of decisions based on personal values. Each person has an inner voice that speaks warnings. *Give each student a copy of Activity 5-18, Not Me!*

5–19 PROTECTING MY SELF-ESTEEM—AND YOURS

Ask students to consider differences between physical and emotional pain. Which is worse—insulting someone or hitting someone? How long does the physical pain last? How long does the emotional pain last? Discuss the fact that physical pain goes away, while emotional pain, which comes from rejection, frowns, put-downs, or insults, burrows deeply and can destroy self-esteem. Write the word EMPATHY on the board and circle it. Then write the words EMOTIONAL PAIN, VIOLENCE, DISRESPECT in a column and across from these write ENCOURAGEMENT, NON-VIOLENCE, and RESPECT. Draw a line between these two vertical columns of words. Have students list some ways in which self-esteem can be built up or destroyed beneath the appropriate words. In that we need and prefer encouragement, nonviolence, and respect from others, ask students to give examples of the kinds of behaviors that would bring about these positive feelings. Elicit from students the meaning of the word empathy, and list examples of how we can fully understand the joy or pain of another person because we have experienced the same kinds of things. Discuss the fact that it is easier to encourage others when someone has encouraged us; it is easier to refrain from violence when people have not been violent with us; and it is easier to respect others when people have shown respect for us. Emphasize that all people feel better and have higher levels of self-esteem when they are valued by others. Ask all students to think of specific ways in which they can spread joy and, in the process, help themselves and other people experience equality, freedom, confidence, and positive self-esteem. (**Note:** Have students share some courtesies, compliments, handshakes, and smiles that they've shown to others: "I opened the door for a classmate on crutches," "James poked me but I laughed it off, rather than hitting him," "Some of the kids called me Crazy Man, but Tom calls me 'The Man.'" *Give each student a copy of Activity 5-19, Protecting My Self-Esteem—and Yours.*

After they have completed the worksheet, have students discuss with peers how actions that build other people up can be implemented throughout the day. Consider keeping a daily account of all the ways that people spread joy.

5–20 SUCCESS ACCORDING TO _____(YOUR NAME)_____

Without self-regard, many other things don't matter. By the mere act of asking teenagers for their opinions, we signal that we consider them important—that we want them around. This activity seeks to raise the self-esteem of young people, while trusting them to do the same for their peers. Have a volunteer define the word *success*. Present to students the idea that things tend to matter more to us when we feel valued by others. Say something encouraging or affirming to students as a group. Then, depending on knowledge of their achievements, compliment students or have them compliment one another. (**Note,** however, that compliments should be sincere.) These exchanges will create a positive atmosphere in which all students feel validated and successful. *Give each student a copy of Activity 5-20, Success According to _____(Your Name)_____.*

5–21 THE BEST THAT I CAN BE

Have students think of specific things that it would take for each person to become the best that he or she can be. Elicit from students the importance of mental as well as physical well-being. The idea here is to have each student assume the responsibility for internalizing the kinds of values that it takes to be a contributor to, rather than a drain on, society. Ultimately, it is important for each student to understand the extent to which his or her life is happier because of attention to such things as obeying laws, consideration of others, resisting immediate gratification, thinking before speaking, loving oneself, recreational outlets, healthful eating, and so forth. *Give each student a copy of Activity 5-21, The Best That I Can Be.*

5–22 TWENTY MINUTES TO PACK

Challenge students to find out more about who they really are by asking what they would choose to take if they had only a few minutes to select. In times of earthquakes, bombing, floods, and so on, authorities have to evacuate affected areas. They usually give people only a little time to locate items that are important for their comfort, health, or that have sentimental value. Ask students to tell why they would choose certain items. Discuss the difference between what people need and what they want, and whether these things change when there is an emergency. *Give each student a copy of Activity 5-22, Twenty Minutes to Pack.*

5–23 WHAT'S HOT? WHAT'S NOT?

Ask a student to explain the term "hot" in the vernacular and have them compare it to "cool." Have them give examples of each and describe the importance to young people. Discuss the role that peer pressure might play in each term. Self-awareness and self-esteem include not having to have someone else define what is good in your life and what is not good. Each person should be able to "call the shots" regarding her or his life choices. Elicit from students their need for guidance from responsible adults in their lives. Have them suggest ways that young people can set parameters in their selections of entertainment. Have them suggest ways that they can learn to discern what is good for them and what is not good for them in the various messages that emerge from the world around them. Discuss the value of getting a good education as foundational to success in their future lives. *Give each student a copy of Activity 5-23, What's Hot? What's Not?*

5–24 WHO ARE YOU IN YOUR SCHOOL?

Elicit from students their willingness to work hard to complete their education. How beneficial is it to each person to make a personal commitment to a goal? Discuss the importance of parental support in providing food, clothing, and shelter while their children learn. Define **literacy** and **illiteracy,** and indicate some of the skills that all people must master if they are to be able to function independently in society: reading, math, writing, map reading, health, speaking, and listening skills. Elicit from students the fact that when individuals have these skills, they are likely to be happier and able to interact with many different people as they go about their daily lives. Ask students to reflect privately on how serious they are about using their time well and doing their best in school. Challenge them to think of school as their job and of success as possible only when they make a personal commitment to put in the necessary time and effort to reach their goals. Discuss the benefits of this approach versus that of being forced to do their best. *Give each student a copy of Activity 5-24, Who Are You in Your School?*

5–25 I PLAN TO WORK AS A . . .

Ask students to share their goals for the future. Identify the number of people who want to go to work right after high school and those who want to attend college. Elicit from them the fact that all honest occupations are valid and valuable to people who need to work. Also, discuss the concept of interdependence in terms of the goods and services that are available to consumers. Make a list of occupations that individual students are interested in. Have students think about and explain the kind of training that will be necessary for their choices. *Give each student a copy of Activity 5-25, I Plan to Work as a . . .*

5–26 REASONABLE PATHS

Ask for students' opinions regarding the criteria for being successful in society. Suggest: planning or goal-setting, staying focused, education, a serious work ethic, mentoring, and others that you consider important. Inquire as to what might happen if a person gets sidetracked and loses focus. Have them indicate the kinds of things that could cause problems for those who want to become successful in life, and elicit from them the importance of personal awareness of those dangers. Ask them to consider, as well, the fact that it's okay for people to change their minds about chosen career paths. Then, have students state personal goals and come up with **one** possible roadblock that could stop them from success. Ask each student to think of a solution for eliminating the roadblock. Talk about how it is possible to get off track, but it is definitely possible to refocus and begin again. Discuss the importance of **responsibility** regarding the choices that individuals make in life. *Give each student a copy of Activity 5-26, Reasonable Paths.*

5–27 SUCCESS IS WITHIN YOUR REACH

Are there certain attitudes and self-images apparent in successful people? Have students name successful people in their families and the larger society. Compare the attitudes, personalities, and character traits of these individuals. Have students share their knowledge of things that would make success possible for anyone. Ask if these people were focused and enthusiastic about the planning, time, and work it took to help them to succeed and realize their dreams. Discuss the various terms that convey that a person wants to succeed in school and in life: attitude, work ethic, perseverance, goals, and so on. Indicate that all people who want success can realize at least some of their dreams, **if they really want to!** Have students relate how enthusiastic they are about their chances for success. Have them set some realistic personal and professional goals. Have them also think about the importance of encouraging their classmates to map out their futures. This action will help students see the value of bringing others along with them as they pursue success. *Give each student a copy of Activity 5-27, Success Is Within Your Reach.*

5–28 THE KEYS TO YOUR SUCCESS

In each student's quest for success, he or she must consider specific actions that will provide him or her with the best opportunities. In addition, young people must think about the various meanings of success. Elicit from students their opinions as to whether fame and glory, riches or material wealth, or happiness and a comfortable living constitute true success. Have them share which one(s) they would want to work toward as they continue their education. Discuss which choice offers the best chance for emotional happiness and stability. Remind students of Activity 2-12, *The Catastrophe of Success*, based on Tennessee Williams' essay, in which he reveals how spoiled he became as a result of fame and fortune. Williams concludes that wealthy people should not wait for others to pick up after them, and that many people only want to be with the rich because of their money. He conveys the idea that "purity of heart is the only success worth having." Discuss Williams's point of view, and ask students how they would apply this to their own quest for success. (**Note:** Tennessee Williams wrote this essay after the success of his play *The Glass Menagerie.*) Discuss the futility of the quest for instant wealth. Compare and contrast the quest for instant fame and wealth with the satisfaction of giving time, energy, food, and clothing, to the poor and homeless. Have students share specific information regarding career goals, plans for college, role models, and existing opportunities that should help them to achieve success. *Give each student a copy of Activity 5-28, The Keys to Your Success.*

5–29 I THINK I CAN, I THINK I CAN, I KNOW I CAN!

Write the words HOPE, DETERMINATION, POSSIBLE, and INSPIRATION, on the board. Have several volunteers give definitions for each word and write their responses near the words. Ask students to share with the class an experience in which they thought something was totally *impossible* to accomplish, but then they found that they were able to do it. Indicate that they will be better able to convey their ideas if they use the words on the board, or others that come to them as they speak. Have them explain the initial reservations they might have had and reveal the catalyst or the source of the inspiration that resulted in their following through and emerging victorious in this experience. (**Note:** Teachers who choose to make themselves vulnerable might want to share a noncontroversial but valuable example with students.) Suggest to students that often we resist most strongly those tasks that provide us with the greatest benefits. Discuss what it takes to get over an aversion to necessary tasks, including doing homework; completing long-term assignments; reading long books; studying for tests; forgiving someone who has offended us; resisting the temptation to cheat or steal; befriending someone of another culture, race, or religion; planning for the future; telling the truth, even though it means trouble; volunteering in a nursing home or hospital; contributing to funds for the needy, and so on. Compare each person's effort of tackling a difficult task to the challenge faced by the *Little Engine That Could.* Remind students of the children's story in which the *Little Engine That Could* climbed a high hill because he had *hope, determination, possibility, and inspiration.* He had hope that he could do it, even though he was frustrated by the monumental challenge. He was *determined* to try, and verbalized his willingness by saying "I think I can" over and over again. An important part of his success was his obvious *inspiration* and positive outlook. Because of his self-imposed high expectations, the Little Engine really believed that it was *possible* to reach the top of the hill. These positive viewpoints filled the Little Engine with the sense of responsibility that he needed to keep trying until he accomplished his goal. Discuss the fact that some tasks that we have to perform are self-serving, while others are for the benefit of the people around us. Have students consider the extent to which individuals must take responsibility for pursuing and accomplishing a personal or social goal. Elicit from students that, in some cases, there will be failure but there is never any reason to give up. Not only in fiction, but in real life, each person must be willing to try his or her best in order to reach desired goals. *Give each student a copy of Activity 5-29, I Think I Can, I Think I Can, I Know I Can!*

5–30 THE EXPERT

Have students share what they think are their strong points—their areas of expertise. Indicate that every person has multiple talents and skills and that it's exciting to discover, develop, and use them. Ask them to indicate ways in which they have discovered, developed, and used their areas of expertise thus far in their lives. Compliment each student regarding his or her talent or skill, whether it's in computers, science, math, sports, art, music, writing, listening, speaking, and so on. Plan a time when they can demonstrate their talents and skills in a classroom performance. Suggest that society needs what they have to offer, but that they have to consider the following things as they mature:

1. Developing their talents and skills to their fullest potential

2. Finding joy in sharing their talents and skills with others

3. Planning to use their talents and skills to help build a better society

4. Passing what they know on to younger people by speaking and/or writing about personal hopes, dreams, and accomplishments

5. Working towards their ultimate goal believing that they can achieve the impossible.

Give each student a copy of Activity 5-30, The Expert.

NAME _____ DATE _____

CHOICES

You're a new actor or actress playing your first role on the stage of life. You're a rookie beginning your first day of spring training in this real-life game. Though you're young, you have to make decisions regarding how you will live and survive on this earth. Some of these decisions will have a great effect on the rest of your life. For example, will you smoke, take drugs, eat junk food every day, or drop out of school? Or will you choose to eliminate those things that can decrease the quality of your life? What about your education? How seriously do you take the need to complete high school and college? How are you preparing for adulthood? Think about whether your eventual success will be connected to how well you care for your physical and mental health while you are young.

Plan to focus on positive actions that contribute to your progress as you develop into adulthood. Make up a list of DO's and DON'TS that will help you to maintain your focus.

MY CHOICES FOR MY FUTURE

Do's	Don'ts

Consider placing this chart on the refrigerator as a reminder.

NAME _____   DATE _____

BREAKING BAD HABITS

Too frequently, overeating, lack of exercise, and a don't-care attitude regarding physical and mental health occur in the lives of teenagers. Old age seems so far away; some young people don't see the connection of taking good care of the YOUNG BODY so that the OLD BODY can be as healthy as possible. How can young people begin breaking bad habits that could make them a high risk for disease? Pretend that you are a counselor. Give teenagers some specific advice for changing risky attitudes and behaviors. Think of ONE negative choice that a teenager might make. Then, write a three-minute speech that would persuade young people to change this negative behavior. Use some of the words listed below to develop your persuasive comments.

FAST FOOD • CIGARETTES • WALKING • RUNNING FUTURE • TIME • HABIT-FORMING • WILL POWER DECISION MAKING • ROLE MODELS • LONG-TERM EFFECTS • HEALTH • DRUGS • MONEY • PEER PRESSURE • INTELLIGENCE • RECREATION RESPONSIBILITY • HOPE • CAREER • ATTITUDE SELF-CONTROL • EDUCATION • TRUTH

LISTEN UP!!

_____
_____
_____
_____
_____
_____
_____
_____
_____
_____
_____

Use the back of this sheet if necessary. Share with peers.

NAME _____ DATE _____

MAKING CHOICES FOR MY LIFE

In life, individuals usually make decisions that are in their own best interest. Trouble results, however, when people make unwise choices regarding their lifestyles and friends. Most decisions impact not only on the decision makers but also on the people with whom they interact, and either positive rewards or negative consequences occur. Read the CHOICES list and, based on your personality and values system, complete the chart by classifying the choices according to the following criteria:

P = POSITIVE   N = NEGATIVE   G = GRAY AREA

A. **Impacts on my present and future life**
B. **Impacts on my family/friends**
C. **Impacts on the people in the community or the larger society**
D. **Has little or no impact on myself or other people**

CHOICE	(CIRCLE ONE)	IMPACT	COMMENT
1. Cursing	P N G	A	I limit my ability to solve my internal/external conflicts
2. Telling the truth	P N G		
3. Eating properly	P N G		
4. Obeying	P N G		
5. Volunteering	P N G		
6. Stealing	P N G		
7. Recycling	P N G		
8. Wearing pants below the waist	P N G		
9. Exercising daily	P N G		
10. Smoking/drugs	P N G		
11. Playing	P N G		
12. Voting	P N G		
13. Working	P N G		
14. Fighting/teasing	P N G		
15. Lying/cheating	P N G		

Discuss what choices are clearly negative or positive, and clarify "gray" areas. Compare and contrast your list with those of your peers. Expand the list of choices, if you wish. Share your classification assessment with family and friends. Which choices contribute to a better life?

NAME _____ DATE _____

DIAMONDS IN THE ROUGH . . .
NEED POLISHING

No one is perfect! Everyone has been faced with situations that require choosing between right and wrong. Even if people make mistakes, they do not have to continue participating in activities that might be physically, mentally, or emotionally destructive. Each person has many opportunities to change negative behaviors to positive ones. If you or someone you know has ever been tempted to become involved in behaviors that might contribute to poor physical, mental, or emotional health, complete the checklist below. Check off (✓)the appropriate categories below. Be prepared to explain your reason for not checking off a category.

THE POLISHING PROCESS

NEVER, EVER WILL I USE OR CONSIDER USING . . .

_____ Inhalants, including glue, aerosols, etc.

_____ Drugs, including uppers, downers, sleeping pills, crack, cocaine, heroin, speed

_____ Cigarettes, cigars, snuff, chewing tobacco, marijuana

_____ Alcohol, beer, and other intoxicating beverages

_____ Violent and/or vengeful sets against others for wrongs against me.

_____ Other _____

There are some things that teenagers might want to discuss with adults. There are other things that teenagers might not want to discuss with adults. Most young people would admit, however, that parents, guardians, or counselors are very helpful when difficult decisions have to be made. Do you think that teenagers should seek adult help, rely on their friends, or just work out all of their problems on their own? Write your response on the lines below:

_____

_____

_____

_____

_____

_____

NAME _____ DATE _____

ABSOLUTE TRUTHS TO LIVE BY

"Let truth EXPLODE asunder"

"Speak the truth"

"Live the truth"

"TRUTH IS INVISIBLE UNTIL SPOKEN"

Each person has a right to conduct his or her life based on certain truths that he or she has learned. On the lines below, list some of the absolute truths that provide a foundation for your life—those things that give you confidence and strength when you're faced with daily moral, social, and emotional decisions. The first one is done for you. Complete the rest:

ABSOLUTE TRUTHS THAT GIVE MORAL STRENGTH

1. Sometimes, following the crowd can result in trouble. Therefore, I think for myself and do what I know is right.

2. _____

3. _____

4. _____

5. _____

6. _____

7. _____

8. _____

9. _____

10. _____

THINK ABOUT THESE THINGS!!!

Is there ever a time when it is appropriate to cheat, or to lie, or to steal? Explain your thoughts about this question.

People—teenagers included—have a right to worship as they please. In your opinion, has this right been diminished?

Sometimes, young people are too hard on each other. What can be done about this reality?

NAME _____ DATE _____

OVERCOMING SHYNESS

If you are shy, chances are that you want to overcome this shyness and to communicate more confidently with other people. Use the chart below to classify the kinds of attitudes and actions you can take to strengthen your self-esteem. Read items 1–15, and decide where they should fit on the chart. Place the numbers in the boxes on the chart. Then use the chart as an action plan for developing a new and higher level of SELF-CONFIDENCE. If you have other ideas, add to the list below:

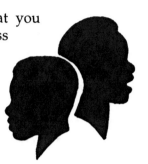 

MY ACTION PLAN

Leadership Qualities	Intellectual Abilities	Creativity and Productivity	A New Attitude and a New Outlook

LIST OF CHOICES FOR THE CHART

1. try using my talents and skills to my advantage
2. become adventurous—within limits
3. write my autobiography
4. initiate conversation with family/friends
5. enroll in creative dramatics classes
6. find a new friend
7. work hard to increase my knowledge of math, science, computers, and English
8. seek help from a teacher or counselor
9. find a hobby
10. volunteer in the community
11. contact distant relatives and family friends
12. find reasons to laugh, sometimes at myself
13. collect information about my early childhood
14. start a club for "shy" teenagers
15. try to ask or answer questions in class more often

NAME _____ DATE _____

I'M TOO YOUNG TO BE STRESSED OUT!!!

How can you take care of yourself so that you do not experience the negative effects of stress? What are some of the things that cause you to get angry, sad, frustrated, or out of control? What are some of the things that comfort you and give you joy and peace? Of course, we prefer those positive emotions that are fueled by success and popularity because they reduce or eradicate stress. On the other hand, negative emotions that lead to unhappiness can cause stress and we seek ways to get rid of it.

From the list below, identify behaviors, actions, and reactions that would help you to remain calm, or bring you happiness, joy, and confidence. Circle those behaviors that help you to avoid stress and maintain joy. Place an X on those behaviors that cause you stress and unhappiness.

TALKING WITH PARENTS

BLAMING OTHERS FOR MY PROBLEMS

REST AND RELAXATION

APOLOGIZING FOR A MISTAKE

VIOLENCE IN TV/MOVIES

DOING HOMEWORK

USING A FAKE ID

CREATING A WORK OF ART

OBSERVING MY RELIGION

VOLUNTEERING

EXERCISE

SHOPPING FOR CLOTHES

COOKING/EATING

GOING ON A BLIND DATE

CHEATING ON A TEST

LAUGHING/ENJOYING THE BEAUTY
  IN LIFE

SILENCE/PERSONAL REFLECTION

PRETENDING TO BE SOMETHING THAT
  I AM NOT

LISTENING TO MUSIC

READING A GOOD BOOK

LYING

FISHING

SINGING/DANCING

TELLING A SECRET

SLEEPING

TELLING THE TRUTH

TOLERANCE OF THOSE WHO ARE
  DIFFERENT

RACISM

EXPRESSING PERSONAL OPINIONS

PLANNING MY FUTURE

NAME-CALLING

ENJOYING MY CULTURAL HERITAGE

To what extent do personal choices cause personal stress? How can you control your own stress levels? How can you increase the positive experiences in your life?

NAME _____   DATE _____

GETTING RID OF THE "BIG BAD WOLVES"

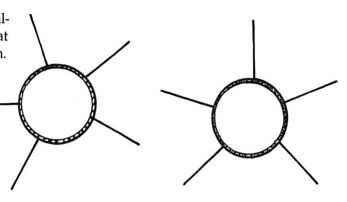

You really don't have to give in to bullies, be afraid of rejection, or tremble at the prospect of making a public speech. The "big bad wolves" in your life can be defeated. First, become aware of your "wolves" and identify personal attributes that can render them harmless. For example, if you are afraid to speak or sing in public, think of the talents that you have and how other people might enjoy what you have to offer. Second, remember that "practice makes perfect." Practice in front of a mirror or family members. Also, remember that even movie stars get nervous and that a little bit of tension is good; it keeps you on your toes. Know your audience. Put a smile on your face. Show what you know! Now, you're in charge!

Look at the many different types of fears that people face every day. Identify those that cause the greatest pain or hinder your progress. Then, develop a plan for overcoming or erasing these fears from your life. Circle the greatest fears, and write your plan for getting rid of them on the next page. Remember, you can control your fear!

1. isolation	16. corruption	31. gluttony
2. abandonment	17. abuse	32. ignorance
3. joblessness	18. prison	33. deceit
4. homelessness	19. confusion	34. ridicule
5. sex too early	20. vengeance	35. wishful thinking
6. alienation	21. negative attitude	36. division
7. guilt	22. poverty	37. stereotypes
8. violence	23. suffering	38. sarcasm
9. no direction	24. uncertainty	39. stubbornness
10. injustice	25. materialism	40. faithlessness
11. pretense	26. rejection	41. impulsiveness
12. divorce	27. manipulation	42. pride
13. power	28. prejudice	43. selfishness
14. laziness	29. arrogance	44. ignorance
15. mental instability	30. greed	45. peer pressure

Now that your fears are going up in steam, never to be seen again, you will need to replace these negative attitudes and attributes with POSITIVE ATTITUDES and PRODUCTIVE ATTRIBUTES. On the back of this sheet or in a notebook, describe these new attitudes and qualities, and explain how you will make them a part of your everyday life. Include comments on how you will expand the effects of these new personal traits, values, and attitudes. From all of the **positive** and **productive** ideas you choose, identify *at least* **two** that would have the most impact on you. Write each positive word in a circle, and then write how your life will improve on the spokes attached to the circle.

NAME _____ DATE _____

RESOLVING A PERSONAL CONFLICT

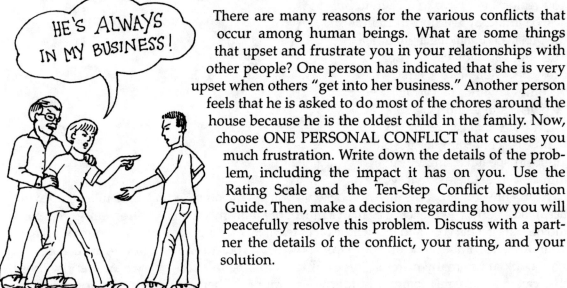

HE'S ALWAYS IN MY BUSINESS!

There are many reasons for the various conflicts that occur among human beings. What are some things that upset and frustrate you in your relationships with other people? One person has indicated that she is very upset when others "get into her business." Another person feels that he is asked to do most of the chores around the house because he is the oldest child in the family. Now, choose ONE PERSONAL CONFLICT that causes you much frustration. Write down the details of the problem, including the impact it has on you. Use the Rating Scale and the Ten-Step Conflict Resolution Guide. Then, make a decision regarding how you will peacefully resolve this problem. Discuss with a partner the details of the conflict, your rating, and your solution.

MY PERSONAL CONFLICT   RATING SCALE 1_____5
                                              (Low   High)

_____

_____

_____

_____

TEN STEPS TO CONFLICT RESOLUTION

1. Hold face-to-face meetings in a positive and neutral environment.
2. State and listen to perceptions of both/all parties on the nature of the problem.
3. Isolate and meet each person's needs so that he or she will achieve wholeness.
4. Set up a partnership/group that has the best interest of both parties in mind.
5. Identify common needs and concerns, and use as a basis for shared power.
6. Avoid getting bogged down in the negatives of the past; agree to forgive.
7. Plan to avoid future conflicts by learning from the past; look toward the future.
8. Steer parties away from conflicts by finding new options.
9. Compliment the other person for a positive trait or accomplishment.
10. Plan to give the other party a gift: a smile, a handshake, a friendship card.

Name _____ Date _____

From the steps listed above, select those that are relevant for your problem. Use these ideas to write how you will peacefully solve your problem. Use the lines below:

MY RESOLUTION TO MY CONFLICT

_____
_____
_____
_____
_____
_____
_____
_____
_____
_____
_____
_____
_____
_____
_____
_____
_____
_____
_____
_____
_____
_____
_____

Share your ideas with a person who can help you solve your conflict.

NAME _____ DATE _____

CHECK YOURSELF

So you really don't like the idea of being frisked by police or security guards in your school, or anywhere? You feel that your human dignity/human rights would be under attack if this were to happen to you, and you want to always be in control of your own life. This is entirely possible because of who you are and what you want out of life. If you are a GIVER and not a TAKER, it will be easy for you to work at keeping your civil rights and making sure that others have theirs. What does this involve? Read the statements representing ways that individuals can be in control of their lives. Indicate whether you Agree or Disagree by writing the letter A or D. Then state a Self-Control idea of your own on the lines.

BEING IN CONTROL OF YOUR OWN MIND AND BODY IS EASY:

____ Do not give in to powerful negative forces whether they are people, addictive substances, or addictive behaviors. They, instead of you, can control your mind if you allow them to.

____ Maintain confidence in yourself as a capable, honest, intelligent individual who can make your own decisions.

____ Always be yourself; don't let the environment or certain people sway your convictions.

____ Never sit on the fence or hover between two opinions or two options. Make a firm, rational, decision and stand your ground. Remember, you are free to choose—so choose.

____ Maintain a high level of expectations for your personal life. Avoid people who make you feel less capable or who discourage you as you try to succeed.

____ Know the rules and obey them. If you feel that some rules are unfair, follow certain procedures to correct them.

____ Be able to laugh at yourself. Don't take yourself so seriously. Also, use laughter to help and heal others—never to mock or ridicule other human beings.

____ Like yourself enough to become your own best friend. Think good, positive thoughts, smile often, avoid gossip, and assume a nonviolent stance as you relate to family, friends, and others.

____ Your body has to last you for a lifetime so you should dictate what happens to it. You don't have to participate in risky behaviors that will bring disease and pain and ruin your body. You dictate!

MY SELF-CONTROL IDEA

_____

_____

_____

_____

NAME _____ DATE _____

THIS FAR AND NO FARTHER

You have a curfew on weekdays, with a one-hour extension on Saturdays. Because you were caught sneaking back into the house at dawn a few weeks ago, you have also endured being completely grounded on Sundays. You can still hang out with most of your old friends, but you have limits. Some of your friends' parents are stricter than yours and these kids rush to get home before their curfews. On the other hand, some of the kids you know try to "get over" on their parents. Until you made up your mind that it would be easier to follow the rules of your household rather than fight them, you were miserable. Now, every day, your friends see your smiling face and wonder why you're finally accepting your parents' limits without protesting. What some of them don't understand is that you have imagined that your life is like a long road with yellow lines on it, and that you know danger awaits you if you cross them; your parents' rules are the yellow lines in your life. You must not cross them. Therefore, you have learned that, in order to be happier, you MUST SET YOUR OWN LIMITS. You have decided to go this far and no farther.

Because everyone has the power to set his or her own limits, use the ideas below to gauge how far YOU will allow yourself to venture into the following experiences (1 is NO WAY and 10 is ALL THE WAY). You can keep the results of your assessment private or share them with family and friends. Most important, use the results to make positive lifestyle choices.

1_____10
NO WAY!   ALL THE WAY!

RATE EACH CHOICE BY USING A NUMBER FROM 1 TO 10

1. ____ dancing
2. ____ cursing
3. ____ premarital sex
4. ____ drugs
5. ____ stealing
6. ____ reading
7. ____ volunteering
8. ____ skipping class
9. ____ buying a fake ID
10. ____ worshipping
11. ____ fighting
12. ____ flirting
13. ____ voting

14. ____ sneaking out of the house
15. ____ playing chess or checkers
16. ____ telling a secret
17. ____ singing
18. ____ having a big ego
19. ____ gossiping
20. ____ lying
21. ____ working after school
22. ____ cheating on a test
23. ____ bullying

24. ____ following dress codes
25. ____ having a bad attitude
26. ____ causing a scene
27. ____ disobeying authority
28. ____ snatching someone's purse
29. ____ copying someone's homework
30. ____ other _____
31. ____ other _____
32. ____ other _____

NAME _____ DATE _____

LIVING THE GOLDEN RULE

When politicians run for office, they have a platform or goals to present to the public. In this platform, they project what they believe in and the plans they have for helping to improve the quality of life if they are elected to office. Listed below are some controversial issues that come up when people are looking for public support:

- Juvenile Crime
- Abortion Issues
- Unemployment
- Homelessness
- Literacy
- The Environment

If you were running for political office or your opinion on certain issues were valued, what would your platform consist of? Give specific examples below:

_____
_____
_____

How would you encourage others to place themselves in the position of people who are unable to care for themselves? ("Do unto others as you would have them do unto you.")

_____
_____
_____

Develop an action plan for one of the issues that you have listed. Include in your plan how to help those that are incapable of caring for themselves.

MY ACTION PLAN

_____
_____
_____
_____
_____
_____
_____
_____

WHEN HATE PREVAILS . . . LOVE MUST ENTER

Communication barriers often prevent understanding among people of various races, cultures, and ethnic groups. The problems might be eliminated if they were broken down and viewed closely, and attempts were then made to correct them.

Place key words for the ten human conflicts on the chart "Breaking Down the Problem." Then identify those that are easily solved, those that are more difficult to solve, and those that will require long, hard study and multi-level plans for resolution. Use numbers to rate the levels of difficulty, identify who is victimized, identify who or what are the causes of the problem, and suggest the people or organizations that should work to solve the problem.

1   Problems easily solved

2   Problems more difficult but possible to solve

3   Problems very difficult to solve, requiring many people and many steps

_____ A school system has many books that depict how much men have contributed to society but very few about the accomplishments of women or minorities.

_____ A television program focuses on the positive images of whites but highlights negative images of blacks, Native Americans, and Hispanics.

_____ Blame for crime against society is placed on individuals just because they belong to a certain racial group.

_____ Certain individuals interpret the law to their own advantage.

_____ A foreign language student was in advanced classes in his own country, but in America he is placed in remedial classes.

_____ Only thin people are asked to appear in the talent and fashion show.

_____ Assumptions are made about people who are identified as learning disabled, and they are often not valued for their skills and talents.

_____ Only certain ethnic groups are presumed to be responsible for the progress of civilization.

_____ More females should be included in male-dominated professions.

_____ Some people are seen as arrogant, aloof, or uncaring, when in reality they are very shy and might suffer from low self-esteem.

NAME _____ DATE _____

BREAKING DOWN THE PROBLEM

	The Problem	The Rating	The Cause	The Victim(s)	The Solution
1.					
2.					
3.					
4.					
5.					
6.					
7.					
8.					
9.					
10.					

Select ONE of these issues to research. Then write a letter to the editor of a local newspaper to offer your suggestions for solving the problem. Keep track of responses to your letter and any indication that improvements are being made, at least in your own community.

NAME _____   DATE _____

GARAGE SALE IN THE YEAR 2020

Take the time to imagine what you will have accomplished and accumulated in terms of career, home, family, and material goods by the time the year 2020 arrives. Possibly, you will own the latest versions of computers, homes, clothing, dishes, gadgets, furniture, cellular phones, microwaves, and whatever new inventions are on the market.

Consider your personality, values, life goals, and the things you possess. Imagine asking yourself this question: "Do I really need all of these MATERIAL things?" Then, think about NONMATERIAL goods and values that are important in your life.

Pretend that you are preparing for a garage sale and record on the chart below the things you need to keep and the things you can get rid of. As you make each decision, record the reasons you have for keeping or getting rid of things. Compare and contrast your list with those of your peers.

PREPARING FOR MY GARAGE SALE

Material or Nonmaterial Possessions	Reason for Selling Reason for Keeping
1.	1.
2.	2.
3.	3.
4.	4.
5.	5.
6.	6.
7.	7.
8.	8.
9.	9.
10.	10.

NAME _____ DATE _____

I CAN REDUCE RACISM, HATRED, PREJUDICE, AND VIOLENCE???

What can you, as a young citizen, do to erase racism, hatred, prejudice, and violence in America and eventually the world? Imagine that as a member of a coalition, your job is to target the main problems and propose strategies for solving them to the group.

Note the PROBLEMS stated above and the SOLUTIONS listed below. Match each identified problem with a solution from the list. Based on your experiences, add other ideas for solving these problems in human relationships. Then, working with your peers, develop programs for reducing or eliminating intolerance in your school and community and increasing understanding, tolerance, and peace. Write the number of the solution(s) next to each identified problem.

RACISM _____

HATRED _____

PREJUDICE _____

VIOLENCE _____

SUGGESTED SOLUTIONS

1. Develop mutual respect.
2. Assume a positive role.
3. Recognize and try to reduce pain among your peers.
4. Contact community social, religious, educational, and recreational agencies.
5. Recognize multiracial and multicultural contributions to the world.
6. Become a voice for peace.
7. Speak up and out, often.
8. Avoid racial arrogance and put-downs.
9. Support freedom and equal opportunity in voting.
10. Always apply concepts of fairness and self-control.
11. Other _____
12. Other _____

NOTE: Work with your peers to develop a plan of action for resolving conflicts. Use the back of this sheet.

Name _____ Date _____

PRO OR CON—WHERE DO YOU STAND?

List your reasons for or against the following controversial issues. Hold class discussions on these and other topics.

ISSUE 1

Parents should pay for crimes committed by their children.

_____

PRO   CON

ISSUE 2

Prayer should be allowed in the public schools.

_____

PRO   CON

ISSUE 3

Public schools should have mandatory dress codes.

_____

PRO   CON

ISSUE 4

Students should have input into the courses that are taught in school.

_____

PRO   CON

ISSUE 5

Curfews are necessary for all teenagers.

_____

PRO   CON

ISSUE 6

Parents must be involved in planning school-based sex education programs.

_____

PRO   CON

Do you have strong, definite opinions on certain issues? People who shift their views depending on whom they are with are luke-warm or "wishy-washy." Always take a firm stand on issues and state your opinions clearly.

NAME _____ DATE _____

FOLLOW THE LEADER? WHY?

A famous athlete publicized that he is not a role model for the young people who observe his life as an athlete and a private citizen. He believes that parents and close family friends must be the ones whom young people emulate. Is this athlete's opinion right? Does he bear any responsibility for the way young people behave, or do parents have sole responsibility for the way their children conduct themselves? At what point do people begin to think for themselves and act on what they know is right and beneficial, no matter what famous or powerful individuals do or say?

Sometimes, dogs run around in circles chasing their tails for no apparent reason. We laugh at this behavior. A species of worms follow their leader around a plate filled with their favorite food, and they all starve to death because not one of them has the drive or intelligence to pull away from the crowd and go toward the life-sustaining substance on the plate. How often do we think of the serious consequences that exist when human beings don't think for themselves and follow misguided, uninformed, ignorant, or uncaring individuals? To what extent do human beings run around in circles, following movie or TV stars, imitating famous people, and accomplishing nothing that would help them to develop their own individual talents and skills? At what point do people learn that it is foolish to follow someone else blindly without considering the dangers of the unknown? At what point should individuals break out of the crowd and think and act independently?

Read the lifestyle choices of some of society's "leaders," and decide how productive or nonproductive their choices are. Write five of the nonproductive choices on the chart, and for every nonproductive choice, substitute an acceptable, productive option. Then, in the process of your assessment, consider the traits a person must develop to become a productive leader. Conclude with a statement that explains whether you would want to lead other people or teach them to be their own leaders—to make the best possible decisions for themselves.

Rate each lifestyle choice from 1 to 4; 1 = always, 2 = frequently, 3 = seldom, 4 = never. Write the ratings on the lines as you respond to the question: How often do you imitate the behavior of a person who would . . . ?

____ stereotype   ____ talk to a stranger   ____ play politics   ____ meddle
____ trust blindly   ____ act without thinking   ____ get revenge   ____ insult
someone   ____ kick another person   ____ laugh at a helpless person
____ look for peer approval   ____ dress inappropriately   ____ listen to rumors
____ manipulate others   ____ fight   ____ tell the truth   ____ treat others with
dignity   ____ make assumptions   ____ lie   ____ beat someone who is already
depressed   ____ display prejudice and hate   ____ make unreasonable requests
____ forgive others   ____ trash talk   ____ promote propaganda or prejudice
____ follow fashion trends   ____ gossip   ____ make unfair accusations
____ threaten those who are powerless   ____ riot   ____ put down others
____ showoff

© 1999 by John Wiley & Sons, Inc.

NAME _____   DATE _____

NONPRODUCTIVE CHOICES	PRODUCTIVE OPTIONS	COMMENTS/IDEAS (FOR BUILDING SOCIETY)
1.	1.	1.
2.	2.	2.
3.	3.	3.
4.	4.	4.
5.	5.	5.

Explore the qualities and responsibilities of a leader on the next page. Then write a paragraph about YOUR leadership qualities on the lines provided.

© 1999 by John Wiley & Sons, Inc.

NAME _____ DATE _____

CHARACTERISTICS OF A LEADER

- ☞ INSPIRATIONAL
- ☞ SETS GOALS FOR THE FUTURE
- ☞ WILLING TO WAIT FOR THE BEST
- ☞ SENSITIVE TO THE NEEDS OF OTHERS
- ☞ CONFIDENT ENOUGH TO LET OTHERS EXPRESS IDEAS
- ☞ FINDS GRATIFICATION IN HELPING OTHER PEOPLE
- ☞ ENJOYS HAVING COMMONALTIES WITH OTHERS
- ☞ OTHER _____
- ☞ OTHER _____

CHARACTERISTICS OF A NONLEADER

- ☞ UNSURE OF HIMSELF/HERSELF
- ☞ TOO AUTHORITATIVE AND CONTROLLING
- ☞ EXPECTS BLIND TRUST AND NO QUESTIONS/CHALLENGES
- ☞ MAKES THE SAME MISTAKES OVER AND OVER AGAIN
- ☞ PROGRESS IS QUESTIONABLE, SPORADIC, ABSENT
- ☞ GOALS ARE NON EXISTENT OR SELF-SERVING
- ☞ OTHER _____
- ☞ OTHER _____

MY LEADERSHIP QUALITIES

_____
_____
_____
_____
_____
_____
_____
_____
_____
_____
_____

NOT ME!

In the span of human experiences, many impulsive or momentary pleasures have the risk of long-term negative consequences. Self-discipline, values, and the ability to refuse with confidence are crucial when human beings are faced with temptations to participate in destructive behaviors. When do you use the words NOT ME to let others know that you want to protect yourself from harm?

From among the choices of behaviors on the chart, rate those that have risks of negative consequences, neutral or harmless consequences, or positive benefits. Use the numbers to indicate your ideas as a teenager who wants the best kind of life possible. Then write NM by all the no. 3 items.

1   **POSITIVE BENEFITS**

2   **NEUTRAL/HARMLESS**

3   **NEGATIVE CONSEQUENCES**

____ Daydreaming

____ Blaming others for your faults

____ Acting silly

____ Getting a detention

____ Shoplifting, robbing

____ Praying

____ Gossiping

____ Driving over the speed limit

____ Chewing gum in class

____ Making sexist remarks

____ Contributing to the needy

____ Reducing responsible, productive behavior

____ Increasing responsible, productive behavior

____ Multiplying positive relationships

NAME _____ DATE _____

_____ Being mean or rude

_____ Maintaining values you've been taught

_____ Joining a gang or a group that promotes violence and/or hate

_____ Putting yourself in someone else's shoes

_____ Assuming the role of victim

_____ Maintaining negative and aggressive attitudes

_____ Getting revenge

_____ Planning for your future

_____ Being kind

_____ Involvement in physical or emotional abuse

_____ Holding hands with someone you love

_____ Getting to know someone of another race or culture

_____ Working hard to achieve success

_____ Threatening another person

_____ Involvement with guns or other weapons

_____ Selling or taking drugs

NAME _____ DATE _____

PROTECTING MY SELF-ESTEEM— AND YOURS

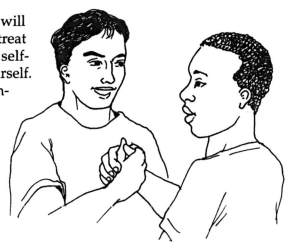

Much of what you are and what you will become as a person depends on how you treat other people. The concepts involving self-esteem include feeling good about yourself. Personal satisfaction is necessary to healthful development. In fact, confident people who have high self-esteem don't mind if other people feel good about themselves, too. People who are really happy with themselves can go even further and treat others better than they treat themselves. This can often be seen in parent-child or best-friend relationships. Rewards are forthcoming for those who esteem others.

Read the list of words. Then, classify them according to whether they BUILD UP or TEAR DOWN people. Circle those words that mean the most to you as an individual who wants to be involved in harmonious relationships with other human beings. Discuss how these things contribute to or prevent feelings of arrogance and false superiority—attitudes that destroy positive human relationships. (**Note:** Change forms of words if necessary, i.e., threats or respectfully.)

- terrorism
- encouraging
- respect
- privileges
- effort
- cooperation

- delight
- regret
- boasting
- swearing
- threatening
- sacrificing

- compliments
- gift giving
- generosity
- excuses
- materialism
- stereotypes

- sympathy
- listening
- eye contact
- put-downs
- sharing
- courtesy

LEARNING TO ESTEEM OTHERS AS IMPORTANT AS MYSELF

Actions That Build Other People Up	Actions That Tear Other People Down

Discuss with peers how actions that encourage or BUILD OTHER PEOPLE UP can be implemented throughout the day. Consider keeping a daily account of all the ways that people spread joy.

NAME _____   DATE _____

SUCCESS ACCORDING TO

(Your Name)

Many people have advice to give to others on how to be successful, including self-confidence, beauty, trust, intelligence, and honesty. These might be fine for some people and not others. What are the criteria for success according to you? What should people do to make others like to be around them? What should they do to succeed in a job? What things are important in achieving self-regard? Write at least five words in each category. Then, explain why you think others can find success with your suggestions.

_____'s Formula for Success
(Your Name)

FRIENDSHIP	JOB	SELF-REGARD
1. _____	1. _____	1. _____
2. _____	2. _____	2. _____
3. _____	3. _____	3. _____
4. _____	4. _____	4. _____
5. _____	5. _____	5. _____

Explanation for your advice: _____

_____

_____

_____

_____

_____

_____

NAME _____   DATE _____

THE BEST THAT I CAN BE

Write down everything that it would take for you to become the best person that you can be. Use the words in the left-hand column of Section A for ideas, then add other ideas in Section B in order to focus your composition on your own personal goals.

A. To become the best person that I can be (*Explain WHY you need these things*) . . .

- Discipline   _____
- Love   _____
- Time   _____
- Values   _____
- Education   _____
- Other   _____
- Other   _____
- Other   _____
- Other   _____

B. Now, write down ten things you need to make your life positive and productive right now:

1. _____
2. _____
3. _____
4. _____
5. _____
6. _____
7. _____
8. _____
9. _____
10. _____

   Now, using ideas from Sections A and B, write a composition describing yourself as the best that you can possibly be. This description can describe you as you are now, or it can describe how you hope to be in the future. You decide.

NAME _____ DATE _____

TWENTY MINUTES TO PACK

What are the most important things to you? Imagine that you live in an area surrounded by beautiful mountains. However, one of these mountains is a dormant volcano that suddenly awakens and begins to erupt. Fire, smoke, and lava begin to pour out of the top, and authorities have ordered all residents within a hundred-mile radius to evacuate the area. You have been given only twenty minutes to select necessary items. What, from among all of your possessions, will you pack in this short amount of time? Which items are most important for your survival and comfort? Make a list of all necessary items and the amount of time it would take to locate and pack each item, and explain the reasons for each selection. Complete the chart below:

NECESSARY ITEM	TIME NEEDED TO LOCATE AND PACK	REASON FOR THIS SELECTION
1.	1.	1.
2.	2.	2.
3.	3.	3.
4.	4.	4.
5.	5.	5.
6.	6.	6.

NAME _____ DATE _____

WHAT'S HOT? WHAT'S NOT?

Only you can tell what's going on in your life that's good or not good. Only you can determine if something will make your life better or worse. Calling the shots over what you will allow to happen in your life is an important skill. What's HOT in your life refers to those things that will help you to set high goals and work to achieve them. What's NOT hot in your life refers to those things that will drag you down and prevent you from achieving success. Identify what's HOT and what's NOT in each category below. It's your call!

WHAT'S HOT?

Your Life: _____

_____

_____

The World: _____

_____

School: _____

_____

The Future: _____

_____

WHAT'S NOT?

Your Life: _____

_____

_____

The World: _____

_____

School: _____

_____

The Future: _____

_____

THINK ABOUT THIS!!!

What adjustments do you need to make to steer your life towards those things that are good for you?

WHO ARE YOU IN YOUR SCHOOL?

Students have a job while they are in school. Your job as a student is to LEARN.

Explain what you are learning in each subject below. Use some of the words on the list in your sentences.

Study	Library	Weekends
Homework	Bedtime	Friends
Weekdays	Practice	Books
Time	Writing	Problems

1. Reading _____
   _____
   _____

2. Foreign Language _____
   _____
   _____

3. Math _____
   _____
   _____

4. Science _____
   _____
   _____

5. Social Studies _____
   _____
   _____

6. Art _____
   _____
   _____

NAME _____ DATE _____

7. Music _____

_____

_____

8. Health _____

_____

_____

9. Computers _____

_____

_____

10. English _____

_____

_____

NAME _____ DATE _____

I PLAN TO WORK AS A . . .

Most teenagers spend some time thinking about what kind of work they want to do in life. What's good about this is that there are so many options to choose from. Look at the list to see if anything interests you. Add your own choices of jobs or professions on the blank lines. Then, according to what you want to do in life, rate these occupations from the most to the least important. Use 1 as the highest rating on a scale of 1–10. Write your ratings next to the jobs/professions.

___ MUSICIAN	___ SECRETARY	___ COMPUTER ANALYST
___ DOCTOR	___ MARINE BIOLOGIST	___ _____
___ SCIENTIST	___ ART RESTORER	___ _____
___ CHEF	___ HERBALIST	___ _____
___ TEACHER	___ ANTIQUE DEALER	

Your No. 1 rating is for the occupation of _____

Explain why you rated this occupation No. 1 _____

_____

_____

_____

_____

_____

_____

NAME _____ DATE _____

Read the information below. Then, circle the kinds of jobs that family members, friends, and acquaintances have. Explain why each of these jobs is important to people who need the services of these workers. You can write your explanation on the back of this page. Also, plan to interview someone whose work experiences would be interesting for others to hear about. Develop at least five questions to ask a person who works as, for example, a grocer.

OCCUPATIONS

If one's job is honest, it has honor. You may choose to be one of these:

Actor	Dressmaker	Management	Priest
Architect	Editor	Consultant	Printer
Astronaut	Electrician	Mathematician	Professor
Athlete	Entertainer	Microbiologist	Rabbi
Baker	Farmer	Milk Deliverer	Railroad Engineer
Banker	Fire Fighter	Minister	Real Estate Broker
Bus Driver	Flight Attendant	Mortician	Repair Person
Businessperson	Grocer	Musician	Reporter
Carpenter	Home Economist	Nun	Salesperson
Chef	Homemaker	Nurse	Scientist
Cleaner	Insurance	Nurse's Aid	Social Worker
Clothier	Salesperson	Optometrist	Sports Announcer
Commercial Artist	Janitor	Packer	Tailor
Computer	Jeweler	Photographer	Teacher
Programmer	Journalist	Pilot	Technician
Counselor	Launderer	Police Officer	Veterinarian
Dentist	Lawyer	Postal Clerk	Window Cleaner
Designer	Maid	Postmaster	Welder
Doctor	Mail Carrier	Plumber	Zoologist

INTERVIEW QUESTIONS FOR _____
(Job/Profession/Occupation)

1. _____

2. _____

3. _____

4. _____

5. _____

6. _____

NAME _____   DATE _____

REASONABLE PATHS

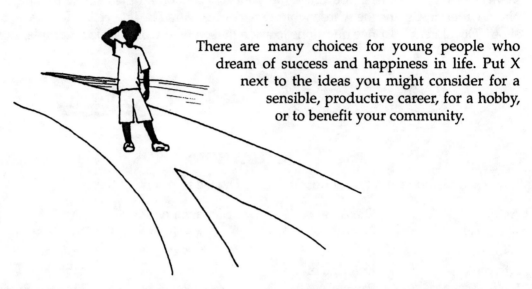

There are many choices for young people who dream of success and happiness in life. Put X next to the ideas you might consider for a sensible, productive career, for a hobby, or to benefit your community.

_____ Fight crime

_____ Organize safe recreation for teenagers

_____ Work in voter registration programs

_____ Volunteer in literacy program

_____ Complete high school or college

_____ Organize meetings to improve race relations

_____ Hold a sale to help the homeless

_____ Apply for a job on weekends

_____ Write letters to support programs for senior citizens

_____ Respect other people in school, at home, and in the neighborhood

_____ Speak up for the rights of immigrants in your school

_____ Find alternatives to violent and sexually explicit entertainment

_____ Report a crime if you are a witness

_____ Take pride in telling the truth

_____ Accept the punishment when you deserve it

_____ Avoid following the crowd

Other: _____

_____

_____

_____

_____

_____

_____

NAME _____ DATE _____

SUCCESS IS WITHIN YOUR REACH

Do you have any personal goals that you want to attain in your life? How will you realize your dreams? What you think, say, do, and believe about your own potential can influence your eventual success or failure. People who are successful usually want it so badly that they set high, realistic goals and then work very hard to achieve them.

Using the ideas below, write several sentences that reveal what you will need in order to have the success you want in your life. Write your own ideas on the blank lines.

IDEAS FOR SENTENCES THAT WILL GUIDE ME TOWARD MY GOALS

- Self-direction
- Self-evaluation
- Adult encouragement
- Moral integrity
- Restraint
- Human relationships
- Social Interests
- Respect (self, mutual)
- Faith
- Motivation

- Plans/strategies
- Parent/guardian
- Consultants
- Personal right to happiness
- Multicultural education
- Tolerance
- Interdependence
- Educational plan
- Positive outlook

- Focus
- Self-confidence
- Cooperative learning
- Human dignity
- Personal interests
- OTHER IDEAS:

_____

_____

_____

Now that you have studied the ideas above, write some sentences that explain what you must do to reach your goals and SUCCESS!

_____

_____

_____

_____

_____

_____

_____

_____

Complete your comments on the back of this sheet.

NAME _____ DATE _____

THE KEYS TO YOUR SUCCESS

King Solomon, a prominent historical figure, was extremely rich and able to buy anything he wanted. However, like many wealthy people in today's world, he found that THINGS like gold and silver left him cold and empty. King Solomon discovered that happiness could not be found in his land, houses, beautiful gardens, pools, cattle, servants, and other treasures. He shows his despair and the futility of having unlimited material goods when he says, "Then I looked on all the works that my hands had wrought and . . . behold, all was vanity and vexation of spirit, and there was no profit under the sun." He had found no joy in his riches.

In today's world, advertisers make people feel that money, success, and fame are all any individual needs in order to know ultimate joy and happiness. How do you feel about this idea? Think of people in today's society who have won the lottery. Reports are that many of them have problems BECAUSE of their riches. Certainly people need adquate funds for survival and comfort. However, do people need an overabundance of MONEY and THINGS in order to be happy or successful?

In the center of the key ring, record the MAIN ELEMENT that you need for success, happiness, and joy. Then, on the lines around the keys, write SPECIFIC ACTIONS that YOU must take in order to achieve REAL SUCCESS for yourself.

_____
_____
_____
_____
_____
_____
_____
_____
_____
_____
_____
_____
_____
_____
_____
_____

NAME _____ DATE _____

I THINK I CAN, I THINK I CAN, I *KNOW* I CAN!

When you were younger than you are now, someone probably read the story *The Little Engine That Could* to you. There were challenges that the main character, the train engine, did not feel that he could meet. However, when he put his mind to it and tried his very hardest, he accomplished his goal. The evidence that he really concentrated on the task (that of climbing a hill) was conveyed in his saying over and over, "I think I can, I think I can, I think I can," even as he was puffing and straining hard to reach the top of the hill. He had a sense of responsibility about what he wanted to accomplish, but he was aware that others had the highest expectations for him, as well. The Little Engine accomplished his goal because he never gave up! To what extent are you like that little train engine? To what extent do you pursue the right course of action in matters concerning your attitude, your behavior, your homework, your goals, and your plans for the future? How far would you go to change negative things in your life to positive ones?

During your work on these activities, you have thought a lot about your goals and what you must do to accomplish them. In addition, you have considered human relationships and what kinds of attitudes and behaviors are necessary for peaceful interaction. Still, there might be times when you and others might have an aversion to certain people or situations. There might be times when you see that you can help someone in need but choose to go the other way instead of becoming involved. America is full of people who need caring, fellow human beings to come to their aid—or at least not go out of their way to hurt them or take their freedom away. At no time are negative feelings of dislike, prejudice, violence, and hate for certain races, colors, nationalities, or cultures justified. How can individuals and groups of people who have these traits change them? Moreover, do they have the responsibility to change them?

Think about the realities of living in a society where some people are at risk because of race, culture, skin color, nationality, and so on. Every person must be able to benefit from the freedoms and advantages of being an American. Every person must have equal opportunities to get an education, find a good job, and live where he or she wants to live without fear of discrimination or harm. No one has a right to take "justice and liberty for all" away from any person or group.

In your relationships with other people, what positive character traits emerge? Based on these attributes, what do you think is the most important thing that you can do to create better human relationships in your home, school, and community? If you knew that someone needed your help and he or she was physically challenged or of a race or culture other than your own, would you go to that person's aid? Use the following criteria to decide the level of responsibility that you would assume in each scenario.

NAME _____ DATE _____

LEVELS OF RESPONSIBILITY

A. YES (I can!)   B. NO (I cannot!)   C. MAYBE (I think I can!)

SCENARIO 1

Tears splashed down his cheeks and his eyes bore into mine—asking for help. I saw him, slouched over and crying quietly, yet I could tell that his pain was deep. My heart jumped when I recognized this boy! Wasn't he among the group of guys who chased me up the stairs to the top of a three-story building and forced me to walk over to the edge? Yes! He was, I remember now, the very one who called me a "nerd" and threatened to push me off the roof if I didn't say "Uncle!" I said it, he called me "Punk," and they all ran away laughing. Now, this bully needed me. I could see blood flowing from his side and he was still looking at me . . . needing my help.

Select a Level of Responsibility   A   B   C

SCENARIO 2

John has asked me, as nicely as he can, I guess, to be his date for the Junior Prom. I've noticed that he is a bit overweight, but he isn't bad looking. Actually, if you look at him from the side, his right profile is quite attractive. But I'd heard some of them saying that he doesn't belong here—that he should go with his own kind. I have a dress, but if I go to the prom with John, people might laugh at me.

Select a Level of Responsibility   A   B   C

SCENARIO 3

Miss Mable is a bit strange. She lives in the corner house and sometimes comes out at night to water her garden. Actually, she has been known to water her neighbors' gardens, even though they had explained to her that they would take care of their own property. Miss Mable is about 85 years old and a little hard of hearing. Very often, she can be seen peering out of her window when the bus drops the school children in front of her house. When she waves at them, some of the kids throw stones at her house and call her an "old witch." In the cold weather, she stays inside and never says anything to the children. But when the weather is nice and warm, she comes outside and shakes her fist and shouts at the children who taunt her. They can never understand what she says because of her heavy accent. As the children run away, Miss Mable limps back into her house with her head down and closes the door. You are Miss Mable's next door neighbor.

Select a Level of Responsibility   A   B   C

SCENARIO 4

Who does Shelley think she is? Every time the teacher gives an assignment, she's the first one saying, "I'm done. What should I do now?" Okay, so she's smart, but other people are too. She got a perfect score on the last test, and the teacher used her paper for the key. Her gloating lasted the whole afternoon. Today, we had to select partners for a special project in which each person has to interview his or her partner and write a paper about his or her best qualities. Guess what? I pulled Shelley's name. We're not allowed to switch names with any one else. I tried.

Select a Level of Responsibility   A   B   C

NAME _____   DATE _____

_____ **THE EXPERT**
             (Your Name)

Although life is not always easy, when people develop their natural talents and improve their skills, chances for success and satisfaction increase. This is true for people of every race, culture, and nationality. While an individual's socioeconomic status can be helpful when he or she plans for the future, it should not prevent him or her from pursuing success. Equal opportunity in education and employment are legal rights for all Americans whether they are lower, middle, or upper class. So, GO FOR IT! Rise above any negativism that would keep you from reaching for the stars—studying, working, and trying to achieve the highest possible goals. Become an expert in some field of work by developing and using your natural abilities. What are your natural abilities? In what areas do you find the most satisfaction and experience the greatest degree of success? How do you plan to use your areas of expertise—your talents and skills to help humanity?

From the list of talents and skills below the chart, select one or more that represent your strong points. Then, think of ways you can contribute to your present and future circumstances and, simultaneously, to society by using these areas of expertise. Complete the chart, accordingly.

YOUR TALENTS/SKILLS/STRENGTHS	HOW YOU WILL USE THEM
1.	
2.	
3.	
4.	
5.	
6.	

WORDS   NUMBERS   DRAWING   ATHLETICS   HUMAN INTEREST
                              SELF-UNDERSTANDING

BIBLIOGRAPHY

Branden, Nathaniel. *The Six Pillars of Self-Esteem*. New York: Bantam Books, 1994.

Comer, James P., and Poussaint, Alvin F. *Raising Black Children*. New York: Plume Books, 1992.

Damon, William. *Greater Expectations: Overcoming the Culture of Indulgence in America's Homes and Schools*. New York: Free Press, 1995.

Edelman, Marian Wright. *The Measure of Our Success, A Letter to My Children and Yours*. Boston: Beacon Press, 1992.

Ellis, Elizabeth M. *Raising a Responsible Child: How Parents Can Avoid Overindulgent Behavior and Nurture Healthy Children*. Secaucus, NJ: Carol Publishing Group, 1996. (A Birch Lane Press book)

Eyre, Linda and Richard. *Teaching Your Children Values*. New York: Simon & Schuster, 1993.

Grevious, Saundrah Clark. *Ready-to-Use Multicultural Activities for Primary Children*. Prentice Hall—Center for Applied Research in Education, 1993.

Kuklin, Susan. *Speaking Out: Teenagers Take on Race, Sex, and Identity*. New York: G. P. Putnam's Sons, 1993.

Lidz, Richard, and Perrin, Linda. *Career Information Center, Sixth Edition*. New York: Macmillan Library Reference, USA, Simon & Schuster Macmillan, 1996.

Powell, Colin, "I Wasn't Left to Myself." p. 34. *Newsweek*. April 27, 1998.

Swann, William B. *Self-Traps: The Elusive Quest for Higher Self-Esteem*. New York: W. H. Freeman and Company, 1996.

Williams, Tennessee. "The Catastrophe of Success," *The Glass Menagerie*. New York: Signet—The Penguin Group, 1972.

Wolfman, Ira. *Do People Grow on Family Trees? Genealogy for Kids & Other Beginners*. New York: Workman Publishing, 1991.

APPENDIX
Ready-to-Use Enrichment Activities

HUMAN DIVERSITY—GREAT!!
HUMAN COMMONALITIES EVEN GREATER!!!

Study the intersecting circles below and think of the importance of your survival into the next century. What do human beings of all races, colors, and creeds have to consider if they are to survive in a world that is now full of warring factions? Since we only have one home, one significant consideration should be that of acknowledging that all human beings are interdependent. Review the list of words beneath the intersecting circles and keep your personal survival, human interdependence, racial and cultural harmony in mind. Select a topic for discussion in your family, among your peers in school, or in your community. You can also use the Topic Word List below, as well as other words, to fill the various areas of the circles. Share the reasons for your selections by explaining whether you agree or disagree with the title of this activity.

FILL THE INTERSECTING CIRCLES WITH WORDS FROM THE LIST
(You do not have to use all of the words)

TOPIC WORD LIST

ACCOUNTABILITY	DESPAIR	KINSHIP	MIXED RACIAL
TRANSFORMATION	DIVERSITY	DIVISION	HERITAGE
TRUTH	COMMONALITIES	STRENGTH IN	INTERDEPENDENCE
STABILITY	DECEIT	NUMBERS	COHESIVE
LOVE	FAMILY	VULNERABILITY	FRAGMENTATION
REALITY	UNITY	CONCERN	ESTRANGEMENT
COMMUNITY	STANDARDS	HUMAN DIGNITY	INTERCULTURAL
MULTIPLICATION	HATE	INDIVIDUALITY	

A SELF-ANALYSIS COMPASS

Based upon your value system and beliefs, how would you gauge your character as you go about your daily life? In your behavior and interactions with others at home, in school, and in the community, do you uphold or violate your values? Does your conscience guide you as you think about how to react to temptations? This is an individual, private matter that does not have to be shared with other people. Identify various responses to daily challenges and score yourself, accordingly. If your scores are too high, generate a list of necessary lifestyle changes that will keep you in the safety zones of your compass!!!

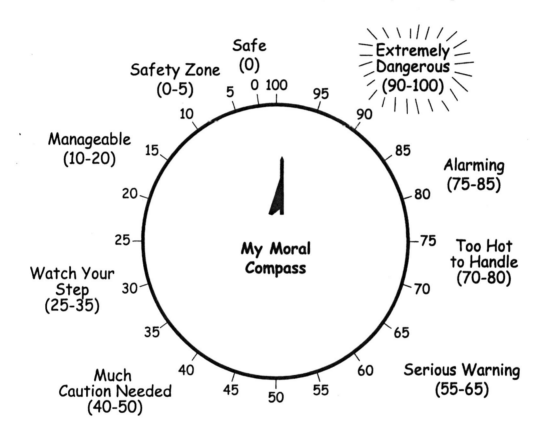

INTERACTIONS DURING A TYPICAL DAY

Home Activity _____ Score _____

School Activity _____ Score _____

Community Activity _____ Score _____

Lifestyle changes that are necessary for safety: _____

_____

_____

_____

_____

8 STEPS TO PEACE

Although you are young, you have ideas that can be very useful in helping peers and adults with whom you interact to find peace. List eight of your own ideas about how human beings might get along better. Then talk to others and find eight more ideas. Starting from the lowest rung on the "LADDER TO PEACE" list all ideas. Then, discuss how you and others can apply these strategies to your daily lives.

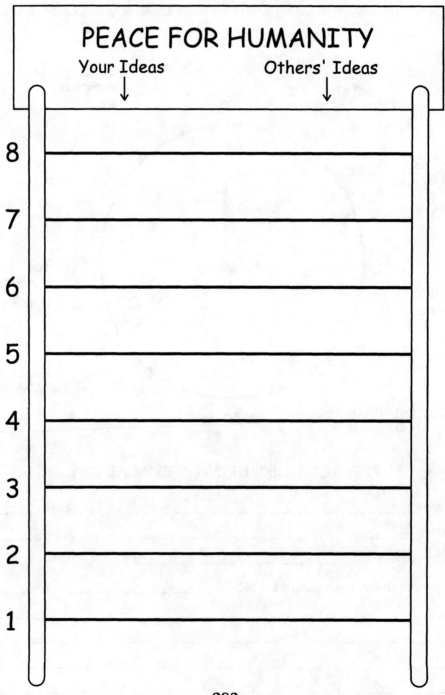

PEACE FOR HUMANITY

Your Ideas   Others' Ideas

8
7
6
5
4
3
2
1

RACIAL AND GENDER STEREOTYPING

What does racial and gender stereotyping look like? What should replace stereotyping? Use the graphs below to view the percentages of racial and gender inequities that exist in America. After interpreting graph #1 on the left, indicate whether you agree or disagree with the percentages by developing your own perspective on graph #2. Finally, in graph #3, formulate percentages that indicate the *ideal* regarding equality of opportunity for all groups of people. Your ideal should show how racial and gender equity in education, employment, business, and housing, should look in America. Your graph should provide a goal and a strategy around which all Americans can mobilize as we work towards ". . . freedom and justice for all" by eliminating injustice and stereotyping.

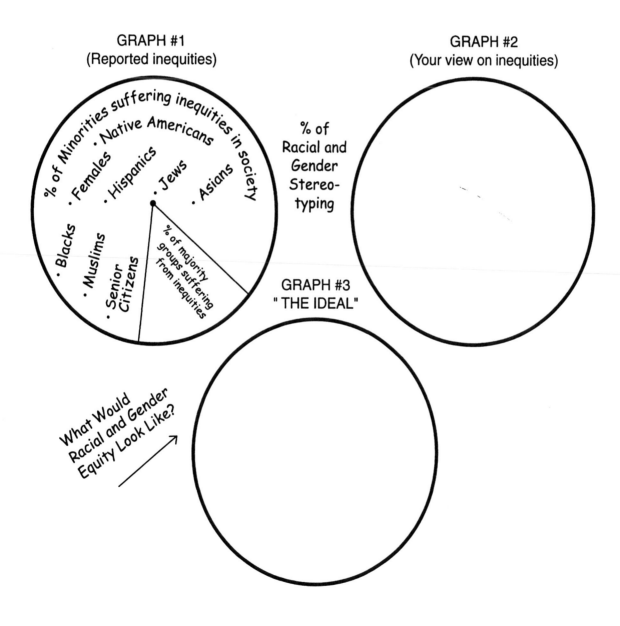

CAUSE-AND-EFFECT RELATIONSHIPS

Most things happen in life for a reason. Sometimes the reasons are good ones, and other times they are not. Nevertheless, the decisions that cause people to participate in certain activities or behaviors have results or outcomes that are directly related to their prior decisions, actions, or conduct. The **cause** or **reason** that people do things is part of the outcome or effect, otherwise known as the **result; cause-and-effect relationships** abound in human society. Look at the areas of concern on the chart below and analyze the reasons and results or the cause-and-effect relationships for each concern. Then, suggest how you would change behavior or what you would suggest for a solution to the problem or concern. Extend this list to include other areas of concern or problematic issues in society. Use your completed chart for discussions of how to change negative results into positive ones. Discussions can be with family, peers, teachers, and community members.

CAUSE AND EFFECT RELATIONSHIPS TO CHANGE

AREAS OF CONCERN	CAUSE (Reason)	EFFECT (Result)
1. **Fighting**	_____	_____
My Solution for Fighting	_____	
_____		
2. **Stereotyping**	_____	_____
My Solution for Stereotyping	_____	
_____		
3. **Prejudice**	_____	_____
My Solution for Prejudice	_____	
_____		
4. **Selfishness**	_____	_____
My Solution for Selfishness	_____	
_____		

COMPARE AND CONTRAST

Think of some of the concepts you have discussed in class or consider some of the people, issues, events, and realities of life that you are aware of. What are some of the similarities and differences in the concepts, people, issues, or events that need to be highlighted? What lessons can be learned from comparing and contrasting aspects of the human condition? Use the chart below to compare and contrast only two of the concepts: people, issues, events, other realities of human existence that are important to you or that your teacher suggests. After completing the comparison and contrast areas of the chart, write an evaluation of your findings on the lines provided.

COMPARE–CONTRAST CHART

List two of the concepts, people, issues, or events to be compared on lines #1 and #2 below:

#1 _____ #2 _____

SIMILARITIES	DIFFERENCES
1. _____	1. _____
2. _____	2. _____
3. _____	3. _____
4. _____	4. _____
5. _____	5. _____

EVALUATION

_____

_____

_____

_____

_____

_____

_____

_____

_____

9 780787 966416